P9-BZL-132

A Learning College for the 21st Century

Terry O'Banion

DISCARDED
JENKS LRC
GORDON COLLEGE

JENKS L.R.C.
GORDON COLLEGE
255 GRAPEVINE RD.
WENHAM, MA 01984-1895

AACC
American Association of Community Colleges

AMERICAN COUNCIL ON EDUCATION ★
ORYX PRESS ★
Series on Higher Education
1997

LB
2328.15
.U6
O33
1997

The rare Arabian oryx is believed to have inspired the myth of the unicorn. This desert antelope became virtually extinct in the early 1960s. At that time several groups of international conservationists arranged to have 9 animals sent to the Phoenix Zoo to be the nucleus of a captive breeding herd. Today the oryx population is over 1,000, and over 500 have been returned to the Middle East.

© 1997 by American Council on Education and The Oryx Press
Published by The Oryx Press
4041 North Central at Indian School Road
Phoenix, Arizona 85012-3397

All rights reserved. No part of this publication may be reproduced or transmitted in any form or by any means, electronic or mechanical, including photocopying, recording, or by any information storage and retrieval system, without permission in writing from The Oryx Press.

Published simultaneously in Canada
Printed and bound in the United States of America

∞ The paper used in this publication meets the minimum requirements of the American National Standard for Information Sciences—Permanence of Paper for Printed Library Materials, ANSI Z39.48-1984.

Library of Congress Cataloging-in-Publication Data

O'Banion, Terry, 1936–
    A learning college for the 21st century / Terry O'Banion.
        p. cm.— (American Council on Education/Oryx Press series on higher education)
    "AACC, American Association of Community Colleges."
    Includes bibliographical references and index.
    ISBN 1-57356-113-4 (alk. paper)
    1. Community colleges—United States. 2. Learning. 3. College teaching—United States. 4. Educational change—United States. I. American Association of Community Colleges. II. Title. III. Series.
LB2328.15.U6033 1997
378'.052'0973—dc21
                                        97-8299
                                          CIP

For Yolande
—the wind beneath my wings

CONTENTS

CONTRIBUTORS

George R. Boggs, Superintendent/President, Palomar College, San Marcos, California

Paul A. Elsner, Chancellor, Maricopa Community Colleges, Phoenix, Arizona

Lee Howser, President, Jackson Community College, Jackson, Michigan

Byron McClenney, President, Community College of Denver, Denver, Colorado

Diane G. Michael, Assistant Superintendent/Vice President of Instruction, Palomar College, San Marcos, California

Jerry Moskus, President, Lane Community College, Eugene, Oregon

David H. Ponitz, President, Sinclair Community College, Dayton, Ohio

Carole Schwinn, Learning Systems Advisor, Jackson Community College, Jackson, Michigan

FOREWORD

K. Patricia Cross
David Pierpont Gardner Professor of Higher Education
University of California, Berkeley

The transition into a new century inevitably provokes reflections on the past and predictions about the future. While any point in time might serve to mark definitive change, the year 2000 seems to promise a heady renewal of the spirit that energized the expansion of community colleges in the mid-twentieth century. This book, *A Learning College for the 21st Century*, provides an exciting model for community colleges of the future.

In the United States during the late 1960s, community colleges were established at the rate of one new college every week. The times were ripe for the creation of a uniquely American institution. Unlike the models of research universities and liberal arts colleges that were imported from Europe, community colleges were designed from the ground up to serve American priorities.

Perhaps because of their unique design as American institutions, community colleges have often been bellwether institutions for change, leading the way into new and unexplored territory. European models of higher education were built with the fundamental assumption that only a certain proportion of the population needed or could profit from a college education. In the United States, that proportion was variously (and erroneously, it turns out) estimated at between 25 and 50 percent by early blue-ribbon study commissions. But as economic and societal pressures changed, so, too, did the demands placed upon higher education. Community colleges anticipated this inevitable need for a well-educated public by opening the doors of educational opportunity to all who wished to come. Once the principle of universal access to higher education had been accepted, community colleges continued to lead the way by devising new programs and adapting practices to meet the needs of previously unserved populations.

Existing models of higher education had assumed that college students were young, full-time students who lived on campus and completed their college education in four years. Community colleges had to devise programs to meet the practical realities of increasing numbers of older, place-bound, part-time students with jobs, families, and other obligations that competed with education for their time and attention.

The access revolution of the 1960s and 1970s also brought new students into higher education who were not prepared to do college work. Community colleges, implementing their "can do" philosophy, set to work to devise remedial and developmental programs to meet the needs of this new population.

Although community colleges have not always received appropriate recognition for their leadership in rising to meet the constantly changing educational needs of the nation, their energy and innovative spirit seem undaunted. This "can do" spirit is fortunate because in many instances change arrives on the doorsteps of the community colleges without fanfare, and they are expected to rise to the challenge. Sometimes, a challenge that seems natural to community colleges becomes a cause celebre for more traditional institutions of higher education.

Because community colleges were committed from the beginning to serving the needs of their local communities, they were early innovators in recognizing the value of diversity as an educational force. Although more traditional colleges struggle to "recruit minorities," community colleges achieve their diversity, on many dimensions, as a natural part of their mission to serve their communities.

Another example of a change that was a natural for community colleges is the current high interest in the teaching of undergraduates. In the 1980s, when higher education was harshly criticized by national study commissions and the public press for failing to give adequate attention to teaching, community colleges were already there with a dedicated faculty whose first priority was teaching.

Now, as we enter the twenty-first century, assessment of student learning outcomes has become a powerful lever nationwide for focusing attention on learning. And once again, it looks as though community colleges will be bellwether institutions if they adopt O'Banion's vision of the learning college.

In this book, O'Banion and his colleagues offer a compelling rationale for focusing the attention of higher education on student learning, i.e., on creating the "learning college." As the long-time executive director of the

League for Innovation in the Community College and as a writer, scholar, and insightful observer of the community college scene, Terry O'Banion has a broad perspective, possessed by few people, of the role of community colleges in education. And because he is a popular speaker and consultant to individual colleges, he also brings to this task a working knowledge of how individual colleges deal with the practical realities and exciting challenges of change.

The challenge that readers will find in this provocative and well-informed book is the contention that the concept of the learning college represents a paradigm shift in the way we think about and plan for a new community college. A "paradigm shift" is a strong concept, and O'Banion is not timid about his call for a *break* with (not merely a change or an extension of) the thinking of the past. O'Banion contends that this change will not be a "natural" for community colleges; it will take great imagination, effort, and energy. But the record of community colleges is strong on meeting new needs, and this book captures a vision waiting to be put into action.

PREFACE

T he publication of A Nation at Risk in 1983 triggered one of the most massive educational reform movements in the history of education. Over 100 national reports and 300 state reports have since been issued to stem the "rising tide of mediocrity" noted in the 1983 report. A wave of educational reform has swept across the country, and there have been many changes: increased requirements for high school graduation, increased standards for teacher certification, increased use of assessment, and increased use of technology. Unfortunately, there has been little or no increase in learning among the nation's students. In retrospect, the first wave of educational reform failed because the proposed solutions only tweaked the current system of education, correcting a process here, adding on a program there—an old pattern of educational reform now impotent in light of the profound changes occurring through-out American and world society.

The failure of this first wave of educational reform led some critics to call for the end of education as we know it. Lewis Perelman (1992) suggested, "The principal barrier to economic progress today is a mind-set that seeks to perfect education when it needs only to be abandoned" (p.24). George Leonard (1992) added, "We can no longer improve the education of our children by improving school as we know it. The time has come to recognize that school is not the solution. It is the problem" (p. 26). And Stan Davis and Jim Botkin (1994) warned, "Over the next few decades the private sector will eclipse the public sector and become the major institu-tion responsible for learning" (p. 16).

These criticisms and threats helped galvanize educational leaders into action. Armed with new insights from brain-based research, Continuous Quality Improvement processes, and new developments in technology, a second wave of educational reform emerged in the early 1990s, preparing the way for the most profound change in education since the invention of the book. The second wave places *learning* as the central value and the central activity of the educational enterprise. *The American Imperative*, published in 1993, ten years after *A Nation at Risk*, is representative of the reports that frame the issues for the second wave of educational reform. *The American Imperative* calls for the "redesign of our learning systems to align our entire educational enterprise with the personal, civic, and work place needs of the 21st century" (Wingspread Group on Higher Education, 1993, p. 19). The report goes on to say that "Putting learning at the heart of the academic enterprise will mean overhauling the conceptual, procedural, curricular, and other architecture of postsecondary education on most campuses" (Wingspread Group on Higher Education, 1993, p. 14). This new wave of reform is not tweaking a system to fix a few broken parts; it is a fundamental overhaul, destruction of much that is traditional and construction of much that is new.

The changes called for will not come easily to education, an institution described as "1,000 years of tradition wrapped in 100 years of bureaucracy" (Moe, 1994, p. 1). But islands of change are emerging across the higher education landscape, and those changes are increasingly evident in some of the nation's leading community colleges.

In this book, I have tried to provide a framework for the reform movements of the past decade and the emerging focus on learning. Chapter 1 is a review of the issues related to the first wave of reform and an analysis of the problems associated with the traditional architecture of education— the time-bound, place-bound, efficiency-bound, and role-bound models that characterize current educational institutions. Chapter 2 is a review of the issues that have emerged in the second wave of educational reform since 1990. The chapter contains perspectives on many sectors of higher education that hold in common the value of "placing learning first." The chapter ends with a review of forces of resistance to change as well as a review of the pressures that are forcing change. Chapter 3 illustrates how the current emphasis on learning is a reflection of earlier attempts to emphasize learning and cites examples from the Progressive Education Movement of the 1930s and 1940s and the Humanistic Education Movement of the 1960s. This key chapter proposes a new model of education for the community college that I call "the learning college," an institution designed to help students make passionate connections to learning. Six key principles that form the emerging definition and character of the learning college are described in detail.

Chapters 4 and 5 explain how to build a foundation for the continuing creation of the learning college. In chapter 4 the potential role of technology in creating the learning college is outlined for educators who are not technologically oriented. Chapter 5 builds further on the foundation by citing recent progress in learning research, outcome and assessment measures, and learning organizations—and by describing how this progress can be applied to the building of the learning college.

Chapters 6 through 11 are descriptions of how six of the nation's leading community colleges are beginning to grapple with changes leading toward more learner-centered institutions. Written primarily by the CEOs of the six institutions, these descriptions provide a realistic snapshot of the early developmental phases of the learning college concept.

Chapter 12 offers a practical guide for community colleges interested in launching a learning college initiative of their own. In the last several years, I have keynoted a dozen national and state conferences and dozens of individual community college conferences on the topic of the learning college. In every case, college leaders and rank-and-file staff want to know how to get started and what to do. This final chapter, gleaned from the experiences of the six colleges and my own experience, should provide a useful point of departure for many colleges.

There are always problems associated with early attempts to frame a new idea, and the reader should be aware of the limitations in this book. The second wave of educational reform to place learning first is still in the early stages of development. There are many unanswered questions regarding how to initiate reform efforts on a campus, how and what changes to make, where resources will come from, how to overcome resistance, how to evaluate progress, and so forth. There is a great deal of interest in the learning college, and some experimentation is already underway, but the future of how this concept will develop and become embedded in community college culture is still quite unclear.

A second limitation is related to the six community colleges I have characterized as emerging models of the learning college. None of the leaders of these colleges claim they have designed the definitive model of a learning college. They are just beginning their journeys, reworking the present to create the future. The stories they tell here may already be obsolete, not only because of publication lag but also because these colleges are leapfrogging toward a vanishing horizon of change. The colleges are different in the way they approach their tasks and design their structures and their outcomes. There is, however, a common bond, a common commitment to placing learning first, for placing learning as the central value and guiding light for everything they do. In their own view, they fall far short of their goal. They are well aware of their limitations and of the difficulty of the long journey still ahead.

Except for a brief review of some of the most important pressures forcing change in education noted in the concluding section of chapter 2, a third limitation of the book is my decision not to include an entire chapter on the social forces and trends that are forcing changes in all institutions, especially in education. This information is so readily available in every article and book on change in education that I felt it would be a repetition of the obvious.

Finally, I caution leaders not to confuse reform efforts to place learning first with all of the other changes going on in higher education. Institutions of higher education can easily claim that they are already deeply involved in placing learning first in their institutions. Many colleges *are* involved in the process of transforming their cultures: marketing to new groups of students, developing assessment and outcome measures, building creative linkages to their communities, applying new technologies to improve teaching and management, increasing standards for students and teachers, flattening organizational structures, decentralizing decision making, building alliances with business and industry, applying Continuous Quality Improvement and Total Quality Management processes, etc., etc., etc. But in many cases these actions have been the usual extensions and add-ons, leading to only modest change in the status quo. In most cases, *what* students learn and *how* students learn have remained relatively unchanged. A great deal of change is going on in higher education, but not much of it is focused on the objective of the second wave of educational reform, which is to place learning front and center in the educational enterprise.

In spite of these limitations, the concept of the learning college is an attractive idea in embryo that, if nurtured properly, can address many of the current problems facing higher education. It even has the potential of changing the entire architecture of higher education. And the community college may be the ideal crucible in which the concept of the learning college can take form. After 100 years of experimentation, the community college has emerged as an institution with a strong penchant for innovation and for risk taking. The community college is not afraid to reach out and explore new ideas and new concepts.

The learning college is a new concept, but it is built on long-established values in the community college, values that place a premium on quality teaching for the purpose of helping students make passionate connections to learning. If the concept of the learning college cannot come to full fruition in the community college, the community college we know today may cease to exist, and the community college we dream of for the future may never come to be.

Terry O'Banion
Newport Beach, California

REFERENCES

Davis, Stan and Botkin, Jim. *The Monster under the Bed: How Business Is Mastering the Opportunity of Knowledge for Profit.* New York: Simon & Schuster, 1994.

Leonard, George. "The End of School," *The Atlantic*, May 1992.

Moe, Roger. Cited in Armajani, Babak et al. *A Model for the Reinvented Higher Education System: State Policy and College Learning.* Denver, CO: Education Commission of the States, January 1994.

Perelman, Louis J. *School's Out: A Radical New Formula for the Revitalization of America's Educational System.* New York: Avon Books, 1992.

Wingspread Group on Higher Education. *An American Imperative: Higher Expectations for Higher Education.* Racine, WI: The Johnson Foundation, Inc., 1993.

ACKNOWLEDGMENTS

T his book has been a joint effort from the beginning, and I owe a great deal to the following friends and colleagues:

- George Boggs and Robert Barr of Palomar College first introduced me to the basic concepts of the new learning paradigm; and their writings and speeches have been a continuing inspiration.
- Donald Berz and Jerry Young of Chaffey College engaged me in hours of rich conversation regarding the learning college. Donald Berz kept my in-box full of the latest information on reform efforts and the learning revolution.
- Don Doucette of Metropolitan Community Colleges edited the first draft of the manuscript and challenged me to think more broadly and more deeply about the learning college.
- K. Patricia Cross wrote the foreword and gently raised several questions that prompted me to reconstruct several key portions of the manuscript.
- The authors of the six chapters on emerging models of the learning college made me realize how difficult it is to translate ideals into reality. If the learning college survives and prospers into the twenty-first century, it will be due to their exemplary leadership.
- Nadine McCarty and Suzanne Lilly of the League for Innovation graciously and competently transcribed, formatted, and edited chunks and pieces of the manuscript until they could create one final document they happily mailed to the publisher.

I owe a special debt of gratitude to the thousands of community college faculty, administrators, and staff who have listened to my speeches on the learning college over the past two years at dozens of national, state, and college conferences; and who have shared their experiences, their criticisms, their hopes and dreams, and their deep commitments to help students make passionate connections to learning. The future of the learning college is clearly in their hands.

Terry O'Banion

CHAPTER 1

Trimming the Branches of a
Dying Tree

I t now appears quite likely that, in the not-too-distant future, visitors from another planet will make contact with planet Earth. It is also quite likely that, if they come soon, a visit to the United States will be included on their itinerary. Once contact has been established and their spaceship has settled in the wheat fields of Nebraska, to the great delight of the Kearney UFO Watchers Club, the visitors will be curious about how we live and function. If the visitors can stay for awhile, they will examine in great detail how we reproduce, how we create structures, how we communicate, how we produce and distribute food, how we wage war, how we practice democracy, and why we watch television.

It will not escape their attention that we are unique organisms who have greatly multiplied in this environment, and they will be particularly interested in how we have adapted and how we learn. They will quickly discover our systems of schooling, and if final reports are to be prepared for their colleagues back home, there will be a summary paragraph something like the following:

> We were intrigued with the great amount of interest shown by the two-legged organisms in the United States in what they refer to as "schooling." It is their most important invention. Everyone does it. Everyone believes in it. Everyone is an expert on it. But there is a peculiar characteristic of the two-legged organisms observed by every member of our entity: They are now and apparently have been for a long time very dissatisfied with how they do this "schooling." We examined records far back in their time range and discovered many annual

reports on how terrible their schools are and how they need fixing. Reforming schooling appears to be their national religion.

SCHOOL REFORM AS A NATIONAL PASTIME

Even a cursory review of the reform literature in education will confirm the accuracy of the views of the visitors from another planet. For each of the last 50 years, the careful scholar can unearth at least one annual reform report on American schooling issued by a commission of eminent Americans, by an agency of the federal or state government, or by a prominent leader. In 1984, K. Patricia Cross noted that in the last few years over 30 national reports on education reform had been issued along with over 300 task reports on reform from the 50 states, not including the individual author reports that crop up on an annual basis (p. 168).

A review of two key reform reports, one issued in 1983 and the other in 1993, provides a snapshot of the nature of education reform efforts and sets the context for key issues in this chapter.

The honorable T.H. Bell, secretary of education appointed by President Ronald Reagan, created the National Commission on Excellence in Education on August 26, 1981, in response to "the widespread public perception that something is seriously remiss in our educational system" (The National Commission on Excellence in Education, 1983, p. 1). In 18 months, the prestigious commission produced a report that triggered one of the most extensive reform movements in the history of education, efforts that are still underway in the latter half of the 1990s.

The commission cast its report as "An Open Letter to the American People" and took a bold position:

> Our nation is at risk. Our once unchallenged preeminence in commerce, industry, science and technological innovation is being overtaken by competitors throughout the world. . . . We report to the American people that while we can take justifiable pride in what our schools and colleges have historically accomplished and contributed to the United States and the well-being of its people, the educational foundations of our society are presently being eroded by a rising tide of mediocrity that threatens our very future as a nation and as a people. (The National Commission on Excellence in Education, 1983, p. 5)

Not satisfied with this call to alarm in the opening statement of the report, the commission became even bolder and suggested that "if an unfriendly foreign force had attempted to impose on America the mediocre educational performance that exists today, we might well have viewed it as an act of war. . . . We have, in effect, been committing an act of unthinking unilateral educational disarmament" (The National Commission on Excellence in Education, 1993, p. 5).

A *Nation at Risk* was issued in 1983. A decade later a similar report was issued that sounded many of the same themes, using the same words "imperative" and "risk." An *American Imperative: Higher Expectations for Higher Education* was published in 1993 as "An Open Letter to Those Concerned About the American Future." Sponsored by four leading private foundations—The William and Flora Hewlett Foundation; The Johnson Foundation, Inc.; Lilly Endowment, Inc.; and The Pew Charitable Trusts—this report focused on higher education whereas A *Nation at Risk* had focused primarily on high schools.

The 1993 report echoed the alarms of the 1983 report:

> A disturbing and dangerous mismatch exists between what American society needs of higher education and what it is receiving. Nowhere is the mismatch more dangerous than in the quality of undergraduate preparation provided on many campuses. The American imperative for the twenty-first century is that society must hold higher education to much higher expectations or risk national decline. (Wingspread Group on Higher Education, p. 1)

Reflecting other themes addressed by the 1983 report, the 1993 report also raised the spectre of competition from abroad. "Education is in trouble, and with it our nation's hope for the future. America's ability to compete in a global economy is threatened. . . . The capacity for the United States to shoulder its responsibilities on the world stage is at risk" (Wingspread Group on Higher Education, p. 1).

Both reports were issued as "open letters" to a key audience; both reports sounded the alarm as an "imperative" for a society at "great risk"; both suggested that education was the root cause of the problem. The similarities in the reports were also reflected in the way each reported the failures of students.

The 1983 commission examined patterns of courses high school students took from 1964-69 compared with course patterns from 1976-81:

- The proportion of students taking "general track" or cafeteria-style curriculum has increased from 12 percent in 1962 to 42 percent in 1979.
- In 1979 only 31 percent of high school graduates completed intermediate algebra, 13 percent–French I, 16 percent–geography, and 6 percent–calculus.
- A 1980 national survey of high school diploma requirements revealed that only eight states required high schools to offer foreign languages, but none required students to take the courses.

- Thirty-five states required only one year of mathematics, and 36 required only one year of science for a high school diploma (The National Commission on Excellence in Education, 1983, pp. 18-20).

The 1993 commission reported outcomes of several major studies as well:

- Of recent bachelor's degree recipients in a 1992 analysis of college transcripts by the U.S. Department of Education, it was discovered that 26 percent did not earn a single credit in history, 31 percent did not study mathematics of any kind, and 58 percent left college without any exposure to a foreign language.
- In a 1993 National Adult Literacy Survey, the largest effort of its type ever attempted, the Educational Testing Service reported that only about one-half of four-year graduates were able to demonstrate intermediate levels of competence in reading and interpreting prose such as newspaper articles, in working with documents such as bus schedules, and in using elementary arithmetic to solve problems involving costs of meals in restaurants.
- The Educational Testing Service reported that 56 percent of American-born, four-year college graduates were unable consistently to perform simple tasks, such as calculating the change from $3 after buying a 60¢ bowl of soup and a $1.95 sandwich.
- In a comment on the survey by the Educational Testing Service, the commission reported, "We note with concern that the 1993 survey findings reflect a statistically significant decline from those of an earlier survey conducted in 1985 (Wingspread Group on Higher Education, 1993, pp. 5-6).

FAILURE OF REFORM

While it is too early to measure the impact of the 1993 report, *An American Imperative*, there is ample evidence in that report that the impact of the 1983 report, *A Nation at Risk*, has been minimal, perhaps even detrimental if the statement in the previous paragraph regarding the decline from 1985 to 1993 is taken into consideration.

Ted Marchese (1995), editor of *Change*, has observed, "Despite the past decade's flood of commission reports, foundation grants, new pedagogies, curricular innovations, and shelves of research, it's hard to say whether American undergraduate education has improved that much. Indeed, looking across years of data on student attainment, it's possible to argue we've slipped a bit" (p. 4). Willard Daggett (1992) has analyzed the changing world of work and the unchanging world of education and has concluded, "Despite 10 years of school reform, high school graduates in 1991 are less prepared for society in general, and the workplace in particular than were graduates of the 1980s" (p. 3).

A number of critics have been quite vocal about the failure of A Nation at Risk to create change and have attacked it as the bellwether of all reform efforts in recent years. In a review of A Nation at Risk, George Leonard (1992) commented, "The painful truth is that despite the spotlight on schooling and the stern pronouncements of educators, governors, and presidents, despite the frantic test preparation in classrooms all over the country and the increased funding, school achievement has remained essentially flat over the past two decades" (p. 26).

In the decade between 1982 and 1991, after adjusting for inflation, funding for K-12 schools increased by $57.2 billion or more than 50 percent. Per-pupil spending increased an average $1,250, or 30 percent, above the level required to keep pace with inflation (Augenblick et al., 1993). In spite of this substantial increase in funding, reform efforts fell far short of their goals. Leonard (1992) concluded that "The failure of this well-intentioned, well-executed movement toward reform summons us to think the unthinkable: We can no longer improve the education of our children by improving school as we know it. *The time has come to recognize that school is not the solution. It is the problem*" (p. 26, emphasis added).

The chairman and CEO of IBM, Louis V. Gerstner, Jr., in a speech to the National Governors' Association reported in *USA Today*, also keyed off on A Nation at Risk by asking, "What's happened since? Lots of hand-wringing; lots of speeches; lots of reports; but little improvement. U.S. students still finish at, or near, the bottom on international tests in math and science" ("Opinion USA," 1995, p. 9A).

In 1989, influenced by A Nation at Risk, the nation's governors created the National Education Goals, later recast as Goals 2000 by the Clinton administration, as a way to invigorate reform efforts. Whereas the first flurry of reform had focused on raising graduation requirements, increasing standards and salaries for teachers, and increasing state assessment programs, the new goals called for restructuring education systems to focus on results instead of processes and regulations. Six years later, the Education Commission of the States (1995, p. 5) indicated that general consensus that efforts to achieve the National Education Goals were not proceeding fast enough to meet the target date of 2000.

The popular press is less oblique in reporting on the results of the federal report on progress in reaching the National Education Goals: "Halfway through the decade, the United States is falling far short of eight ambitious goals it aimed to reach by the year 2000. By most measures, the nation has slipped or only managed to stay even, with improvement limited to a few areas" (Garcia, 1995, p. 1).

Perhaps the large number of similar reports in the daily press have contributed to the public's perception that schools are getting worse, not better. In 1994, 51 percent of Americans felt that schools had deteriorated, while only 16 percent felt they had improved. In 1995, 71 percent of the public gave the nation's schools an overall grade of "C" or worse. Even more disturbing, only 2 percent of the public gave the nation's schools an "A" (Education Commission of the States, 1995, pp. 16-17).

In *The Monster under the Bed* (1994), Davis and Botkin declared, "Over the next few decades the private sector will eclipse the public sector and become the major institution responsible for learning" (p. 16).

More pointedly, Lewis J. Perelman (1992) observed the following: "So contrary to what the reformers have been claiming, the central failure of our education system is not inadequacy but *excess*: Our economy is being crippled by too much spending on too much schooling. . . . The principal barrier to economic progress today is a mind-set that seeks to perfect education when it needs only to be abandoned" (p. 24). Even within the educational establishment, no punches are pulled when describing the current situation: "Our education system is in crisis; business-as-usual is a formula for national disaster" (Wingspread Group on Higher Education, 1993, p. 19).

A year after *A Nation at Risk* was published, Cross (1984) warned us not to expect too much: "The pattern of educational reform has been to generate a lot of enthusiasm, reform the curriculum, raise standards, restore prestige to teaching—and then somehow have the improvements swept away again by the *rising tide of mediocrity*" (p. 168, emphasis added).

There are some indications, however slight, that reform efforts since 1983 are contributing to improved schools (Pipho, 1986; Weinman, 1995; and Education Commission of the States, 1995). The overwhelming perception, however, of the public, leading critics, business executives, policy makers, and educators themselves is that the reform effort launched by *A Nation at Risk* in 1983 has been a spectacular failure.

THE HORTICULTURE OF REFORM

The authors of education reform have a penchant for garden analogies that seem entirely appropriate as a way of characterizing the growing pains of reform, as well as a way of illustrating the decay and decline of reform. For example, in a special report on reform in the *Phi Delta Kappan*, Pipho (1986) noted the beginnings of the current reform movement. "Academic standards made no visible turn upwards in the Seventies, and the seeds of the reform movement were sown. Its green shoots broke ground in 1983 when a plethora of proposals made the need for reform visible to the American public" (p. K2).

Another gardening analogy was advanced by an observer of a series of Higher Education Roundtables supported by The Pew Charitable Trusts, in which education leaders discuss the problems their institutions face and how they can initiate academic and administrative reform. This observer reported in *Policy Perspectives* (1993) that "he felt himself in the company. . . of gardeners who had pruned and weeded without changing the garden itself. All the plants remained fixed, the layout unchanged, the walls hardly breached" ("A Call to Meeting," p. 1A). Later, the same observer noted, "Many institutions are discovering, however, that in maintaining their gardens they are trapped between the proverbial rock and the hard place—between the need to restructure and the insistence of faculty and staff that any change be minimal" (p. 1A).

Community college leaders have also used garden analogies in reviewing education reform. In an article in the *Community College Journal*, Baker and Reed (1994) discussed current reform efforts in terms of the role of the community college in creating a world-class workforce and reviewed a number of proposed solutions to the "serious illness" that plagues the country. They concluded, "All of these solutions work toward trimming the branches, when attacking the root is the only viable source of action" (p. 32).

Baker and Reed are right on target. The primary problem of education reform triggered by *A Nation at Risk* is that solutions have been proposed as add-ons or modifications to the current system of education. Tweaking the current system by adding on the *innovation du jour* will not be sufficient. Fixing what is broken by repairing the pieces or grafting on a prosthetic technology will not address core issues. "The reform movement of the past decade has been trimming the branches of a dying tree" (O'Banion, 1995, p. 1).

There have been plenty of branches to trim in the blackboard jungle of American education. As Roger Moe (1994), majority leader of the Minnesota State Senate, remarked: "Higher Education is a thousand years of tradition wrapped in a hundred years of bureaucracy" (p.1). This observation reflects the perceptions and frustrations of elected officials who are trying to institute educational reform. But these same elected officials have also contributed to the problem along with educators and other social architects who for over a century have been building a great tangle of structural elements that form the architecture of education.

THE HOUSE THAT CARNEGIE BUILT

The "Carnegie unit" is a metaphor for the vast array of traditional structural elements that have provided the framework of American schooling
for generations of students. The Carnegie unit is equivalent to the one
credit students receive for a year-long course in high school, an early
attempt to codify accumulated learning. Ideally, students earn five credits
in each of the last four years of high school, and the accumulated 20 credits
earn them a high school diploma.

The Carnegie unit is but the tip of a very large iceberg that has frozen
education into a structure created for an earlier social order. The current
architecture of education was created at the end of the last century, when
90 percent of the population left school after the eighth grade and when the
industrial revolution began to replace an economy built on agriculture.

In an agricultural society, students were needed by their families to work
on the farms. Schools were designed to end in the middle of the afternoon
so that students could be home before dark to milk the cows, gather the
eggs, and feed the hogs. On weekends school was out. Saturday was a full
work day on the farm for larger projects such as mowing the hay, repairing
fences, and harvesting corn. On Sunday agricultural and theological values
combined to create a day for rest and religion. Summers were set aside for
major farm chores: harvesting crops, tilling new land, building barns, and
repairing tools and fences. In Plant City, Florida, a major strawberry-
producing center, the schools, as late as the 1940s, were referred to as
"strawberry schools" in recognition of their adaptation to an agricultural
economy. This anachronism was noted by Clara Lovett (1995): "Everyone
recognizes it [the academic calendar] for what it is: a relic of an agrarian
society in which all able-bodied men and women were needed in the fields
at certain times of the year" (p. B1).

When the nation changed from an agricultural to an industrial economy,
the old school structure remained but was updated and streamlined to fit
the new industrial model. "Scientific management" and hierarchical organization, the bedrock principles of bureaucracy, were introduced in the
schools, in part to socialize youth in the virtues of order and discipline.
More importantly, the modern factory, pioneered by Henry Ford in the
production of automobiles, appeared ideally suited to schooling that up to
this point had flourished in the cottage industry of one-room schoolhouses.
Schools could be operated like factories with students as products moving
through an assembly line. Teachers were the workers who turned out the
products, and they were, in turn, managed by principals and presidents, the
management bureaucracy.

Reformers have been consistent in their criticism of the constraints on learning imposed by this industrial model of schooling. John and Evelyn Dewey (1962), earlier reformers, said, "Nature has not adapted the young animal to the narrow desk, the crowded curriculum, the silent absorption of complicated facts" (p. 15). And Mario Savio, speaking for a generation of college students, launched the Free Speech Movement at Berkeley in 1964 when he described education as a machine designed to grind the bones of students to make societal bread. At the time, students across the country closed a number of institutions of higher education in response to Savio's lamentation.

> There is a time when the operation of the machine becomes so odious, makes you so sick at heart that you can't take part; you can't even tacitly take part, and you've got to put your bodies on the gears and upon the wheels, upon the levers, upon all apparatus and you have got to make it stop. And you've got to indicate to the people who run it, to the people who own it, that unless you're free, the machines will be prevented from working at all. (1964)

K. Patricia Cross, a leading advocate for educational reform throughout her career, observed. "After some two decades of trying to find answers to the question of how to provide education for all the people, I have concluded that our commitment to the lock-step, time-defined structures of education stands in the way of lasting progress" (1984, p. 171). More recently, Alvin and Heidi Toffler (1995) have noted that "America's schools . . . still operate like factories, subjecting the raw material (children) to standardized instruction and routine inspection" (p. 13).

Today this inherited architecture of education places great limits on a system struggling to redefine and transform itself into a more learning-centered operation. The school system, from kindergarten through graduate school, is time-bound, place-bound, efficiency-bound, and role-bound. (See Figure 1-1.) There is almost universal agreement that these bonds must be broken if the schools are to be redesigned and reengineered to place learning first. "Putting learning at the heart of the academic enterprise will mean overhauling the conceptual, procedural, curricular, and other architecture of postsecondary education on most campuses" (Wingspread Group on Higher Education, 1993, p. 14). There are many other factors, of course, that must change if the schools are to be transformed, but the transformation of the structural elements is essential. Changes to the educational structure will provide highly visible testimony to changes in policy, governance, funding, mission, and values.

Time-Bound	Place-Bound
• class hours	• campus
• semester course	• classroom
• school year	• library
Efficiency-Bound	**Role-Bound**
• linear/sequential	• expert
• ADA/FTE*	• lecture
• credit/grade	• sole judge

*Average Daily Attendance (ADA), Full Time Equivalent (FTE)

STRUCTURAL/TRADITIONAL LIMITS ON EDUCATION

FIGURE 1-1

Time-Bound

"Hurry up, the bell's going to ring." Every teacher who has ever lived knows full well the tyranny of time forced on the system by the creation of the "class hour." "Unyielding and relentless, the time available in a uniform six-hour day and a 180-day year is the unacknowledged design flaw in American education. By relying on time as the metric for school organization and curriculum, we have built the learning enterprise on a foundation of sand" (National Education Commission on Time and Learning, 1994, p. 8).

Herding groups of students through one-hour sessions daily in high schools and three days a week in college, flies in the face of everything known about how learning occurs. No one believes that 30 different students arrive at the appointed hour ready to learn in the same way, on the same schedule, and all in rhythm with each other.

Recognizing that the schools suffer from a time-bound mentality, the United States Department of Education appointed a national commission in 1992 to study the issue. Members of the commission concluded "Learning in America is a prisoner of time. For the past 150 years, American public schools have held time constant and let learning vary. . . . Time is learning's warden" (National Education Commission on Time and Learning, 1994, p. 7).

The time framework is particularly pernicious when it is extended to credit hours per course. "The vast majority of college courses have three or four hours of credit. Isn't it a coincidence of cosmic proportions that it takes exactly the same billable unit of work to learn the plays of Shakespeare and the differential calculus? Or maybe the guest has been amputated to fit the bed" (Peters, 1994, p. 23). The National Education Commission on Time and Learning (1994) reports that no matter how complex or simple the school subject—literature, shop, physics, gym, or algebra—the schedule assigns each an impartial national average of 51 minutes per class period, no matter how well or poorly students comprehend the material (p. 7).

The reliance on time as a unit of measure must be changed to reflect mastery of a subject instead of time on task, recognizing what is universally understood: human beings learn at different rates. Students should not have to serve time. Time should serve them.

Place-Bound

School is a place. It is a schoolhouse, a schoolroom, a campus, or a college. Sometimes schooling occurs off-campus, but it is obviously defined in relationship to "campus." Young students go *to school*. Young adults go *off to college*. Incorrigible students are kicked *out of school*. School/college, and the learning that occurs in that context, is over "there." It is external to everything else that goes on in the learner and the society. It is cloistered, private, sacrosanct territory. Speed zones control its outer edges, and liquor stores cannot be built within its perimeters. School is an ivory tower on the hill; it nestles in the gated groves of academe. Its residents do not mix with "townies." School is a place.

School as a place is deeply embedded in the collective unconscious of Americans who made great sacrifices to construct their first college in 1636. This early pattern of school and schoolrooms has been stamped indelibly on each successive generation as the natural order of the world of education. "[T]he design and practices of our childhood schoolrooms tend to be reproduced in most education and training settings, even those that aspire to be nontraditional or 'radically innovative.' Despite decades of experience with models, demonstrations, and experimental programs, the 'New American School' persistently gravitates back to our familiar models of school, classrooms, and teaching" (Perelman, 1992, p. 125).

Schools are as place-bound as they are time-bound, and together these two traditions constitute a formidable barrier to change. Leonard (1992) says, "[T]he conventional classroom . . . is the isolation cell, the lock-up" (p. 28). If the student is to be freed for more powerful learning experiences and if the teacher is to be freed to facilitate that learning in a more powerful way, then the walls must crumble, the boundaries made limitless. "The metaphor of a classroom is a powerful one. This most basic and fundamental unit of academic life—the sanctity of the classroom and the authority of the teacher within it—is about to be turned inside out" (Plater, 1995, p. 27).

If reform efforts are successful, the campus, the classroom, and the library will be turned inside out. A few structural elements will remain to serve the needs of those students who learn well in a place-bound context.

But for the most part, these place-bound constructs will be artifacts, abandoned by the majority of students and faculty who will learn to use the open architecture created by new applications of technology and by new knowledge about how human beings learn.

Efficiency-Bound

The adoption of business values and practices in education, the efficiency model, started in about 1900 and was based on Frederick Taylor's system of "scientific management." The great business barons of the time also had great influence on American culture, especially education, including Andrew Carnegie, John D. Rockefeller, and J.P. Morgan.

In *Habits of the Heart,* Robert Bellah and his associates (1985) noted that "The bureaucratic organization of the business corporation has been the dominant force in this century" (p. 45). President Calvin Coolidge set the stage in 1925 when he said, "The business of America is business."

One example of the influence of American business on American education is William C. Bagley's *Classroom Management,* which was saturated with business terminology. Bagley, a leading educator in the early 1900s, stated that the problem of classroom management was principally a "problem of economy: it seeks to determine in what manner the working unit of the school plan may be made to return the largest dividend upon the material investment of time, energy, and money. From this point of view, classroom management may be looked upon as a 'business' problem" (quoted in Callahan, 1962, pp. 6-7). Bagley's book was so popular among American educators at the time that it was reprinted 30 times.

Of all the traditional architectural elements of schools, critics have been most vocal about the negative influence of the efficiency model. Perelman (1992) wrote, "Education developed in scale and bureaucratic density to mimic the industrial bureaucracy it was styled to serve. Education in its less than two-century-old modern form is an institution of bureaucracy, by bureaucracy, for bureaucracy" (pp. 118-19). Perelman believes that the bureaucratic nature of schools will lead to their ultimate downfall as the society in general moves to less bureaucratic models of social interaction. "[T]he disappearance of education is inevitable, not only because education itself has become a huge socialist bureaucracy, but because it is a bureaucracy designed for a bureaucratic society. Reformers who aim to free schooling from bureaucracy are trying to free an aircraft from air. An aircraft for airless transport is, in fact, a spacecraft not a 'reformed' aircraft but a whole different thing" (p. 119).

Leonard (1992) made much the same observation, "From the beginning it was an administrative expediency, an attempt to adapt the tutor-learner system to mass education, a crude way of handling a large number of learners with a much smaller number of teachers. We were able to get away with it in the past chiefly because our society required few academically or technically educated citizens" (p. 26).

Theodore Sizer (1984) noted a decade ago that the hierarchical bureaucracies of contemporary schools are "paralyzing American education. The structure is getting in the way of children's learning" (p. 206). And Peter Drucker (1992) weighed in with the astute observation that, "Nothing is less productive than to make more efficient what should not be done at all" (p. 29).

The negative effects of the bureaucratic efficiency-bound model can be seen in clear relief in the educational code that regulates the California community college system. For 100 years, state and federal laws and structures have been added piece-meal to regulate the delivery of education to California residents; the cumulative effect is mind-boggling. In the California Education Code alone, there are currently over 1,200 statutes that directly regulate and affect the affairs of community colleges. This ponderous code doesn't even include the 640 regulations adopted by the board of governors, and the hundreds and hundreds of federal statutes and regulations that govern the specific activities of colleges (Nussbaum, 1992).

Vice chancellor and general counsel for the California Community Colleges, Thomas Nussbaum (1992), has observed "The California Community Colleges are micro-managed as much or more than any other higher education institution in the country. The combined effect of the multitude of federal, state, and local laws leaves most of us in the system feeling frustrated, confused, and sometimes resentful. Even worse, as we devote more and more time, energy, and money to complying with these laws, we are losing the capacity to serve the very students who seek educational opportunity in our colleges" (p. 1).

Dianne Van Hook (1995), president of the College of the Canyons in Santa Clarita, California, noted the deleterious effects of this kind of regulation, "Instead of lifting senseless and outdated rules which are costing us millions of dollars to monitor, we initiate 400 to 500 new bills a year, to pass more laws. Most of these laws serve as disincentives as to cooperation, innovation, to economies of scale and to redesigning how and what we do. We have far more reasons why we can't than why we can!" (p. 5). More regulations from the state and federal governments mean more offices and more staff to respond to the new requirements. The bureaucracy grows. The focus on the learner and learning, if ever front and center, fades to the background as leaders struggle to become more efficient as a way to survive. There is no time to pay attention to root causes. All the energy is expended in trimming the branches of a dying tree.

Role-Bound

By the end of the sixth grade a typical student has experienced at least 6 different teachers. With high school graduation, assuming 6 teachers a year for six years, the number climbs to 42. With a bachelor's degree, assuming 124 units divided by three, the number of teachers for a typical student now totals 83. Ten courses for a master's degree, the minimum level of school achievement for the great majority reading this book, bring the total number of teachers experienced by a student to 93, not including a vast array of teachers encountered in preschool, scouts, 4-H, Sunday school, and summer camp.

Therefore, most students with a master's degree have spent 17 or more school years under the tutelage of approximately 93 different teachers. Considering the advanced training of teachers, considering their strong commitments to teaching, considering their great dedication to a calling that provides so little financial reward—and considering the powerful influence of 17 years of concentrated education provided by 93 different teachers in the most crucial years of a student's life—why do students, even after 17 years, know so little? The fault is not in the teachers. The fault is in the system.

Teaching is the one profession that expects so much of its members and requires and pays so little. Teachers are expected to be knowledge experts, assessors, evaluators, managers, data controllers, artists, group facilitators, counselors, information processors, lecturers, problem analysts, problem solvers, coaches, mentors, behavior controllers, and value clarifiers. Their formal education is ill-designed to prepare them for these multiple roles; waiters and airline stewards receive more on-the-job training. New teachers are not inducted into the profession, except sometimes in an internship as part of preteaching exercises. Teachers are thrown into the profession, dumped into the classroom to sink or swim on their own. No wonder they fall back on the models they know too well. They teach as they were taught, repeating the dull catechism that is passed on generation after generation. They remain bound in a role that requires them to be knowledge experts when knowledge is expanding too rapidly for anyone to be an expert, that endorses the lecture method as the primary tool of teaching, and that demands that each teacher serve as sole judge and jury over the lives of the students under his or her tutelage.

In addition to changing the architecture of time and place, educational reform must release teachers from their traditional roles to focus their talents and abilities on the learner as their raison d'être. "Restructuring the role of faculty members will, at first, prove to be a monumental undertaking. All of the incentives seem against doing so—except, in the end, survival" (Guskin, 1994, p. 16). As schools are being reengineered to increase productivity, the prevalent model for faculty restructuring is to increase the number of courses taught or to increase the number of students in a course. Most legislators and many school and college administrators want faculty to do more of what they are currently doing to more students. Another popular solution is to reduce the number of faculty and the number of courses. Once again, these solutions are trimming the branches of a dying tree, although the latter option may extend the life of the institution a bit longer than the former.

The core problem related to teacher role is the implicit assumption that the basic purpose of education is to transmit a society's culture from one generation to the next. This purpose is often listed in community college catalogs as part of the general education objectives, but it tends to be much more pervasive in actual practice. The essential meaning of *instruction*— "knowledge or information imparted"— suggests a model in which the knower, the teacher, delivers knowledge to those who do not know, the students. It is a model that actually worked for Neanderthals. *Pedagogy* is derived from a Greek verb meaning "to lead." And *education* is from the Latin meaning "to lead forth"—both suggest an active leader herding a passive flock.

Perelman (1992) described the basic model of education in vivid terms: "There may be no more common and erroneous stereotype than the image of instruction as injecting knowledge into an empty head. Whether in a typical schoolroom, or a congressional hearing, or a corporate training session, the same one-way process is acted out. In each, the teacher or expert faces the learners, taking on the critical role of 'fountain of knowledge.' The learner plays the 'receiver of wisdom,' passively accepting the intelligence being dispensed, like an empty bowl into which water is poured" (p. 135).

If the dominant role for teachers has been that of a conveyor of information, the conveyor belt has been the lecture. "Lecturing is the overwhelming method of choice for teaching undergraduates in most institutions" (Terenzini and Pascarella, 1994, p. 29). Despite a large body of evidence gathered over many years regarding the inadequacies of the lecture method, the current architecture supports and encourages its continuing and widespread use. One study (Pollio, 1984), for example, found that teachers in the typical classroom spent about 80 percent of their time lecturing to students who were attentive to what was being said about 50 percent of the time.

In a 1992 benchmark study of the education reform movement conducted by the American Association of Medical Colleges, investigators were disappointed that the findings were remarkably similar to those in a 1932 study: "Faculty members are hesitant and insecure about meeting their education responsibilities in a new way and about becoming facilitators of the learning process rather than only transmitters of information to students. . . . Lectures are the quickest and easiest way for faculty to deal with students" (Braslow, p. M6). Lecturing has its value and its place but not as the dominant mode of teaching, especially if the full impact of 93 teachers over a student's school lifetime is to be brought to bear more productively on the development of learners.

On the surface, the system does appear to work. How else can a society educate the masses if not in some linear and sequential order in which a student moves through grade levels, amassing credits that are exchanged for diplomas and degrees as signs of achievement? It is, after all, the most remarkable and largest system of schooling ever created, and it is infused with a sense of democratic values.

The entire structure, however, is built on a shaky foundation—the course grade. Grades are the coin of the realm in the education factory; they undergird all other exchanges. According to Paul Dressel (1983), the course grade is "an inadequate report of an inaccurate judgment by biased and variable judges of the extent to which a student has attained an undefined level of mastery of an unknown proportion of an indefinite material" (p. 1). No amount of efficient accounting of accumulated credits can overcome the messy point at which grades begin.

A NEW WAY OF THINKING

A great deal of reform effort in the past decade has focused on the traditional architecture of education: increasing hours in the school day, increasing the number of days in the school year, decreasing the ratio of students to teachers, delivering regular courses over television and through the Internet, increasing the number of courses required to enter or exit the system, and using computers to manage grading and reporting—efforts that add up to nothing more than trimming the branches of a dying tree.

The 1993 reform report on higher education, An American Imperative, recognized the impotency of these structural reform efforts set in motion by the 1983 report, A Nation at Risk, and called for refocusing reform efforts on core issues. "The nation that responds best and most rapidly to the educational demands of the Age of the Learner will enjoy a commanding international advantage in the pursuit of both domestic tranquillity and economic prosperity. To achieve these goals for our country, we must educate more people and educate them far better. That will require new ways of thinking" (Wingspread Group on Higher Education, p. 7, emphasis added).

At the start of this decade, a new way of thinking about education began to emerge from a great variety of sources, a way of thinking that places learning as the central aim of the education enterprise. This new way of thinking about learning appears to reflect a major transformation in American society. As noted by Drucker (1992) in *Managing for the Future*: "Every few hundred years throughout Western history, a sharp transformation has occurred. In a matter of decades, society altogether rearranges itself—its world view, its basic values, its social and political structures, its arts, its key institutions. Fifty years later a new world exists . . . our age is such a period of transformation" (p. 95).

Drucker (1992) believes that education will play a major role in this transformation and will also be transformed in the process. "[I]t is a safe prediction that in the next 50 years schools and universities will change more and more drastically than they have since they assumed their present form 300 years ago when they organized themselves around the printed book" (p. 97).

For 300 years, the printed book has been an organizing force for education. For 150 years, the needs of an agricultural society followed by an industrial society have been organizing forces in shaping education. It remains to be seen whether or not a new way of thinking that places the learner first will uproot the established system of education and replace it with a new model, especially in only 50 years.

REFERENCES

"A Call to Meeting," *Policy Perspectives*, section A. Philadelphia, PA: Institute for Research on Higher Education, February 1993.

Augenblick, John et al. *How Much Are Schools Spending? A 50-State Examination of Expenditure Patterns over the Last Decade*. Denver, CO: Education Commission of the States, 1993.

Baker, George A., III and Reed, Lester W., Jr. "Creating a World-Class Work Force," *Community College Journal*, April/May 1994.

Bellah, Robert N. et al. *Habits of the Heart*. New York: Harper and Row, 1985.

Braslow, Ken. "Radical Treatment Needed for U.S. Med Schools," *Los Angeles Times*, July 9, 1995.

Callahan, Raymond E. *Education and the Cult of Efficiency*. Chicago: The University of Chicago Press, 1962.

Cross, K. Patricia. *Accent on Learning: Improving Instruction and Reshaping the Curriculum*. San Francisco: Jossey-Bass, 1976.

———. "The Rising Tide of School Reform Reports," *Phi Delta Kappan*, November 1984.

Daggett, Willard R. "Preparing Students for the 1990s and Beyond." Unpublished paper from the International Center for Leadership in Education, January 1992.

Davis, Stan and Botkin, Jim. *The Monster under the Bed: How Business Is Mastering the Opportunity of Knowledge for Profit*. New York: Simon & Schuster, 1994.

Dewey, John and Dewey, Evelyn. *Schools of Tomorrow*. New York: E.P. Dutton and Company, Inc., 1962.

Dressel, Paul. "Grades: One More Tilt at the Windmill." In *Bulletin*, edited by A.W. Chickering. Memphis State University Center for the Study of Higher Education, 1983.

Drucker, Peter T. *Managing for the Future: The 1990s and Beyond.* New York: Penguin, 1992.

———. "The New Society of Organizations," *Harvard Business Review*, September/October 1992.

The Education Commission of the States. *The Progress of Education Reform–Draft*. Denver, CO: Education Commission of the States. November 1995.

Garcia, Joseph. "U.S. Is Far Short of Goals for Education, Report Says," *The Dallas Morning News*, November 9, 1995.

Guskin, Alan E. "Restructuring the Role of Faculty," *Change*, September/October 1994.

Leonard, George. "The End of School," *The Atlantic*, May 1992.

Lovett, Clara M. "Small Steps to Achieve Big Changes," *The Chronicle of Higher Education*, November 24, 1995.

Marchese, Ted. "Getting Smarter about Teaching," *Change*, September/October 1995.

Moe, Roger. Cited in Armajani, Babak et al. *A Model for the Reinvented Higher Education System: State Policy and College Learning.* Denver, CO: Education Commission of the States, January 1994.

The National Commission on Excellence in Education. *A Nation at Risk: The Imperative for Educational Reform*. Washington, D.C.: U.S. Government Printing Office, April 1983.

National Education Commission on Time and Learning. *Prisoners of Time.* Washington, D.C.: U.S. Government Printing Office, April 1994.

Nussbaum, Thomas J. "Too Much Law. . .Too Much Structure: Together We Can Cut the Gordian Knot." Paper delivered at the 1992 Annual Convention of the Community College League of California.

O'Banion, Terry. "School Is Out—Learning Is In," *On the Horizon*, June/July 1995.

"Opinion USA." *USA Today*, August 22, 1995.

Perelman, Lewis J. *School's Out: A Radical New Formula for the Revitalization of America's Educational System*. New York: Avon Books, 1992.

Peters, Roger. "Some Snarks Are Boojums: Accountability and the End(s) of Higher Education," *Change*, November/December 1994.

Pipho, Chris. "States Move Reform Closer to Reality," *Phi Delta Kappan*, December 1986.

Plater, William M. "Future Work: Faculty Time in the Twenty-First Century," *Change*, May/June 1995.

Pollio, H. *What Students Think about and Do in College Lecture Classes*, Teaching-Learning Issues, no. 53, Knoxville, TN: University of Tennessee, Learning Research Center, 1984.

Savio, Mario. Unpublished paper. 1964.

Sizer, Theodore R. *Horace's Compromise: The Dilemma of the American High School*. Boston: Houghton, 1984.

Terenzini, Patrick T. and Pascarella, Ernest T. "Living with Myths: Undergraduate Education in America," *Change*, January/February 1994.

Toffler, Alvin and Toffler, Heidi. "Getting Set for the Coming Millennium," *The Futurist*, March/April 1995.

Van Hook, Diane. "California Community College Funding: A Case for Redesign," *Community College Week*, November 6, 1995.

Weinman, Janice. "The Challenge of Better-Prepared Students," *The Chronicle of Higher Education*, October 27, 1995.

Wingspread Group on Higher Education. *An American Imperative: Higher Expectations for Higher Education*. Racine, WI: The Johnson Foundation, Inc., 1993.

CHAPTER 2

The Student Is First

The early 1990s was a time of realignment for the educational reform movement that followed fast and furious on the heels of the 1983 release of *A Nation at Risk*. There was growing recognition that tweaking the established system of education by adding on new programs or by reorganizing existing programs would not create an educational enterprise capable of addressing the increasingly complex issues developing in American society.

THE VISION TO PLACE LEARNING FIRST

A new vision for the schools began to emerge in this period, a new way of thinking that placed learners first. Many leaders and organizations had held this vision for decades, but in the early 1990s, for the first time in the history of education, "placing learning and the learner first" became the universal cry of commissions, professional organizations, business leaders, policy makers, and increasingly, educators from every sector of the educational landscape.

Organizations and Foundations

The Association of American Colleges and Universities (AACU) has been a champion of liberal learning for decades, encouraging its member institutions and all of higher education to ensure that liberal learning forms the core of undergraduate education. Established in 1915, AACU includes over 700 institutional members. Liberal education has a long and honored tradition in higher education, and the AACU has become a guardian of

that tradition. Leaders at AACU are not easily influenced by new movements and reform cycles because they believe that the core values of liberal
learning provide a sound basis for education even when, and perhaps
especially when, there are major changes in society.

It was testimony, therefore, to the importance of the emerging focus on
learning when the AACU distributed a paper entitled "The Direction of
Educational Change: Putting Learning at the Center" (1995). In this
paper, AACU contrasted the "contemporary ferment and rethinking of
undergraduate education" with earlier academic revolutions and suggested
that liberal education needs updating in terms of "Putting Learning at the
Center." The paper included a listing of the emerging curricular designs
and practices related to general education, suggested there is a value in
integrating learning across the curriculum, and provided a preliminary
analysis of major principles, many of which reflect a new emphasis on
learning.

The Education Commission of the States (ECS) is a nationwide, interstate organization formed in 1965 to help governors, state legislators, and
state education officials develop policies to improve the quality of education at all levels. ECS has played a critical role in keeping the states
informed about reform efforts and has provided a continuing national
forum for state leaders to review and assess the impact of reform. ECS has
noted that "Nationwide, political, civic, and business leaders are pressing
state governments and local school districts for radical alternatives to
current operations" (Armajani et al., 1994).

ECS has actually provided support for one such "radical alternative" in
*A Model for the Reinvented Higher Education System: State Policy and College
Learning* (Armajani et al., 1994). The authors of this model echoed views
held by many other leaders: "[W]idespread evidence suggests a societal
paradigm shift is occurring, yet all too frequently higher education clings to
its nineteenth-century toolbook, intent on repairing the old bureaucratic
system" (Armajani et al., 1994, p. 1). Instead of tweaking the current
system for a little more change, the authors proposed an "enterprise model"
in which the focus is on the customer, there is accountability for outcomes,
and there are positive assumptions about student and employee motivation. The focus is on the learner, here referred to as the customer because
as the authors explained, "[W]e prefer and use the word *customer* because
we believe it is an important reminder that higher education is in business
to serve others, not to perpetuate itself or to make self-interested choices"
(Armajani et al., 1994, p. 2). In the enterprise model, the student is clearly
first.

In late 1995, ECS released a special progress report on education reform
and concluded "The difference between the expanding skill needs of the

future and the slow, uneven progress of student achievement is creating a performance gap that will widen over time if solutions are not found" (p. 1). It was noted that a majority of states are pursuing the implementation of new standards and that the performance of students is slowly improving but that the public believes the schools are getting worse, not better. In studies cited in the report, it is clear that progress occurs when schools are involved in institutionwide efforts that place the learner at the center of the enterprise. When partial changes are made, however—adding on a new program here or revising a practice there—high-quality schools are not the result. "While [the piecemeal implementation of reforms] may lead to progress, it will not be of the same magnitude as a systemic strategy focused on student learning" (The Education Commission of the States, p. 29).

The Pew Charitable Trusts has played a key role in assisting institutions of higher education to respond to changing times. Through the Higher Education Roundtables (sponsored by Pew), representatives from colleges and universities committed to reform have been meeting over several years to develop strategies for reform. The reform efforts at Maricopa Community Colleges (see chapter 9) were initiated with assistance from the roundtables.

The roundtables began with a proposition that "[C]olleges and universities have become less relevant to society precisely because they have yet to understand new demands being placed on them" ("To Dance with Change," 1994, p. 1A). "What is being demanded is not just greater efficiency but a willingness to consider new ways of doing business in order to better serve customers" ("A Call to Meeting," 1993, p. 5A).

Here again, the call is for a major change in education that places learning and the learner first. The reformers meeting in the roundtables have not been shy about what is needed. They have called for outsourcing some instruction to gain access to pedagogies and technology not available in the institution. They have recommended using a wider range of "learning products" to help students master basic competencies. They have urged a reduction in the number of courses offered. They have proposed that departments, as the basic building blocks of academic institutions, become accountable for the quality of instruction and related services and that individual faculty compensation be tied to the department's collective performance. And finally, these reformers advocate, in no uncertain terms, that the size of the faculty must be reduced so that salaries and benefits amount to approximately 50 percent of educational and general funds, rather than the 80 percent common to most institutions of higher education. The overall goals, though yet to be implemented, are clear: "make institutions less labor-intensive; simplify the curriculum; transform the departments into instructional collectives" ("A Call to Meeting," 1993, p.

11A). This reform actually has teeth, and interestingly enough, it has emerged from educators themselves. The underlying goal is to realign institutions of higher education to place the student first.

The Autodesk Foundation, incorporated in 1991, was created by Autodesk, Inc., the world's leading supplier of design automation software and the fifth-largest PC software company in the world. The primary purpose of the Autodesk Foundation is to design and develop new models for education. The foundation was established just in time to catch the current wave of reform in American education and has done so by reintroducing some of the views of John Dewey and the Progressive Education Movement, especially the notion that people "learn by doing."

Project-Based Learning (PBL) is the umbrella under which the Autodesk Foundation unfurls its ideas for improving education. To date, the program has involved a small number of middle schools in a national network, but many more schools are becoming partners in these efforts to place learning and learners first. The definition of PBL reflects a strong emphasis on learning. Project-Based Learning involves:

- Learning structures that tap students' inherent drive to learn, and their inherent capability to do important work.
- Learning experiences that engage students in complex, real-world projects through which they develop and utilize new skills and knowledge.
- Learning in which the ultimate results are not predetermined or fully predictable.
- Learning that enables students to draw from many disciplines in order to solve problems.
- Learning that develops students' ability to make decisions related to the allocation of valuable resources as with time, materials, and facilities (Oakey, 1995).

In an extensive assessment of PBL in four schools that had been using the approach for two years, teachers provided some special insights about the centrality of learning:

- The learning needs to go out of my hands into the kid's—they take charge, control, describe, and drive their learning.
- Students learn more than you expect them to learn.
- I am constantly learning from my mistakes—what works and what doesn't.
- Letting go of the idea that I have to do it all, and giving more to the kids is the main thing I have learned.

- If you organize the learning environment so the student is the problem solver, planner, manager, students are motivated and take responsibility for learning (Oakey, 1995, p. 15).

By undertaking this process, the teachers had also become learners, learning more about how students learn and how they can better facilitate learning.

Project-Based Learning is a powerful approach to improved learning that is effective in the middle schools. It could also be effective in colleges and universities and is reflected, in part, in "learning communities" and "collaborative learning" models that are already well established in some community colleges. The Autodesk Foundation is playing a major role in revising an earlier vision of learner-centered education and is updating it as an important element in reform efforts.

The Western Governor's Association (WGA)—an independent, nonpartisan organization of governors from 18 western states—is taking a very active position in addressing educational issues. The association is creating its own *Virtual University*. In February 1996, Simon and Schuster, the world's largest educational publisher, made a major grant to the WGA to design the technology-based institution. Among other goals, the Virtual University will 1) provide a means for learners to acquire an education at home or on the job; 2) shift the focus of education to the actual competence of students and away from "seat time" and similar measures of instructional activity; and 3) create high performance standards that are widely accepted.

Individual governors, commenting on this unprecedented action, reflected the new way of thinking emerging across the country that places the needs of the learner first and that rejects the constraints that have bound education in the past. The chair of the Western Governor's Association, Ben Nelson of Nebraska, said, "As the document spells out, the barriers of time and place are eroding, and opportunities to learn are everywhere" (Media Advisory, 1996, p. 1). Utah governor, Mike Leavitt, observed, "There was a time when if you wanted a college education you went to a college campus because that's where the professors and information were, but technology is changing all that. Education no longer has to be bound by place. In the Knowledge Age, the knowledge will go where the people are" (Media Advisory, p. 1). The 18 governors have unanimously supported the creation of the Virtual University, and when their resources are matched with those of Simon and Schuster, the outcomes are likely to be substantive and long-range. Placing the learner first is rapidly becoming a reality as governors and other leaders prepare for the twenty-first century.

Commissions and Task Forces

In addition to statements and programs supported by prestigious organizations and foundations, a number of special commissions and task forces have been created since 1990 which place great emphasis on the importance of the learner and the improvement and expansion of learning processes. The Wingspread Group on Higher Education (1993) created a self-assessment checklist for institutions of higher education to determine if they were "putting student learning first" and "creating a nation of learners" (pp. 30-31). The goal of the Wingspread Group is to transform American education into "a seamless system that can produce and support a nation of learners, providing access to educational services for learners as they need them, when they need them and wherever they need them" (p.19).

While the Wingspread Group focuses on higher education, the Committee for Economic Development (CED) focuses on elementary and secondary education; their interests and their message, however, are the same: the student is first. The goal of this private, nonpartisan, research and educational organization is to study and seek solutions to pressing social and economic issues that most affect the long-term health of the nation's economy. Its 250 trustees are mostly top business executives and presidents of major universities.

Concerned that the schools are being asked to take on too much responsibility for the nation's social ills and cultural conflicts, the CED issued a key report entitled *Putting Learning First: Governing and Managing the Schools for High Achievement* (1994). Addressed primarily to the local leaders who govern and manage the schools, the report strongly recommended that these leaders should "First and above all state clearly that learning is the fundamental goal of schools" (Committee for Economic Development, p. 3).

This report was not related to the current reform movement. It was an attempt to extricate the schools from the tangle of social service functions that have been added to schools in recent years. In calling for schools to return to their basic mission of learning, however, the report reaffirmed the calls of other groups and agencies to place the student first.

The American Council on Education (ACE) appointed a task force on distance learning that issued its report in May 1996. *Guiding Principles for Distance Learning in a Learning Society* is bursting with the language of "learners and learning providers," an example foreshadowing future documents that are likely to intensify a focus on learning. The principles developed in the ACE document on distance learning strongly affirm the new emphasis on placing learning first:

- We are becoming a society in which continuous learning is central to effective participation as citizens and wage-earners (p. 2).
- The diversity of learners, learning needs, learning contexts, and modes of learning must be recognized if the learning activities are to achieve their goals (p. 3).
- The learning experience is organized over the time, place, and pace of instruction (p. 4).
- The development of a learning society may require significant changes in the roles, responsibilities, and activities of provider organizations and personnel as well as of the learners themselves (p 4).

Another key group underscoring the new value placed on learning is The National Policy Board on Higher Education Institutional Accreditation (NPB). Established in 1993 by the leaders of the nine regional accrediting associations and seven higher education associations to consider major problems facing accreditation, the NPB recognized that accreditation must extend beyond evaluating resources, processes, governance, institutional objectives, and institutional missions. For accreditation to be effective in the future, uniform eligibility criteria and meaningful course standards common to all institutions must be established. Most importantly, "To elevate the importance of student learning . . . . core standards should emphasize student learning" (*Independence, Accreditation, and the Public Interest*, 1994, p. 17).

Accreditation has been a powerful force in American education, and if it continues, as is likely, it will play a key role in requiring all educational institutions to place more emphasis on learning. If new core standards emphasizing student learning are adopted by accrediting associations, institutions will begin to place the student first on a more careful and consistent basis.

Community College Leaders in the Trenches

The foregoing proclamations are not unusual. All major movements and reforms are accompanied by reports and spokespersons claiming the value of their particular perspective. What is unusual about the current reform effort is the diversity of groups and the common view they hold regarding the centrality of the learner. What is more unusual is the extent to which this view has captured the attention of one particular sector of higher education, the community college.

In the last five years, there has been a groundswell of interest in the learner from community college presidents, trustees, faculty, researchers, and state policy makers. Between the lines, community colleges have always been student-centered institutions; the current reform efforts have helped flush out their student-centered values, which now appear in their opening statements, their central theses, and their concluding arguments. Myran, Zeiss, and Howdyshell (1995) provided an eloquent framework for this more visible perspective on the centrality of learning:

> There is something magical about the year 2000. We hear, as you do, the siren call of new beginnings and new possibilities. We feel we are entering a period of profound and fundamental change for community colleges, the most sweeping period since the 1960s. Then, we transformed campus-based colleges into community-based colleges; today we are becoming learner-based colleges. As we enter the new century, we will combine the forces of learner-based and community-based education to shape a powerful new definition of the community college. (p. i)

Among the earliest advocates of the new emphasis on learning are George Boggs and Robert Barr of Palomar College in California. They have been leaders in transforming their own institution and in advocating change through numerous speeches to community college groups across the nation. Much of their work contrasts the teaching paradigm with the learning paradigm. Boggs (1993) noted, "The new paradigm says that community colleges are learning, not teaching, institutions. The mission is student learning. The most important people in the institution are the learners. Everyone else is there to facilitate and support student learning" (p. 2). Barr and Tagg (1995) made much the same point: "In the Instruction Paradigm, the mission of the college is to provide instruction, to teach. . . . In the Learning Paradigm the mission of the college is to produce learning" (p. 15).

Many other community college leaders have also articulated the need to place a new emphasis on learning. A trustee at the San Diego Community College District, Fred Colby (1995), has noted the difficult challenges facing community colleges and remarked, "To meet the challenge, we must develop new instructional methodologies which focus on learning, not teaching, and make use of new technologies at every level of education" (p.4). Larry Toy (1995), a community college faculty member who has been the president of the Faculty Association of California Community Colleges and the president of the California Community College Board of Governors, recently investigated reform efforts in the public schools and concluded, "[I]t has been the most profound experience in my 27-year professional teaching career. It has caused me to fundamentally question what I do and how I do it. To question what is teaching and what is learning" (p.1).

Many of these individual perceptions and a number of updated documents have coalesced into a basic agenda for the California Community Colleges—*The New Basic Agenda: Policy Directions for Student Success* (1995). This agenda is the major policy-setting document of the Board of Governors of the State of California. It is designed to provide direction to the chancellor and staff of individual colleges in the areas of legislation, budget, and work plans. This key document will influence the 107 community colleges in California for some time in the future, and the focus on student learning is clear and unequivocal:

> Student learning is essential to the social and economic development of multicultural California. Consequently, the Board of Governors' policy directions for the community college are based on improving student learning. To focus on successful learning, the Board proposes that *The New Basic Agenda* include ways for colleges to (a) help all students determine their educational needs; (b) adapt to the rapidly changing demographic, economic, and social conditions of California so that the educational services colleges provide are relevant and timely; and (c) manage and deliver these services, and monitor their results in the most effective way possible. (p. 2)

This sampling of perspectives from organizations, foundations, commissions, task forces, and individual community college leaders—all recorded in the last five years—is confirmation that the learner and the learning process have emerged more clearly than ever as the key priorities of education. These priorities have always been assumed; now they are articulated as the most visible cornerstone of reform efforts in policy, program, and practice.

Armed with a potent perspective on the student as central to the educational process and supported by critics, researchers, and policy makers, the community college appears well-positioned to lead the revolution to create a new kind of learning enterprise. In contrast to other institutions of higher education, the community college has always taken great pride in its commitment to teaching as its highest value. Community college faculty and administrators take great pride in describing the institution whose values and culture they champion as "the teaching college." At one time or another most community college advocates have compared their institution with the university by declaring their commitment to teaching over research. To drive the point home, community college advocates often note the university's propensity to use graduate students to staff large lecture sessions, while they, more committed to quality teaching, make teaching the priority of professional staff.

The community college literature, not unexpectedly, is full of references to the importance placed on teaching in the community college. One of the most significant documents ever written on the community college, *Building Communities* (1988), the Report of the Commission on the Future of Community Colleges, echoed this view over and over: "Building communities through dedicated teaching is the vision and the inspiration of this report"(p. 8). "Quality instruction should be the hallmark of the movement" (p.25). "The community college should be the nation's premier teaching institution"(p. 25).

This strong emphasis on teaching in the community college has led some reformers, including this author in several earlier articles, to cast "the teaching college" as an obstacle to transforming community colleges into more learning-centered institutions. But the interest in teaching is really a reflection of the interest in learning. In the final analysis, the great majority of community college faculty believe that "The purpose of teaching is to help students make passionate connections to learning" (O'Banion, 1994, p. vii).

The student has always been the first priority in the community college, and the current interest in learning is the next evolutionary step in the continuing quest for quality education. Reform efforts may be signals of dissatisfaction with current practice and progress, but they are also natural responses to new information, new needs, and new opportunities. The current reform efforts have sharpened the focus on learning and have created an opportunity for substantive institutional change—change that will always be met with considerable resistance.

FORCES OF RESISTANCE

Resistance to change is a hallmark of higher education. It has been said that changing a college is a lot like moving a cemetery—you don't get a lot of help from the residents. In this case the residents include the education bureaucrats, the faculty, the administrators, the students, and the parents—all stakeholders in the status quo.

Education Bureaucrats

As the education enterprise grew into a multibillion dollar business, a complex structure developed to support and manage that business. There are tens of thousands of specialized educational personnel at the federal, regional, state, and county level managing and coordinating educational programs and practices. Each specialist has a vested interest in maintaining his or her territory, and any suggestion of change is a threat to the established order.

Federal and state programs are difficult to dismantle, as every newly elected politician soon learns. The California education system is a prime example. In January 1995, Governor Pete Wilson announced that he would work to abolish the California Education Code—7,745 pages of rules and regulations—and replace it with a set of rules based on student performance. Later that same year, California's superintendent of public instruction, Delaine Eastin, proposed that schools be granted greater flexibility in exchange for real accountability for boosting student achievement. To date no changes have been made, and the bureaucracy is still in place.

To understand why such sweeping changes are so hard to make, it helps to examine the whole system. The governor and legislature enact the laws; they are interpreted and enforced by an appointed state board that overseas an elected superintendent who manages a state department of education. The laws are implemented by a superintendent of schools and often a board of education in each of California's 58 counties. Within the counties are 1,002 school districts, each with a superintendent and an elected board. As the president of the Los Angeles Board of Education has said, "The mountain of control, distrust, and micromanagement stifles the very innovation we now need to help improve our schools. California's system creates incentives based on compliance with rules rather than on the actual academic achievement of students" (Slavkin, 1995, p. M4).

The bureaucracy of education is what perpetuates the time-bound, place-bound, efficiency-bound, and role-bound architecture reviewed in chapter 1. If learning is to become the primary focus of restructuring educational systems, the educational personnel who maintain the bureaucracy will have to be enlisted or they will have to be bypassed or eliminated. Some critics such as Perelman and Leonard would eliminate them. Some new forms of distance education would bypass them. The charter school movement would enlist them. In any case, these educational specialists constitute a formidable force for resisting any movement toward a new paradigm of education that places learning first.

The Faculty

In most institutions of education, and especially in community colleges, there are small groups of maverick faculty who will try any new idea—the early adopters of innovations. But the faculty as a whole can be highly resistant to change. Their allegiance to the discipline guilds and their unification under the protective mantle of academic freedom are twin pillars of conservatism fortified against change. Faculty, first "schooled" as students then inducted into a system in which they become the gatekeepers of educational tradition, do not embrace alternative ideas with enthusiasm, despite their own deep cynicism about the current system.

Virginia has been "restructuring" its system of higher education for the last several years on order of the state legislature. At the University of Virginia, there have been a number of changes in administrative structures but few in academic affairs. Polly McClure, the university's vice president for information technology said, "The culture here is small classes, with regular faculty teaching undergraduates. That's very nice and it's very expensive, but faculty members don't want to hear about reaching more students through technology. Their view is 'That's what we do here, and if students don't want that, let them go someplace else'" (Trombley, 1995, p. 1).

This same disregard for what students want is echoed in a statement by Washington, D.C., teachers' union president, Barbara Bullock, "It doesn't matter what students say. We still have rights" (Hancock and Brant, 1995, p. 81). The statement was made in response to students who were protesting the union's reversal in a change in schedule enthusiastically endorsed by most teachers, administrators, and students. Two teachers complained that the new schedule sliced a few minutes from their contractually mandated free planning periods, and the school was forced to follow the rule book. If the National Education Association with 22 million members and the American Federation of Teachers with 885,000 members were to merge, as some have predicted, they would become the largest single labor union in the world. The authors of a *Newsweek* article on the power of teacher unions noted, "[T]here are times when education reform is only as innovative as the union contract allows"(Hancock and Brant, 1995, p. 81). Teacher unions can certainly mobilize organized resistance to any changes in education, including those designed to place learning first.

The unions provide a visible structure for the communication of resistance to change, but the more invidious resistance is often hidden in the values and perceptions of individual faculty members. Donald Berz, executive vice president of Chaffey College in California, has tapped into these individual forces of resistance and made them visible. On September 11, 1995, Berz launched a project to institutionalize a "learner-centered" environment at Chaffey and appointed an institutionwide task force charged with "Advancing the 'focus of learning' or 'placing learning first' agenda" (p.1). He encouraged faculty members to respond to the creation of the task force by sharing their views in writing.

A number of the faculty rejected the need for the task force, claiming they had always placed learning first:

- As faculty we always have been, and continue to be, primarily focused on learning. It is an insult to suggest otherwise.
- To suggest we need too *create* a learner-centered environment is to suggest that we, the faculty, aren't centered on learning needs.

- We are already doing many if not most of what the literature purports we are not doing.
- My classroom is a "learning environment."

Others viewed the new project as an administrative ploy designed to reduce costs:

- This whole agenda smacks of budget reductions or ways in which administration can justify their not hiring more faculty.
- The emphasis on technology is an attempt to displace, reduce, or downgrade the role of the faculty.
- The focus on the learning agenda is an undertaking to ask faculty to do more with less.

Still others defended the role of teaching and teachers in traditional terms:

- You cannot have quality learning without quality teaching.
- Students cannot learn without the teacher.
- I like being the sage on stage and students want to hear me lecture.
- You cannot produce learning without providing instruction.
- The knowledge I provide is not necessarily otherwise available.

Several faculty members questioned whether or not there was evidence the old way was wrong and the new better:

- Who is to say what we are doing and the way we are doing it is not working?
- Not all that we do in terms of affecting learning outcomes is measurable.
- What evidence exists that students learn any better via distance learning on their own, or by other means than that which comes from motivation, inspiration, and departing of knowledge through a teacher? (Berz, 1995)

These viewpoints are shared by pockets of faculty in almost all community colleges, and probably in almost all educational institutions. Given the opportunity in faculty meetings or in sessions with outside speakers, most of these viewpoints will be aired if the topic under discussion has anything to do with change. The views are often presented by the most articulate faculty members and are usually applauded by large numbers of faculty. In this way the views of a small group can become the views of "the faculty," and a kind of collective resistance to change emerges to protect the status quo.

There are certainly valid positions stated in some of the views of faculty resisters, and they must be addressed by leaders, especially faculty leaders.

The extent and validity of the resistance will depend on the culture of the institution, and in some cases substantive change will not be possible.

The Administration and Support Staff

Administrators, expected to be leaders, are not as often criticized for resistance to change as the faculty. They are not as given to joining unions where a collective voice of resistance can be made visible, and they can't speak out in faculty meetings against change lest they be viewed as toadying up to the faculty. Nevertheless, many administrators are as resistant to change as the faculty. Berz (1990) remarked on this issue in his work at Chaffey: "I can easily understand the inherent conservatism of the faculty, but what is surprising at Chaffey is the resistance to change exhibited by managers whose styles manifest authoritarian or otherwise undemocratic practices, and those who focus on the rule or procedure and the bureaucratic orientation of 'doing business'" (p.2).

Upon further analysis, however, it is easy to see why administrators may be resistant to change. Administrators also have territories to protect, and because they are almost always directly involved in creating the structures—the rules and procedures—related to their "span of control," they are not comfortable changing their architecture. Moreover, suggested changes hint at something wrong with how business has been conducted.

Even administrators who pursue change are not particularly well-equipped to become the risk takers they are urged to become: most want to be loved by the faculty, many do not have the security of tenure, and few can find sanctuary in the discipline guild. Administrative survival is fragile compared to that of faculty; it is a wonder that administrators can muster any courage to lead, especially to lead an institution toward a new learning paradigm.

First-line administrators in community colleges—department and division heads who interact directly with faculty—are probably more aware than any other group of administrators of the need for change because of their close-up view of the teaching and learning process. At the same time, they are probably the most important group of administrators needed to bring about change. Unfortunately, they occupy a particularly stressful position trying to negotiate between the faculty and administration, a band in which they can find no safe haven or affiliate group. Negotiating the selection of textbooks and constructing the class schedule is often challenge enough for the brave souls who carry one of the major burdens in an educational organization. Some colleges have abandoned all hope for leadership from their front-line administrators and have turned the management over to faculty who occupy the post on a rotating basis and who are expected to provide only the minimal necessities of coordination.

Presidents also are not always the most reliable leaders when it comes to making changes. In the Virginia reform efforts cited earlier in this chapter, University of Virginia President John T. Casteen III tried to organize the other Virginia college and university presidents to oppose the restructuring efforts. That strategy failed when the governor and legislature threatened budget cuts, but Casteen may prevail in the long run. Efforts to restructure at the University of Virginia have been combined with a self-study for a ten-year reaccreditation coordinated by 67 committees with 856 members. This approach will almost certainly guarantee that no disruptive change comes to the University of Virginia.

As in other institutions of higher education, community college presidents are often selected for their abilities to secure funds, work with the legislature, or represent the college to the community. Many community college presidents are challenged when there are buildings to be constructed, programs to be developed, and partnerships to be forged. Restructuring an institution to place learning first is a challenge many community college presidents are not prepared to take on, either because they do not feel academically prepared for the task and/or because they know such change is too difficult and too time consuming when weighed against the value of the long-range outcomes.

The support staff—custodians, secretaries, bookstore clerks, technicians—who operate key components of the school's infrastructure can also be resistant to change. While the philosophies of Total Quality Management and "learning organizations" subscribe to flattened organizations that empower all stakeholders, including support staff, these staff do not always gravitate to new power easily. Placing learning first may change the roles of support staff (as is recommended in chapter 3), making them more visible partners with the professional staff. In a new learning paradigm, support staff will be called upon to help manage and coordinate learning activities as faculty are freed to take on new roles as learning facilitators. While some will resonate to opportunities to take on new roles, many will feel unprepared to take on new assignments and will need encouragement, training, and recognition to overcome the natural resistance that will emerge.

Students and Parents

The greatest resistance to placing learning first may come from students and their parents. Parents often indulge in a nostalgic yearning for the "good old days" when schools taught basics, and they are often vocal about a "return to the basics." Parents also know what school means as do students who have recently experienced at least 12 years of schooling. School means attending classes on time, studying for the exam, doing your homework, taking the tests, and being awarded the As. Students who have figured out the system of schooling and who excel in this system certainly do not want it changed.

If learning is placed first, the role of the student will change from a passive receptor to an active participant. At each step of the educational enterprise, from the first point of engagement to graduation, students will be active learners, fully responsible for their own choices and for their own activities—a far cry from the current system. The current system has created a nation of passive learners who will resist with all the might of their passivity any changes that suggest more active behavior—and they will be supported by vocal parents.

IMPERATIVES FOR CHANGE

Despite admittedly strong forces of resistance lined up to support colleges and universities as we know them, there are equally or more powerful imperatives insisting that change is inevitable. Even though the model for higher education for most students, parents, and educators remains Harvard or a similar institution, strong economic, technological, and demographic forces for fundamental restructuring of higher education are at work in the land. These forces converge to make one key demand on education: more learning for more students at lower cost.

Economic Pressures

Some economists and economic historians point to the crumbling of the Berlin Wall and the Iron Curtain as yet another demonstration of the "economic imperative," the irresistible power of economic forces to ultimately overcome forces resistant to change. If the economic failure of the Communist Eastern Bloc could not be countered by one of the most powerful authoritarian and military regimes in the history of the world, why should we expect that the higher education establishment will be able to resist the economic forces that demand fundamental change in the system? The economic pressures pushing for change in higher education cannot be ignored, as Carol Twigg and Don Doucette (1992) noted: "There is universal agreement among all sectors of American society that improving education and training is essential if the United States is to remain competitive in the world economy" (p. 1).

Kay McClenney and James Mingle (1992) argued that the 1990s have seen the confluence of three salient factors: high expectations for the future, growing public distrust for institutions, and concern about the future. "The dilemma is that the challenges of meeting the expectations of society are coming at a time when the costs are on the rise and traditional sources of support—state tax dollars—are shrinking" (p. 1).

While the economies of most states have improved since the recession during which McClenney and Mingle wrote, the basic facts have not changed: business and political leaders expect higher education, increasingly community colleges, to provide the training and retraining that will be required for nearly all Americans if they are to compete in a global economy and maintain standards of living. The problem is that these same business and political leaders believe that colleges and universities have been treated well with state appropriations for decades, and they are demanding better results without corresponding increases in resources. "The good news is that community colleges are coming into their own as respected players in the educational system and the economic infrastructure. The bad news is that they will not be able to meet the demands that society continues to make upon them unless they develop new ways to serve new students—with no new resources" (Doucette, 1992, p. 16).

Adding to the conclusion that the current model of higher education has become economically unsustainable is the growing public dismay over spiraling tuition costs. With the operating costs of colleges and universities rising rapidly and public support steady or declining, users have been asked to pay an increasing share of the costs. These factors have led to tuitions amounting to $1,000 per week in many private colleges and universities ("Those Scary College Costs," April 1996) and tuition increases of 50-100 percent in many public universities since the beginning of the decade. Unfortunately, these tuition increases have taken place in a changing economy that has created ever greater uncertainty in the job market for college graduates. "One of the most serious problems facing the country is the seemingly inexorable rise in the cost of education, with no apparent increase in benefits. In colleges and universities, in particular, the trend is for students to be paying more and receiving less" (Twigg and Doucette, 1992, p. 1).

Economic pressures are forcing a fundamental reconsideration of the model for higher education, and fundamental—not incremental—change is inevitable.

> The current model of higher education will inevitably change because it is economically unsustainable. . . . The key to success is the transformation of the teaching and learning process from one that is teacher-centered to one that is learner-centered, to transform the paradigm of the "community of scholars" to one that is defined by "communities of learners." Still, shifting from a system of higher education in which the learner replaces the faculty member at the center is equivalent to replacing the earth in the center of the Ptolemaic universe with the sun of the Copernican. (Twigg and Doucette, 1992, p.2)

Technological and Competitive Pressures

Companion to the economic forces pushing change in higher education are equally compelling technological and competitive forces. The most direct pressure placed upon higher education to integrate information technology in its curriculum and instructional practices comes from business and industry. Technology has been so thoroughly infused into the world of work for which colleges and universities prepare their students, and from which many now draw a significant proportion of their enrollments, that institutions of higher education, most specifically community colleges, have no choice but to use and upgrade regularly the technology they use to reflect new developments and applications in the workplace.

Another aspect of the current technological revolution that has already thoroughly transformed corporate America is the expansion of telecommunications to become a dominant player in how business is transacted. With the continued refinement of video technologies and the growth of the telecommunications infrastructure, including the Internet, most experts agree it is only a matter of time before commercial video-on-demand technologies are available to most businesses and private homes. The delivery of education and training directly to consumers will place enormous competitive pressures on colleges and universities.

It is fashionable to dismiss such scenarios by pointing to the dreadful "talking head" lectures provided by Mind Extension University during the past decade as proof of the bankruptcy of distance education by the home television model. It is foolhardy, however, to believe that these pressures will not be very real when Disney and Microsoft team up with higher education experts to develop high quality and accredited courses and programs for the higher education market. Stories of business meetings at which Bill Gates and Michael Eisner trade barbs about which one of the two will dominate the education and training market (not if) are too prophetic to be ignored.

The fact is that a certain portion of the market for higher education and postsecondary education and training will embrace video-on-demand and will compete directly with more traditional providers stuck in time-bound and place-bound delivery models. Community colleges and other nonselective colleges and universities may be most directly affected, especially as their roles shift increasingly to education and training for older adults and workers.

The availability of new technology, however, doesn't necessarily mean employing it will automatically solve all of an institution's problems. Those universities with inflated notions of lucrative markets for the graduate courses they hope to export via the Internet to users all over the world should reconsider whether they have the resources to compete with Disney,

Microsoft, or a partnership venture of Time-Warner and MIT. On the other hand, community colleges may have a perfect niche in a higher education world defined by video-on-demand technology: providers of support services including assessment, advising, tutoring, remediation, and counseling to learners in their service areas who have access to information from multiple sources.

Eli Noam, professor of finance and economics in the Graduate School of Business at Columbia University, tackled this convergence of economic and technological trends in his analysis of their effect on the university in his *Science* article, "Electronics and the Dim Future of the University." He argued, "Change the technology and economics, and the institutions must change eventually" (Noam, 1995, p. 247). Noam analyzed the principal functions of the university to be three: 1) the creation and validation of new knowledge, 2) the preservation of knowledge and information, and 3) transmission of this knowledge to others, that is, teaching. His assessment of the prospects for the current university model, however, are not encouraging to its supporters: "Thus, while new communications technologies are likely to strengthen research, they will also weaken the traditional major institutions of learning, the universities. Instead of prospering with the new tools, many traditional functions of the universities will be superseded, their financial base eroded, their technology replaced, and their role in intellectual inquiry reduced" (Noam, 1995, p. 247).

Noam conceded that many of his colleagues believe that the failed promises of previous technologies to effect change in the university will be repeated with the latest set of technologies, but he argued that this time the forces are different: "[T]he fundamental forces at work cannot be ignored. They are the consequence of a reversal in the historic direction of information flow. In the past, people came to the information, which was stored at the university. In the future, the information will come to the people, wherever they are" (Noam, 1995, p. 249).

Demographic Pressures

Finally, there are immutable demographic forces at work that call for fundamental change in the current higher educational model. One of these forces is the next generation of students. The so-called Nintendo generation is at the door, and these students are accustomed to not only eye-catching visuals, but also interactive toys, games, and instructional materials. Many have routine access to personal computers and the Internet. Perhaps even more significant, these students are the products of schools that have been stressing critical thinking, collaborative problem solving, and consumerism as part of the last wave of educational reforms. While technology has not penetrated the nation's elementary schools to any consistent degree, active learning, collaborative learning, brain-based research, and applied academics have. As the current generation of elementary students moves into higher education, colleges and universities will find a generation that will simply not put up with traditional lecture formats and professors who teach in the "great person" tradition. Rather, the next generation of students will be demanding consumers who expect active engagement in the learning process, and the number of these students (18- to 24-year-olds) will increase by 15 percent in the next ten years.

The second major demographic trend of significance for higher education is one that is increasingly evident—the return of older adults and workers with aspirations to improve their employment prospects, change careers, and update job skills in a fast-changing and scary workplace. Although the absolute number of these 25- to 34-year-old students will decline, their impact on the system of higher education, especially on community colleges, will only increase. And like their younger counterparts, these adult consumers demand results and are impatient with unresponsive organizations. A conversation with any dean in any college in this country will confirm the increasingly demanding nature of the current generation of students—who insist on methodologies that meet their needs, who insist on accountability from their professors, and who want their money back when they get neither. The days of in loco parentis and passive students to be tamed and socialized by a paternalistic system of instruction and governance are over.

CONCLUSION

The education bureaucrats, the faculty, the administrators and support staff, and the students and their parents all have a stake in maintaining the current architecture of education. Collectively, these groups present a formidable obstacle for the reformers who are committed to making learning and the learner the central focus of the educational enterprise. Leaders who plan to engage their institutions in reform efforts to place learning first will have to understand and address the concerns of each of these key groups and involve their representatives as active participants in all restructuring plans and programs. Whether they will participate as strong defendants of the status quo or as curious onlookers of change initiatives depends, in part, on the quality of overall leadership of the reform efforts and, in part, on the validity and attraction of the philosophy and practices associated with more learning-centered approaches.

Arrayed against these constituents, however, will be the leaders of business and industry, large and small, who insist on and will only support a system of higher education that produces students with the kinds of skills their companies need to remain competitive in a global economy. In the business roundtables, they will insist not only on the integration of applied academics but also on the assessment of student skills and learning that are the intended outcomes of a college education. They are the scions of the business and industry interest groups that so profoundly influence public support for higher education at both the state and local levels, and they are the representatives of the irresistible economic and technological pressures that are forcing fundamental changes in higher education. It is the business leaders of this country who will confront the academy and prevail. While hardly educators, they are becoming the most powerful advocates of learning. Unfortunately, their solutions are often simple minded and business based. If educators are not to settle for these simple solutions, they must not be so resistant to change and must apply their efforts to create a system of education that works better than the present one. Making learning the central focus for all activity is a very promising direction.

REFERENCES

American Council on Education. *Guiding Principles for Distance Learning in a Learning Society.* Washington, D.C.: The American Council on Education, May 1996.

Armajani, Babak et al. *A Model for the Reinvented Higher Education System: State Policy and College Learning.* Denver, CO: Education Commission of the States, January 1994.

Barr, Robert B. and Tagg, John. "A New Paradigm for Undergraduate Education," *Change,* November/December 1995.

Berz, Donald. "The Challenge of Change: The Leadership Challenge at Chaffey." Unpublished paper, 1990.

————. "Focus on Learning Task Force." Unpublished paper, September 11, 1995.

Boggs, George R. "Community Colleges and the New Paradigm," *Celebrations.* Austin, TX: National Institute for Staff and Organizational Development, September 1993.

"A Call to Meeting," *Policy Perspectives,* section A. Philadelphia, PA: Institute for Research on Higher Education, February 1993.

Colby, Fred. "Breaking Down the Walls in Education," *Community College Week,* August 28, 1995.

Commission on the Future of Community Colleges. *Building Communities: A Vision for a New Century,* Washington, D.C.: American Association of Community Colleges, 1988.

Committee for Economic Development. *Putting Learning First: Governing and Managing the Schools for High Achievement. Executive Summary.* New York: CED, 1994.

The Direction of Educational Change: Putting Learning at the Center. Washington, D.C.: Association of American Colleges and Universities, 1995.

Doucette, Don S. "Now That the Technology Problems Are Solved," *Community College Week,* October 12, 1992.

The Education Commission of the States. *The Progress of Education Reform–Draft.* Denver, CO: Education Commission of the States. November 1995.

Hancock, LynNell, and Brant, Martha. "Town to Unions: Drop Dead," *Newsweek,* November 27, 1995.

Higher Education Information Resources Alliance. "Executive Outlook on the Transformation of Higher Education," Report #7, July 1996.

Independence, Accreditation, and the Public Interest. Washington, D.C.: National Policy Board on Higher Education Institutional Accreditation, Ocotober 1994.

McClenney, Kay and Mingle, James. "Higher Education Finance in the 1990s: Hard Choices for Community Colleges," *Leadership Abstracts*, September 1992.

Media Advisory, "Western Governors Announce Plans, Funding for Western Virtual University," Denver, CO: Western Governors' Association, February 6, 1996.

Myran, Gunder, Zeiss, Anthony and Howdyshell, Linda. *Community College Leadership in the New Century: Learning to Improve Learning.* Washington, D.C.: American Association of Community Colleges, 1995.

A New American Urban School District. Denver, CO: Education Commission of the States, 1995.

The New Basic Agenda: Policy Directions for Student Success. Sacramento, CA: Board of Governors, California Community Colleges, September 14, 1995.

Noam, Eli M. "Electronics and the Dim Future of the University," *Science,* October 13, 1995.

O'Banion, Terry. "Community Colleges Lead a Learning Revolution," *Educational Record,* Fall 1995.

O'Banion, Terry and Associates. *Teaching and Learning in the Community College.* Washington, D.C.: American Association of Community Colleges, 1994.

Oakey, Joseph H. Foreword to *Learning About Project-Based Learning* by Rudie Tretten and Peter Zachariou. San Rafael, CA: The Autodesk Foundation, July 1995.

Slavkin, Mark. "Lift the Education Code Dead Weight," *Los Angeles Times,* December 31, 1995.

"Those Scary College Costs." *Newsweek,* April 29, 1996.

"To Dance with Change," *Policy Perspectives,* section A. Philadelphia, PA: Institute for Research on Higher Education, April 1994.

Toy, Larry. "Out of the Box: Restructuring the Curriculum of the Community Colleges." Unpublished paper, March 10, 1995.

Trombley, William. "Ambitious Reform Agenda: Restructuring in Virginia Higher Education," *Crosstalk,* October 1995.

Twigg, Carol A. and Doucette, Don. "Improving Productivity in Higher Education—A Paradigm Shift Needed," *Leadership Abstracts,* August 1992.

Wingspread Group on Higher Education. *An American Imperative: Higher Expectations for Higher Education.* Racine, WI: The Johnson Foundation, Inc. 1993.

CHAPTER 3

Back to the Future

If Jung is right and there is a collective unconscious for the human race, surely a feature of that great stream of knowing is reflected in the basic philosophy that human beings learn best by doing. This philosophy is deeply embedded in the cultures of the world, most evident in the practices related to becoming an adult male in primitive cultures in which a boy engages in behaviors (performing acts, not just listening and memorizing) that will test his readiness for manhood; successful completion of the behaviors provides the bridge into adulthood. It is passage into a new world of knowing, one described by Jung himself at the age of 14: "Yes, this is it, my world, the real world, the secret, where there are no teachers, no schools, no unanswerable questions, where one can be without having to ask anything" (1989, p. 78).

A LONG STREAM OF CONSCIOUSNESS

There are truths self-evident in primitive and modern cultures. Children learn to walk by walking, to talk by talking. Children learn to hunt by hunting, to farm by farming. Children learn to swim by swimming, to drive by driving. Children learn to write by writing, to read by reading. These are self-evident truths noted by Aristotle as an example of the long stream of the collective unconscious long before the process was named by Jung: "For the things we have to learn before we can do them, we learn them by doing them."

With the formation of the modern school, the self-evident knowledge that human beings learn best by doing was often repressed or forgotten. For periods of time, schools encouraged and rewarded more passive behaviors in which students took in information and parroted it back without doing anything with or to that information. Learning by doing, however, appears to be so natural to human behavior that it cannot long be repressed. In recent times, learning by doing has broken through to the surface in great outbursts of creativity in the 1930s and the 1940s in the form of Progressive Education, in the 1960s in the form of Humanistic Education, and in the late 1980s and early 1990s in a renaissance of innovation still to be named.

John Dewey was one of the major architects for what became the Progressive Education Movement, and his ideas influenced education for decades. In a key passage from *My Pedagogic Creed,* Dewey (1929) referred to the long stream of human consciousness and noted the central value of the natural educative process:

> I believe that all education proceeds by the participation of the individual in the social consciousness of the race. This process begins unconsciously almost at birth, and is continually shaping the individual's powers, saturating his consciousness, forming his habits, training his ideas, and arousing his feelings and emotions. Through this unconscious education, the individual gradually comes to share in the intellectual and moral resources which humanity has succeeded in getting together. He becomes an inheritor of the funded capital of civilization. (p. 3)

Dewey felt that traditional schools impeded the natural processes of learning embedded in every child. "Our first teachers. . . . are our feet, hands, and eyes. To substitute books for them does not teach us to reason; it teaches us to use the reason of others rather than our own; it teaches us to believe much and to know little" (Dewey and Dewey, 1962, p. 8). The need for learning, he said, resided in the child, not in the school. "If we want, then, to find out how education takes place most successfully, let us go to the experiences of children where learning is a necessity, and not to the practices of the schools where it largely is an adornment, a superfluity, and even an unwelcome imposition" (Dewey and Dewey, 1962, p. 2).

Dewey was a prolific writer but not a very readable one. His ideas were not always clearly expressed, and for this and other reasons, he was often misinterpreted and oversimplified, sometimes by his most zealous supporters. The following excerpt expresses his central philosophy.

I believe that:

- Education is a process of living and not a preparation for future living.
- The school must represent present life—life is as real and vital to the child as that which he carries on in the home, in the neighborhood, or on the playground.

- Education which does not occur through forms of life, forms that are worth living for their own sake, is always a poor substitute for the genuine reality, and tends to cramp and to deaden (Dewey and Dewey, 1962, pp. 6-7).

A.S. Neill's Summerhill was the idealized version of the progressive school later to be lampooned in the play and movie *Auntie Mame*. Summerhill was founded by Neill in 1921 in the village of Leiston in Suffolk, England, and was very influential in the United Kingdom and the United States as a prototype of the applied theories of Progressive Education. "When my first wife and I began the school, we had one main idea: to make the school fit the child—instead of making the child fit the school" (Neill, 1960, p. 4). Neill's views regarding traditional education made him one of the great iconoclasts of his time. "We have no new methods of teaching, because we do not consider that teaching in itself matters very much" (Neill, 1960, p. 5). Eighteen years after the founding of Summerhill, another popular book, Harold Benjamin's *The Saber-Tooth Curriculum*, echoed many of Neill's and Dewey's ideas and provided in its title and content a conscious recognition of what Progressive Education owed to more basic and ageless concepts—a clear case of back to the future.

In the Humanistic Education Movement of the 1960s and early 1970s, Carl Rogers, Arthur Combs, Sidney Jourard, Abraham Maslow, and others battled against the behavioristic and psychoanalytic views that reduced human beings to passive animals governed primarily by their past experiences. The humanists opted for a more liberated view of human beings, one in which people were innately good and innately self-directing. The role of education, in the eyes of the humanists, is to free the human spirit to become all it is capable of being, by providing opportunities for the practice of new behaviors.

Carl Rogers is best known for creating the theory and practice of client-centered therapy, and many of these concepts were transported directly into educational practice. In 1969, Rogers summed up his observations on education in *Freedom to Learn for the Eighties*.

> We have shown that very diverse individuals, working at various educational levels, with different intellectual interests, can bring into being a learning environment in which there is responsible freedom. These facilitators of learning create a humane planet in which, being themselves real persons, they also respect the personhood of the student. In this climate there is understanding, caring, stimulation. And we have seen students respond with an avid interest in learning with a growing confidence in self, with independence, with creative energy. (p. 307)

Rogers felt strongly that traditional education was a failure and urged teachers and administrators to develop new roles. He may have been the creator of the term "learning facilitator," which is gaining currency in today's learning paradigm. "We had found a way of being with students that was sharply different from conventional education. It did not involve teaching so much as it involved us in a process that we came to think of as the facilitation of learning" (Rogers, 1969, Back cover).

Arthur Combs was the leading advocate for phenomenological psychology that helped provide a theoretical base for Humanistic Education. His book with Donald Snygg, *Individual Behavior,* was a seminal work that significantly influenced education in the 1960s and presaged the constructivist theories that undergird much of the current reform movement. For most of his professional life, Combs worked closely with the influential Association of Supervision and Curriculum Development. One of his last major projects for the association included chairing a national committee on the assessment of Humanistic Education. The preface of that book could well serve as the preface to this book.

> If education is to place high priority on the development of humane people, it must utilize and expand those methods and practices that are known to facilitate positive growth and eliminate those administrative structures, policies, and teaching procedures that make the achievement of humanistic goals difficult. (Combs, 1978, p. vii)

The book also included the basic tenets of Humanistic Education which echo earlier concepts of Progressive Education and portend concepts expressed in today's new learning paradigms.

> Humanistic education:
>
> 1) Accepts the learner's needs and purposes and develops experiences and programs around the unique potentials of the learner.
> 2) Facilitates self-actualization and strives to develop in all persons a sense of personal adequacy.
> 3) Fosters acquisition of basic skills necessary for living in a multicultural society, including academic, personal, interpersonal, communicative, and economic proficiency.
> 4) Personalizes educational decisions and practices. To this end it includes students in the process of their own education via democratic involvement in all levels of implementation.
> 5) Recognizes the primacy of human feelings and utilizes personal values and perceptions as integral factors in educational processes.
> 6) Develops a learning climate which nurtures growth through learning environments perceived by all involved as challenging, understanding, supportive, exciting, and free from threat.

7) Develops in learners genuine concern and respect for the work of others and skill in conflict resolution. (Combs, 1978, pp. 9-10)

Community colleges, developing rapidly in the 1960s and struggling to create their own forms of education free from the constraints of traditional practices, provided a natural crucible for the development of Humanistic Education.

As a young zealot for Humanistic Education, the author of this book railed against the educational conventions of the day:

> In the dehumanizing production model of education, we have developed a society in which the old are plagued by heart attacks and the young by heartbreaks. Our noncognitive capacities have atrophied like an appendix. But no man is so diminished, so emaciated, so retarded or polluted that he can escape responding to be himself, to be natural, to be more fully human when others call to him to be so and allow opportunities for him to answer that call. And there is a clear call today across the land for a new kind of education. . . .We are at the crest of a new humanistic education, and if the junior college will but respond to this call, this demand, for human liberation, it will live up to its claim of being 'the people's college.' (O'Banion, 1971, pp. 170-71)

This excerpt from a passionate speech conveys some of the fervor that accompanied the Humanistic Education Movement. This reformer, and many others in community colleges in the 1960s and early 1970s, in more rational moments, created and instituted some of the most humanistic practices of the day, including learning communities, encounter groups, cross-functional teams, life-skills training, and an elimination of the D and F grades.

In the late 1980s, a renaissance of innovation in education once again focused on the learner and the age-old notion of learning as doing. The theories of collaborative learning and learning communities were put into practice in collectives where students worked with each other to achieve their goals. "The kind of challenging, integrated learning, offered in these communities, when combined with the experiences of cooperating with a diverse group of fellow students and teachers, helps prepare students for the real world beyond the classroom and beyond the college" (Matthews, 1994, p. 199).

Service learning, pioneered at Antioch College decades earlier, found new life in the late 1980s as a way of linking the campus to the community by providing special internships and "real-life" experiences for students in local social and service agencies. School-to-work and tech-prep were hailed as new applications of work-based learning, applying the concepts of contextual and applied learning. Project-Based Learning (PBL), rooted in the Progressive Education Movement and renewed in the public schools of the 1980s, is the epitome of learning by doing: "Using hands-on projects, learners have the freedom to actively experiment and explore ideas" (Quesada, 1995, p. 3).

These innovations and others were heralds of a resurgence of interest in learner-centered education in American schools and colleges in the late 1980s and early 1990s. The age-old wisdom about how learning occurs, stored in the collective unconscious, is percolating to the top once again as described by Dede (1993): "In post-industrial models of institutional functioning, just-in-time learning-while-doing targeted to authentic, novel problems is displacing the classroom-based, discipline-focused, learning-by-listening approaches characteristic of schooling and of workplace training in industrial organizations" (p. 3).

TOWARD A NEW WAY OF LEARNING

The learner-centered innovations—along with the new research about learning, the breakthroughs in technology, the focus on outcome measures, and the application of business concepts such as Total Quality Management (TQM) and learning organizations—has created a crucible of opportunity that comes along about every two decades. Paul Privateer, a professor at Arizona State University who characterizes himself as "a new kind of teacher who can bring technology, management, and content into some new formations," has described this crucible of opportunity as follows: "American education in general is at a strategic anxiety moment in its evolution. We're at a very odd midpoint between the death of one kind of paradigm of learning and the yet-undefined formation of an entirely new way of learning" (In Gales, 1994, p. 22).

A rich ferment of yeasty ideas is being put forward to define "an entirely new way of learning" for American education. In the latter half of the 1990s, unless there is some cataclysmic social change to redirect attention, there will be hundreds of commission reports, local and state plans, and individually authored books on what many will call a new paradigm for learning. The community college, because of its central role in American higher education, and because of its long history of commitment to teaching and learning, will be a key playing field for experimenting with and testing out models of new approaches to learning. Community colleges are often the first institutions to feel the impact of change because they are positioned so closely to mainstream values in American society. Through experience, they have become responsive to new needs and new opportunities, developing a well-deserved reputation for innovative and entrepreneurial solutions. Given these characteristics, it is not surprising to find community colleges in the vanguard of exploring new approaches to learning.

At the moment, most community colleges are struggling to operate, as Privateer has said, within an established paradigm that is dying. The response has been to bolt on new programs and activities, often at in-creased cost, to old structures. Community colleges have been national leaders in the efforts to improve the traditional system by applying informa-tion technology, developing collaborative learning models, and incorporat-ing assessment and outcome measures. These innovative applications *have* improved teaching and learning in community colleges, and they should be encouraged; but there will be a limit on improving learning outcomes when these innovations are applied in the context of traditional practices.

The community college needs a new model of education, a model that incorporates the best practices and philosophies of its past with the expand-ing base of new knowledge about learning and technology. "The learning college" is a model tailor-made for the community college and one that holds great promise for helping students make passionate connections to learning.

THE LEARNING COLLEGE

"The learning college places learning first and provides educational experiences for learners anyway, anyplace, anytime" (O'Banion, 1995-96, p. 22, emphasis added). The model is based on the assumption that educational experi-ences are designed for the convenience of learners rather than for the convenience of institutions and their staffs. The term "the learning college" is used as a generic reference for all educational institutions.

The learning college is based on six key principles:

- The learning college creates substantive change in individual learners.
- The learning college engages learners as full partners in the learn-ing process, with learners assuming primary responsibility for their own choices.
- The learning college creates and offers as many options for learning as possible.
- The learning college assists learners to form and participate in collaborative learning activities.
- The learning college defines the roles of learning facilitators by the needs of the learners.
- The learning college and its learning facilitators succeed only when improved and expanded learning can be documented for its learn-ers.

Principle I

The learning college creates substantive change in individual learners. The need for colleges to support this first principle is a self-evident, general truth easily verifiable in personal experience by anyone reading this page. It is so elementary that it is often unstated and overlooked. This first principle must be stated and restated until it becomes an embedded value undergirding all other principles.

Basic human experience easily confirms the validity of the first principle. Consider the joy and release of energy that accompanies the first steps of a baby learning to walk. The new walker paddles off in all directions, teetering forward on toes used differently for the first time, teetering backwards on bottoms that cushion repeated falls. The new walker is a joyous learner excitedly testing out new boundaries and excitedly exploring objects seen from a new vantage point. In this situation, learning is clearly a powerful process that brings about substantive change in the individual; there is also substantive change in all the other players connected to the new walker's environment!

These special learning experiences are moments of discovery, natural processes used by every human being to move forward from the first breath of life. The developmental tasks that frame the various milestones of growing up provide the most dramatic moments for discovery, but the smaller steps tucked away in the nooks and crannies of everyday life are key components in constructing a full picture of a complex, growing human being. Learning kindles new ways of seeing, thinking, and doing—in dramatic events and incrementally in day-to-day experiences.

First day at school is one of the dramatic events. First song before the class is a dramatic event. First crush on a classmate, first fight, first trip to the principal's office, first A on a research paper, and first prom are all dramatic learning experiences leading to new discoveries about self and others.

Formal schooling provides an extraordinary laboratory for learning about self and others, but most importantly, it provides an extraordinary opportunity to learn about things and ideas, about changes in the past and hopes for the future, about where and how others live and die, about cultures and civilizations, and about ways to examine and arrange all this information to make sense of it. And it can provide opportunities to acquire new skills in writing, speaking, listening, information processing, analyzing, and creating. Formal schooling can also provide training for a learner to become a special person—a nurse, physician, salesperson, teacher, lawyer, automotive technician, cosmetologist, nanny, stockbroker, or computer analyst.

At its best, formal schooling is every society's attempt to provide a powerful environment that can create substantive change in individuals. But formal schooling is no longer at its best. In the learning college, this first principle must form the framework for all other activities. The learners and the learning facilitators in the learning college must be aware of the awesome power that can be released when learning works well. Learning in the learning college will not be business as usual. Powerful processes will be at work; substantive change will be expected. Learners will be exploring and experimenting with new and expanded versions of what they can become.

In *The Once and Future King*, Merlyn provides perspective on learning as a powerful process in his advice to the young King Arthur:

> The best thing for being sad . . . is to learn something. That is the only thing that never fails. You may grow old and trembling in your anatomies, you may lie awake at night listening to the disorders of your veins, you may miss your only love, you may see the world about you devastated by evil lunatics, or know your honor trampled in the sewer of baser minds. There is only one thing for it then—to learn. Learn why the world wags and what wags it. That is the only thing which the mind can never exhaust, never alienate, never be tortured by, never fear or distrust, and never dream of regretting. Learning is the thing for you. (White, 1939, pp. 185-86)

Principle II

The learning college engages learners as full partners in the learning process, with learners assuming primary responsibility for their own choices. At the point a learner chooses to engage the learning college, a series of services will be initiated to prepare the learner for the experiences and opportunities to come. Until there is a seamless system of education for lifelong learning based on the principles of the learning college, these services will be heavily focused on orienting the learner to the new experiences and expectations of the learning college, which are not usually found in traditional schools. Two key expectations will be communicated to new learners at the first stage of engagement: 1) learners are full partners in the creation and implementation of their learning experiences, and 2) learners will assume primary responsibility for making their own choices about goals and options. These same expectations work for fourth- and fifth-grade students in the Autodesk Foundation's Tinkertech Schools; they will also work for community college students.

The services will include assessing the learner's abilities, achievements, values, needs, goals, expectations, resources, and environmental/situational limitations. A personal profile will be constructed by the learner in consultation with an expert assessor to illustrate what this learner knows, wants to know, and needs to know. A personal learning plan will be constructed from this personal profile, and the learner will negotiate a contract that outlines responsibilities of both the learner and the learning college.

As part of the contract, the learner will purchase an appropriate number of initial learning vouchers to be used in selecting from among the learning options provided by the learning college. The assessment information, terms of the contract, historical records from previous learning experiences, and all pertinent information will be recorded on the learner's "smart card," which serves as a portfolio of information, a lifelong record of lifelong educational experiences. The "smart card," similar to an automated teller machine (ATM) card already widely used by banks, will belong to the learner, who will be responsible for keeping it current with assistance from specialists in the learning college.

The state of Ohio is currently developing a prototype of the "smart card." By the end of 1996, every high school senior completing a vocational program in Ohio will receive a "Career Passport." The passport will include a personal profile, competencies, transcripts, attendance records, agency guarantees, letters of recommendation, and more. It has been designed as a "living document" to reflect future career changes and competencies achieved. The Ohio State Board of Education is encouraging employers to require the Career Passport from all job applicants who have completed the vocational programs. The student guide for preparing the passport declares, "It puts you in control of your life and allows you to make decisions concerning your achievements and future career goals" (Miami Valley Career Technology Center, 1995, p. 2).

The learning college will also provide orientation and experimentation for learners who are unfamiliar with the new learning environment of the learning college. Some learners will need training in using the technology, in developing collaborations, in locating resources, and in navigating learning systems. Specialists will monitor these services carefully and will be responsible for approving a learner's readiness to fully engage the learning opportunities provided.

It will be the learning college's responsibility to provide clear and easily accessible information in a variety of formats. This information should include guidelines for making decisions about dates, work loads, resources, and learning options; details about processes and options new to the learner; and agreements regarding expectations and responsibilities. It will be the learner's responsibility to review and provide information, experiment with processes and options, make choices, and commit to full engagement in the choices made.

K. Patricia Cross (1984) made this point over a decade ago, long before it became currently popular. "If schools are to meet the foreseeable demands of the learning society, they will have to. . . gradually put students in charge of their own learning, so that they can make wise choices from among the many learning options that will confront them as adults in the learning society" (p. 172). Cross said "gradually," and she is correct. The goal is to help students become independent, lifelong learners, but many community college students are dependent, first-generation college students who will require careful attention and support. They will require even more attention and support in the model of education suggested here, and community colleges will have to provide the support at the front end if students are to have any hope of succeeding in this unfamiliar territory.

The process of engagement between a learner and an educational institution is usually given short shrift. Historically, universities have done a better job than community colleges, sometimes requiring new students to participate in a week-long, on-campus orientation before classes begin. Community colleges are notoriously weak in the engagement process, despite their recognition that many of their students are first-generation college students in great need of more orientation. The orientation process in community colleges is usually voluntary and short, often scheduled for only two hours or a half day. Overall, it does not have much of an impact on inducting students into what should be a powerful process that will create substantive change in their lives.

In the learning college, the engagement process will take as much time as required to meet the needs of each individual learner. Some learners seeking minimal learning experiences about which they are very clear can begin their activities immediately following their first point of engagement. Some learners will want to participate in the process for a few days or a few weeks. Some learners may be engaged in the process for several months. Since there will be no restrictions on time and place for the engagement, there will be no limitations governing the activities except the needs of the learner. There will be many options for learners to engage the learning college, including self-guided print and video modules, group-based activities—face-to-face or through the Internet—classes and laboratories "on-campus," and individual consultations with a variety of specialists. Continuing learners will learn to navigate the learning college system and use it to their full advantage, but not without a great deal of initial support and attention at the beginning and well into the system.

Principle III

The learning college creates and offers as many options for learning as possible.
"The student is best served by a program that accommodates individual

differences in learning styles, learning rates, aptitudes, and prior knowledge while maintaining educational quality" (Berz, 1995). New research on "multi-intelligences," learning styles, and information processing confirms common wisdom: Human beings are highly complex and unique individuals who learn differently from one another. It follows that the best educational enterprise will be one that best responds to those individual differences.

In the learning college, there will be many options for the learner in initial engagement and in educational programs—options regarding time, place, structure, and methods of delivery. After the learner has reviewed these options and experimented with some that are unfamiliar, entry vouchers will be exchanged for the selected options and exit vouchers will be held for completion.

Each learning option will include specific goals and competency levels needed for entry, as well as specific outcome measures of competency levels needed for exit. Learning colleges will be constantly creating additional learning options for learners, many of them suggested by learners from their own experiences. Some possible learning options may include:

- Prescribed, preshrunk portable modules in such areas as general education core courses or specific skills training. These will be universally recognized packages developed by national knowledge organizations such as the American Medical Association or major companies such as AT&T.
- Stand-alone technological expert systems that respond to the idiosyncrasies of a specific learner, guiding and challenging the learner through a rich maze of information and experiences. IBM's *Ulysses* and Philips Interactive Media of America's *The World of Impressionism* are prototypes that show the potential of such systems.
- Opportunities for collaboration with other learners in small groups and through technological links. Learning communities developed in the state of Washington, The Electronic Forum developed by Maricopa Community Colleges, and Project-Based Learning supported by the Autodesk Foundation are examples.
- Tutor-led groups, individual reading programs, school-to-work, service learning, lectures, and laboratories—all of the established learning options, since many of these still work well for many learners. These established learning options will not be constrained, however, by the limits of time and place, but will be designed for the needs of learners and framed by specific goals and competency levels needed for entry and specific outcome measures of competency levels needed for exit.

A major goal of the learning college is to create as many learning options as possible in order to provide successful learning experiences for all learners. If the learner's goal is to become competent in English as a Second Language (ESL), a dozen or so learning options should be available to achieve that goal, and the learner should be able to use any combination of those options.

Figure 3-1 lists a number of options to assist the learner in learning English. Several of the options provide stand-alone technological expert systems for the learner who wants to work on an individual basis and who does not need assistance from learning facilitators or interaction with other learners. There are also options that provide opportunities for students to work in small groups with other students, some led by tutors, and some working independently under the direction of the learners themselves. There is also an opportunity for learners to engage others on the campus not usually included in the list of professional educators. In these options, learners may take a part-time job at the college and receive direct instruction and support from a custodian or from a secretary. If one option does not work, the learner should be able to choose an alternative learning option or a combination of options at any point, with considerable guidance from learning facilitators.

- stand-alone video and audio tapes
- stand-alone interactive expert system
- distance education courses
- self-guided small group
- tutor-led small group

- one-on-one mentoring with a custodian (includes part-time job)
- regular classroom
- community volunteer project
- live in home of college secretary

LEARNING OPTIONS
GOAL: LEARN ENGLISH AS A SECOND LANGUAGE

FIGURE 3-1

If a learning college had to develop such a full array of options from scratch, the task would be overwhelming and too costly. Fortunately, there are a tremendous variety of resources available, many of them field-tested and free. Thousands of individual faculty members have designed improved or alternative learning materials on their sabbaticals, on released time during regular terms, or on summer projects. Many of these projects have been supported with innovation grants from various institutions and with grants from the federal government and various foundations. Individual colleges have also initiated programs to design and develop new learning opportunities for students, sometimes with a considerable commitment of college resources. Colleges have initiated consortia to work with each other and with other agencies and companies to produce new learning programs. State and federal agencies, especially the military, have created hundreds of learning options that are free for the asking. Business and industry have spent billions on training materials. Educational entrepreneurs such as book publishers, testing agencies, information networks, training organizations, and computer corporations are in the specific business of developing training materials, which are often available to educational institutions for a fee paid by the students.

These educational materials are already available in every delivery method imaginable, on every topic, and for many different levels of competency; and the future will bring more choices. The learning college will inventory this tremendous array of learning options and will begin to select and organize them to provide as many learning options as possible for its learners. Some enterprising individual or agency will eventually provide inventories of the available options, providing important data so the staff of the learning college can make informed decisions regarding selection and use. When faculty are no longer role-bound to provide all of these learning options directly themselves, the learning college will be free to secure learning materials from whatever sources are available. When learners are treated as full and respected partners in the learning enterprise, they, too, will search for options to meet their needs, and current technology will provide access.

To "manage" the activities and progress of thousands of learners engaged in hundreds of learning options at many different times, at many different levels, and at many different locations, the learning college will rely on expert systems based on early developments such as General Motors' Computer-Aided Maintenance System or Miami-Dade Community College's Synergy Integrator. Without these complex technological systems, the learning college cannot function. These learning management systems are the breakthroughs that will free education from the time-bound, place-bound, and role-bound systems that currently "manage" the educational enterprise.

Principle IV

The learning college assists learners to form and participate in collaborative learning activities. To transform a traditional institution into a learning college is to turn the university ideal of a "community of scholars" into a new ideal of "communities of learners." More than just cute word play, the focus on creating communities among all participants in the learning process—including not just students but also the faculty and other learning specialists—on creating student cohorts, and on developing social structures that support individual learning is a requirement of a learning college.

The focus on creating learning communities is characteristic of a learning college because such communities have been demonstrated to improve learning. Lewis Perelman (1992, p. 156) cites over 80 studies by David and Roger Johnson of the University of Minnesota which show that students not only master subject matter better in cooperative settings than they do working in isolation, but that they also develop better social skills and self-esteem.

Uri Treisman's research (1985) demonstrated that a principal factor in the high achievement levels of Asian American students in higher education is their consistent and effective use of the study group. While there might be some cultural factors at work in the tendency of Asian American students to form such groups, Treisman was able to demonstrate similar learning improvements among African Americans who formed effective study groups. The notion that there is something about some kinds of group interactions that encourage and support individual learning is intuitive to most educators, and is perhaps at the core of the sentimental attachment to the classroom as an effective learning environment that many in higher education do not wish to abandon.

Practitioners as well as researchers know that group interaction can be very helpful to individual learning. There are examples of effective collaborative learning models at all levels of education. We also know from experience that programs which are designed to build cohorts of students and then to engage them in a common experience or curriculum greatly increase retention, and ultimately program completion. Nursing programs in community colleges have some of the highest success rates in all of education, at least in part because a cohort is guided together through a rigorous competency-based curriculum. Nursing students study together and support each other, and there is no disincentive for all to succeed at high levels because students are not graded relative to each other (as on a Bell curve) but relative to a set performance standard.

There are numerous examples of successful cohort-based programs. The Community College Leadership Program at The University of Texas at Austin has very high completion rates among the doctoral students enrolled in its "block program," which continues year after year to produce community college leaders. The Program for Adult Continuing Education (PACE) is an associate of arts degree program at Longview Community College, one of the Metropolitan Community Colleges in Kansas City, Missouri, that has formed adult students into cohorts who supplement televised delivery of courses with weekend conferences. Once each month, an interdisciplinary core of faculty meet for a day and a half with the cohort of students, who come to know each other and support each other to degree completion. Degree completion rates for PACE students are consistently higher than for any other college programs, except for nursing and similar well-defined, cohort-based occupational programs.

The most widespread form of collaborative learning in the community college takes place in "learning communities." "Learning communities" is a specific term for a curricular intervention that enhances collaboration and expands learning. "Learning communities . . .purposefully restructure the curriculum to link together courses or coursework so that students find greater coherence in what they are learning as well as increased intellectual interaction with faculty and fellow students" (Gabelnick et al., 1990, p. 5). These structures are also referred to as learning clusters, triads, federated learning communities, coordinated studies, and integrated studies; but "learning communities" has emerged as the favorite descriptor. When the same 30 students enroll for nine credit hours in a sequence of courses under the rubric of "Reading, Writing, and Rats," they have enrolled in a learning community.

There have been numerous variations on the learning community in higher education for the last 70 years. The first learning community was offered in the Experimental College at the University of Wisconsin in 1927. Early experiments in a community college occurred at Santa Fe Community College (Florida) in 1966. More recently, Daytona Beach Community College (Florida), LaGuardia Community College (New York), and community colleges in Washington state have been leaders in developing new and expanded forms of learning communities.

There is a growing body of research on the impact of learning communities. Vincent Tinto and others (1993) have confirmed that learning communities increase academic performance and persistence; help students bond to the broader social communities of the college and engage them more fully in the academic life of the institution; and add an intellectual richness to student experience that traditional pedagogies do not. Tinto and others have also noted that the positive outcomes of learning communities are also present in nonresidential settings. In fact, these communities may be the commuter students' only viable alternative for increased student involvement.

Learning communities and other forms of collaborative learning provide alternative models to traditional structures and processes. Tinto and his colleagues(1993) have said, "Our research also suggests that we need to give serious attention to the argument that the attainment of the goals of enhanced student involvement and achievement is possible only when institutions alter the settings in which students are asked to learn" (p. 21).

In the learning college, some learning communities and collaborative learning activities will not look very much like classrooms, and many will have dynamics defined by characteristics of pace, distance, membership, and means of communication. For instance, as the number of adult workers returning to college for education and training continues to grow, a most likely venue for establishing learning communities will be in the workplace. Workplaces that value and encourage lifelong learning—whether because of altruism or enlightened self-interest—will make ideal sites for communities of learners, as common interest may be easier to determine and as the level of resources available to support the community is potentially very high. For instance, video-on-demand can distribute information, and even interactive training modules, directly to the desktop of employees; information resources can be concentrated at a common work location; and assessment services or learning specialists can be housed at the work site as desired.

Powerful networking technology can also help nurture a learning community by assisting its members to communicate with each other regularly in both synchronous and asynchronous modes. Certainly if courtship can be accomplished in cyberspace, then learning communities can be formed there. The Electronic Forums established in the Maricopa Community Colleges are pioneering efforts to create communities of learners through electronic networks.

The roles that college educators will play in forming and supporting learning communities are yet to be thoroughly defined, but some basic suggestions can be made based on the learning college model. In a learning college, staff will form and recruit students into cohorts of common interests or circumstances. Process facilitators will orient individuals and form them into groups or communities of learners. Resource specialists will attend to the resource needs of both individuals and groups of learners. Learning facilitators will design experiences that build upon and use group strengths and other dynamics. Assessment specialists will design and implement authentic assessments that can occur both individually and in the context of the learning community. The learning college will be designed not only around the unique needs of individual learners but also around their needs for association. The learning college will foster and nourish learning communities as an integral part of its design.

Principle V

The learning college defines the roles of learning facilitators by the needs of the learners. If learners have varied and individual needs that require special attention, then it follows that the personnel employed in this enterprise must be selected on the basis of what learners need. Community college staff are usually selected on the basis of needs of an administrator, a department, a center, or a course. All too often these staff are role-bound by established job descriptions or by traditional expectations, especially for teaching faculty.

Figure 3-2 is a beginning list of specific functions that a learning college will need to provide if it is to serve learners well. This list or a similar one could free leaders to review the kinds of personnel needed to staff the college. The list suggests a number of alternatives.

- encourage and facilitate enrollment
- assess student needs
- encourage attendance and participation
- design learning experiences
- locate resources
- provide technical assistance
- provide content expertise
- develop feedback mechanisms
- lecture
- lead discussions
- coordinate field trips

- arrange work-based learning
- arrange service learning
- nurture interpersonal relationships
- create connection activities
- guide, tutor, coach
- create standards and outcome measures
- conduct research
- maintain attractive environment
- coordinate systems
- provide vision
- award credentials

ROLES FOR STAFF AND FACULTY

FIGURE 3-2

Everyone employed in the learning college will be a learning facilitator, including categories formerly designated administration and support or clerical staff. Trustees will also be considered learning facilitators as they exercise their responsibilities for governance and policy development. Every employee will be directly linked to learners in the exercise of his or her duties, although some activities, such as accounting, may be more indirectly related. The goal is to have every employed person thinking about how his or her work facilitates the learning process.

The learning college will contract with many specialists to provide services to learners. Specialists will be employed on a contractual basis to produce specific products or to deliver specific services; some will work full-time, but many will work part-time, often from their homes, linked to learners through technology. A number of specialists will be scattered around the world providing unique services and special expertise. Learners in the learning college will need specialists who can

- Assess learner abilities, achievements, values, needs, goals, expectations, resources, and environmental/situational limitations; create personal profiles and personal learning plans; negotiate learning contracts; and assist in developing a personal portfolio on a "smart card."
- Design and create learning options in a variety of formats based upon the latest learning and adult development theories.
- Design and create expert systems to manage and track the activities of learners.
- Train learners in the use of a variety of technologies and systems.
- Select, update, and repair software and hardware.
- Assist in creating and convening collaborative networks of other learners.
- Access, synthesize, and update constantly expanding databases of knowledge.
- Establish and clarify skill levels, competencies, goals, and outcomes.
- Establish and maintain a clean and attractive environment for those who elect to participate in learning "on location."
- Guide and coach learners needing individual assistance.
- Arrange new options for new needs.
- Challenge learner assumptions, question their values, and encourage their explorations.

The groundwork is already being prepared for these new roles to emerge. A 1996 report by the Ohio Technology in Education Steering Committee recommended the term "learning consultant" to best describe the educator of the future. "As learning consultants, educators will play many roles:

- Learning consultants will be mentors—guiding each learner to his or her own chosen goals.
- Learning consultants will be facilitators of inquiry—coaching learners and helping them remove barriers as they move toward discovery.
- Learning consultants will be architects of connection—observing the needs of individual learners and joining them to information experiences, resources, experts, and teams.
- Learning consultants will be managers of collaboration and integration—combining the needs and abilities of *their* learning communities with the needs and abilities of *other* learning communities" (p. 13).

Learners will also participate as learning facilitators, and this role could be made part of the expectations negotiated in the engagement process. Some learners will not have time, but others will welcome the opportunity to offer their experience and knowledge to assist other learners. Colleges already use students as lab assistants and tutors to facilitate learning. In the learning college, these roles and opportunities will be expanded to capitalize on the resources students bring, to free professional staff for other roles, and to reduce personnel costs.

Principle VI

The learning college and its learning facilitators succeed only when improved and expanded learning can be documented for its learners. "What does this learner know?" and "What can this learner do?" provide the framework for documenting outcomes, both for the learner and for the learning facilitators. If the ultimate goal of the learning college is to promote and expand learning, then this will be the yardstick by which the learning college faculty and staff are evaluated. Conventional information may be assembled for students (retention rates and achievement scores) and for faculty (service and observation by students, peers, and supervisors), but the goal will be to document what students know and what they can do and to use this information as the primary measure of success for the learning facilitators and the learning college.

All learning options in the learning college will include the competencies required for entrance and for exit. These competencies will reflect national and state standards when available, or they will be developed by specialists on staff or on special contract. Assessing a learner's readiness for a particular learning option will be a key part of the initial engagement process and thereafter a continuing process embedded in the culture of the institution.

Learners will negotiate and sign contracts for overall programs (general education core, basic skills, workplace skills, etc.) and a specific contract for each learning option, whether part of a program or not. Learners will be encouraged to add competencies and goals beyond those established in the standards.

Portfolio assessment, a form of authentic assessment, will be the primary means by which learning is documented. A portfolio will be a systematic and organized collection of evidence of what the learner knows and what the learner can do. It will build on prior information, will be in constant use through revision and updates, and will provide continuity into future learning activities. Specific benchmarks of achievement may be applied to determine credits earned, if that continues to be the coin of the realm for moving learners along a seamless path of education.

The learner will be a full partner with learning facilitators in creating, monitoring, and assessing the information in the portfolio. As long as certification is a function of educational institutions, the learning college will retain final authority for certifying outcomes such as competencies achieved and credits earned, but certification will be based on more indices than time served and grades given. The portfolio, in the form of a "smart card," will include a summary of assessment information gathered at the point of initial engagement; the learning contract; competencies achieved; samples of work; experience logged; external evaluations by employers, supervisors, and collaborators; grades and test scores if applicable; evaluations and observations by learning facilitators and other specialists; self- and peer-evaluations; and a log by the learner continually analyzing the portfolio process.

The portfolio assessment process will be one of the primary functions of learning facilitators. Since many of the learning options will not include the traditional classroom, learning facilitators will have more time for the portfolio assessment. It may be possible to codify some of the assessment process for easier management, and advances in technology will provide some assistance.

In any case, there has been sufficient experimentation with portfolio assessment in the last decade to affirm its value. It is well-designed to support the goals and structures of the learning college and will become one of its key features.

CONCLUSION

The six principles outlined in this chapter form the core of the learning college. They refer primarily to process and structure, and are built on the basic philosophy that the student is central in all activities within the scope of the educational enterprise. There are certainly other principles that must be considered in creating a new paradigm of learning. Content, funding, and governance are examples of key issues that must be addressed and for which principles must be designed. In these six principles, there is at least a beginning direction for those who wish to create a learning college that places learning first and provides educational experiences for learners anyway, anyplace, anytime. Such a college is designed to help students make passionate connections to learning.

REFERENCES

Berz, Donald. Personal communication. December 14, 1995.

Combs, Arthur W. et al. *Humanistic Education: Objectives and Assessment.* Washington, D.C.: Association for Supervision and Curriculum Development, 1978.

Cross, K. Patricia. "The Rising Tide of School Reform Reports," *Phi Delta Kappan*, November 1984.

Dede, Chris. "Beyond Distributed Multimedia: A Virtual Forum for Learning," Unpublished paper. Fairfax, VA: Center for Interactive Educational Technology, August 1993.

Dewey, John. *My Pedagogic Creed*. Washington, D.C.: The Progressive Education Association, 1929.

Dewey, John and Dewey, Evelyn. *Schools of Tomorrow*. New York: E.P. Dutton and Company, Inc., 1962.

Gabelnick, Faith et al. *Learning Communities: Creating Connections among Students, Faculty, and Disciplines*. New Directions for Teaching and Learning, Number 41. San Francisco: Jossey-Bass, Inc., Spring 1990.

Gales, Ron. "Can College Be Reengineered?" *Across the Board: The Conference Board Magazine*. March 1994.

Jung, C. G. *Memories, Dreams, Reflections*. New York: Vintage Books, 1989.

Matthews, Roberta S. "Enriching Teaching and Learning Through Learning Communities." In *Teaching and Learning in the Community College* by Terry O'Banion and Associates. Washington, D.C.: American Association of Community Colleges, 1994.

Miami Valley Career Technology Center. *The Career Passport: Your Personal Success Story*. Dayton, OH: The Center, 1995.

Neill, A. S. *Summerhill*. New York: Hart Publishing Company, Inc., 1960.

O'Banion, Terry. "The Junior College: A Humanizing Institution." In *A Day at Santa Fe*, edited by Joseph W. Fordyce. Gainesville, FL: Santa Fe Junior College, 1971.

O'Banion, Terry. "A Learning College for the 21st Century," *Community College Journal*. December/January 1995–96.

Ohio Technology in Education Steering Committee. *Technology in the Learning Communities of Tomorrow: Beginning the Transformation*. Ohio Board of Regents, March 1996.

Perelman, Lewis J. *School Is Out: A Radical New Formula for the Revitalization of America's Educational System*. New York: Avon Books, 1992.

Quesada, Arli. "A Mind-Set for the Future," *The Technology Teacher*, October 1995.

Rogers, Carl R. *Freedom to Learn for the Eighties*. Columbus, OH: Charles E. Merrill Publishing Company, 1969.

Tinto, Vincent, Goodsell-Love, Anne, and Russo, Pat. "Building Community," *Liberal Education*, Fall 1993.

Treisman, Uri. "A Study of the Mathematics Performance of Black Students at the University of California, Berkeley." Doctoral dissertation, University of California, Berkeley, 1985.

White, T.H. *The Once and Future King*. New York: G.P. Putnam's Sons, 1939.

CHAPTER 4

How Firm a Foundation

The Promise of Technology

The traditional education system is based, as has been noted, on an architecture that is time-bound, place-bound, efficiency-bound, and role-bound, undergirded by a grading system that assigns only 5 of 26 possible letters in the alphabet to designate amount and kind of learning achieved. As the National Education Commission on Time and Learning (1994) has indicated, "We have built the learning enterprise on a foundation of sand" (p. 8).

The learning college must be built on a firm foundation, a foundation of strong building blocks that can support the many new programs and practices required to operate a learning college. Those building blocks are beginning to be put in place. New applications of technology, new research on learning, progress with assessment and outcome measures, and experimentation with reengineering educational institutions to become learning organizations are already being used by progressive institutions to create more learning-centered environments.

TECHNOLOGY: MAGIC BULLET OR BROKEN ARROW?

The Magic Bullet

There is always a certain kind of euphoria connected to the introduction of new ideas and inventions, a natural expression of hope that the new will correct or at least mitigate the negative effects of the old. For the past several decades, that euphoria has been expressed in a "rapture of the technologies," a belief of society in general that technology will cure our ills; after all, technology did make it possible for human beings to walk on the moon. In education circles, there are numerous advocates of technology who view technology as the magic bullet.

IBM's William Geoghegan cites Patrick Suppes of Stanford University, who in 1967, made this euphoric forecast:

> Both the processing and the uses of information are undergoing an unprecedented technological revolution. Not only are machines now able to deal with many kinds of information at high speed and in large quantities, but it is also possible to manipulate these quantities so as to benefit from them in new ways. This is perhaps nowhere truer than in the field of education. One can predict that in a few more years millions of schoolchildren will have access to what Phillip of Macedon's son, Alexander, enjoyed as a royal prerogative: the services of a tutor as well-informed and as responsive as Aristotle. (1995, p. 2)

The failure of such predictions to come true appears to have little influence on other prognosticators. The literature of education is steeped in similar predictions about the value and power of technology as the following random sample of predictions illustrates:

- "What the interstate highway system did for personal travel in the 1950s and 1960s, the electronic information highway is doing for the distribution of information and images in the 1990s" (Institute for Research on Higher Education, 1995, p. 42).
- "Technology is the primary vehicle by which institutions of higher education are going to re-engineer the teaching and learning process" (Heterick, 1992, p. A17).
- "New technologies will create new philosophies and new concepts and new ideologies" (Privateer, 1993, p. 13).
- "Technology makes it possible for us to create what we want, not settle for what we have" (Baker, 1994, p. 1).
- "The eventual transformation of higher education and the integration of instructional technologies is inevitable" (Gilbert, 1995, p. 47).

These claims for technology are made by some of the leading and most respected educators of our time and are grounded in considerable experience. Technology is having a profound influence on our society and on education, and that influence is growing rapidly and penetrating deeply. "One can no longer afford to ignore technology and still maintain institutional health" (Ehrmann, 1995, p. 24).

Few educational institutions are ignoring technology these days. In a recent survey of 112 higher education institutions participating in the Pew Higher Education Roundtable Program, respondents were asked to identify the issues most important on their campuses. Among the nine issues repeatedly mentioned by campus leaders, technology was the one noted most frequently. Eighty-four percent of the campus leaders indicated "more effective use of technology in teaching and learning" was the most important issue on their campuses and especially so among the 21 community colleges in the study. The second most important issue noted by 62 percent of campus leaders was "becoming a more learning-centered or student-centered institution" (Institute for Research on Higher Education, 1995, pp. 43-44). The institutions participating in the Pew program might not be entirely representative of higher education, but they do represent a broad cross-section of American higher education. These institutions form a critical mass of innovation by exploring key issues; their concern with technology and learning-centered education may serve to influence the rest of higher education in the coming years.

A Broken Arrow

Technology does not always hit the mark with educators, however, and while many see technology as a magic bullet, just as many view technology as a broken arrow. In spite of claims that technology can transform teaching and learning, that transformation is not likely to take place unless faculty actually use technology. "The consensus in some recent surveys seems to be that no more than about 10 percent of faculty are doing very much with technology in the classroom, despite a national ownership rate for PCs of about 50 percent among college and university faculty" (Geoghegan, 1994, p. 13). One community college futurist has observed that even when faculty use technology they use it primarily to do the same old things faster. "Much as bookkeepers have used both quill pens and computers to keep ledgers, too many faculty use technology to track attendance, score tests, record grades, or perform other traditional tasks. Few faculty desire to use technology to change the concept of the classroom" (The Institute for Future Studies, 1992, p. 13).

Technology to expand and extend learning may not be in widespread use at the moment, but teacher unions are increasingly concerned about the growing impact of technology. Unions have tended to view technology more as a broken arrow than as a magic bullet. *The Chronicle of Higher Education* reported on a 1995 meeting in Seattle of 200 union members on the role of technology on college campuses. The conference was sponsored by the American Federation of Teachers' (AFT) community college affiliates in the Pacific Northwest. "Delegates said that, after a slow start, faculty unions needed to work hard to catch up with changes that *threatened* (emphasis added) to revolutionize the teaching profession" (Monaghan, 1995, p. A17).

Concerns about technology explored by the delegates included loss of jobs, compensation for time spent in learning to use technology, intellectual property rights, institutional support for new projects, and workloads. Distance education came under careful scrutiny by the delegates who suggested it was designed by administrators to "provide more services for less money."

Another key concern that surfaced among delegates and speakers focused on the personal interaction between students and faculty. One speaker said that faculty members had a duty to insist on "the right of students to have a human being teaching them." Some faculty are seriously concerned that technology will depersonalize their interactions with students, and this issue will be used for ill and good in continuing discussions on technology.

It is a powerful issue and one that played a part in the decision of the chancellor of the California Community Colleges to announce his retirement. The chancellor, David Mertes, had pushed innovative changes in the system, particularly the use of technology as a cost-effective way to serve California's growing and diverse constituency. Faculty groups were quite vocal in their criticism of Mertes, charging that technology would reduce their personal contacts with students. The chancellor of the University of Maine also resigned in 1995, in part because of a firestorm with the faculty over his decision to seek accreditation for the Education Network of Maine. The network was designed to use video and computer networks to provide degrees to learners in Maine's rural areas. Faculty argued these degrees would be of lesser quality because they failed to provide the intimate contact students received from faculty in regular degree programs.

In a new position paper on the role of technology in education, the AFT comes out clearly against technology and especially distance education. "All of our experience as educators tells us that teaching and learning in the shared human spaces of a campus are essential to the undergraduate experience and cannot be compromised too greatly without rendering the education unacceptable" (Blumenstyk, 1996, p. A20). Mitchell Vogel, chair of the AFT task force that prepared the paper, said of technology, "We do embrace these new things. We're skeptical of it as a replacement for the more traditional forms of education. Face-to-face meetings with professors and actually going to a library to conduct research is better for students" (Blumenstyk, 1996, p. A20).

The AFT opposes courses taught on the Internet, through videoconferencing, and with other technologies unless they meet standards of quality set by faculty. Credit can be granted only for courses approved by faculty on the home campus and taught by faculty who are appointed and evaluated through a traditional process. The AFT also urges its members to seek restrictions on the number of distance education credits granted to students and to oppose programs that are taught entirely with technology. Furthermore, the AFT advises its unions to bargain for contracts that will protect the jobs of professors who choose not to use the new technologies (Blumenstyk, 1996, p. A20).

Even when faculty use technology and there is no organized resistance, there is still the issue of whether or not technology increases productivity. The technology advocates have promised that information technology will "a) allow the same number of faculty to teach more students at the current (or at an enhanced) level of learning or b) allow campuses to serve the same number of students with fewer faculty and with no loss in learning (either what is learned or the number of students who learn it)" (Green and Gilbert, 1995, p. 10). In a nutshell, that is the productivity argument supported by many administrators and other leaders who are trying to use technology to cope with declining resources, but resisted by some faculty and some unions who view technology as having deleterious effects on students, on the campus, and on themselves. Green and Gilbert, two of the most knowledgeable information technology experts in higher education today, concluded that " . . . relatively few would claim—even after a dozen years into the 'micro' revolution—any real gains in *instructional productivity*. In that realm, as ever, we're still left with the 'promise' of technology" (Green and Gilbert, 1995, p. 10).

The Changing Battlefield

Whether technology is viewed as a magic bullet to hopeful educators looking to improve a process they know is not working as well as it should or as a broken arrow to faculty unions fighting fearfully to protect their current status and jobs, there is not much question that the battlefield, and perhaps the rules of engagement, are changing rapidly. It is certainly true that technology has yet to fulfill its promise to improve education or to improve instructional productivity, but there is mounting evidence that the promise will be kept.

Doucette, in his 1993 review of nearly three decades of instructional uses of computers in community colleges, argued that "how to transform the teaching and learning process with technology is becoming known" (Doucette, 1994 a, p. 203). He offered a two-part typology for characterizing instructional uses of technology in community colleges: those that improve current practice by automating processes or by otherwise helping faculty and students do better what they already know how to do, and those that actually transform the process—the way faculty teach and students learn. The vast majority of current uses of technology fit firmly in the

former category, ranging from the nearly universal use of personal productivity tools such as word processors and spreadsheets to instructional
management systems and computerized instrumentation. However, another set of commonly applied technologies, including multimedia presentations, simulations, and computer adaptive testing, begin to edge into the
transformational category. "While a number of technology applications
have potential to transform the teaching and learning process, it seems only
those that actually change the nature of the interaction between students
and faculty qualify as transformational" (Doucette, 1994 a, p. 215).

Doucette argued that educators know quite a lot about how technology
has been used in instruction in community colleges. We not only know the
most important ways technology assists us to improve current practice, but
we also know how to transform the teaching and learning process. First,
technology can greatly enhance communication between students and
faculty, students and students, and all participants in the learning process.
Second, technology can provide access to rich and recent sources of
information; and third, technology allows instructors to tailor educational
resources to the diversity of learning styles, cultural differences, skill levels,
motivations, disabilities, and educational objectives of an increasingly
pluralistic student body. With this knowledge, we have learned the key to
transforming processes from those that are teaching-centered to ones that
are learner-centered:

> The key is shifting the locus of control from the teacher to the student.
> In best-of-practice applications, faculty retain critical control over the
> content, design, standards, and assessment of student learning. How-
> ever, they give up control over the delivery mechanisms to students
> and empower them to choose the ways they acquire information and
> the learning activities they find effective. The emphasis is on the
> assessment of student learning, not on teaching methodology. The
> focus is not on content but on the transferable skills that are the
> learning outcomes of courses and programs—the ability to gain access
> to information, to interpret it, to give it context, to use information to
> solve problems, and to collaborate with others in problem solution.
> (Doucette, 1994 b, p. 23)

Perhaps the best single example of how technology has actually accomplished transformation of the teaching and learning process is in the area of
writing instruction. Not long ago, college composition classes consisted of
the study of perfect examples of great writers exercising their command
over a mode of rhetoric—classification, contrast and comparison, persuasion, or some other form. Students would study great writing and then
attempt to imitate it. Word processing has made possible a process approach to writing which is not a study of good writing crafted by well-

known authors, but a study of the inner workings of a student's own writing. Students work on single pieces of writing for extended periods of time, taking each through recursive stages of prewriting, editing, feedback, rewriting, and so forth. With the advent of electronic communications and collaborative writing environments, writing instruction has added an emphasis on new audiences, including both peers in the classroom and readers across the country and around the world. At least in part because instructors using a technology-assisted process approach have documented dramatic improvements in the length, quality, and complexity of students' writing (Kozma and Johnson, 1991), writing instruction in community colleges has been fundamentally transformed, both in form and in content, from a teacher-centered lecture and discussion class into a learner-centered, collaborative experience.

Finally, we have learned that the primary issues involved in applying information technology to improve teaching and learning are not technical in nature; the principal issues are educational and those related to human organization. Now that technology is available to perform nearly any instruction-related task, the focus has turned to basic (and long standing) educational issues: What are the intended learning outcomes of a higher education? of a general education? of each course and program offered? How is student learning measured with respect to these intended outcomes? (Kozma and Johnson, 1991, p. 24).

Even as substantial progress has been made in understanding how to use technology to improve or transform teaching and learning, there has been little or no progress in improving instructional productivity with this technology. Thus far, rather than improving efficiency, using technology has been almost always an add-on cost. The explanation for this situation is not hard to come by; the problem is that technology has been applied to extend the old model of education rather than to reengineer a new model using the transforming power of technology.

The skepticism that many still have about the real impact that technology will have on colleges is justified, for technology has disappointed far more than satisfied the need for assistance. Yet some of that skepticism is surely a product of human beings' tendency to overestimate the impact of any innovation in the short run but to underestimate it in the long run. The important fact is that the knowledge learned about how to use technology to improve or transform teaching and learning has come very quickly. So much more is known today than even a year or two ago, when most of those writers referenced in this chapter made their thoughtful assessments. In fact, even Green, one of those early thinkers on the subject, has recently noted how much has changed in just one year (from 1995 to 1996):

But something significant is happening. Fueled by more than four decades of aspirations and a dozen years of sustained (if often ad hoc) experimentation, information technology has finally emerged as a permanent, respected, and increasingly essential component of the college experience. New data from the annual Campus Computing Survey, now in its sixth year, indicate a major gain in the proportion of college courses (and by extension, college faculty) using information technology as an instructional resource. These data reveal that the use of information technology in instruction is finally breaking past the innovators and early adopters and into the ranks and experience of mainstream faculty. (1996, p. 24)

TECHNOLOGY AND THE LEARNING COLLEGE

Computer and electronic technology is neither a magic bullet nor a broken arrow; it is simply a tool, albeit one of the most sophisticated and complex tools human beings have ever invented. Technology is like a Swiss army knife; in adept hands, it has many uses including that of opening a "can of worms." In education, technology is a flexible tool that can enhance and expand learning when it is used to support a potent pedagogy and a content-rich curriculum. "Communications media and other technologies are so flexible that they do not dictate methods of teaching and learning" (Ehrmann, 1995, p. 24).

The learning college places learning first and provides educational experiences for learners anyway, anyplace, anytime. Technology is a key building block in creating a firm foundation for the learning college; it has many characteristics that support the goals and principles of the learning college.

Technology is ubiquitous in American culture, a way of life for the young and increasingly a way of life for older adults. The Committee for Economic Development reported in 1995 that more than two-thirds of American families with incomes over $50,000 and college-educated parents have a computer at home (p. 2). *Newsweek* dubbed 1996 the "year of the Internet" and reported that the World Wide Web doubles every 53 days and currently is used by 24 million North Americans (Levy, 1995-96, p. 27). "The Internet revolution is sweeping the globe with such swiftness that companies are desperately trying to understand what is occurring, what it all means, where it is going, and how to leverage their new opportunity" (CommerceNet/Nielsen, 1995, p. 1).

In a 1995 interview, Microsoft's Bill Gates said the Internet is becoming the ultimate market, the world's central department store "where we social animals will sell, trade, invest, haggle, pick stuff up, argue, meet new people, and hang out" (p. 60). Furthermore, Gates predicted that "the information highway is going to break down boundaries and may promote a world culture, or at least a sharing of cultural activities and values" (p. 66). This prediction is supported by Peter Schwartz in his book, *The Long View,* in the phenomenon he describes as the "Global Teenager." There will be over two billion teenagers in the world by the year 2001. With a high technological awareness, and high use of technology they "will have a more global identification than their parents and will embrace peers from other countries" (Jobe, 1995, p. 2).

Rapid changes in the expansion of technology are occurring in all aspects of American society and increasingly in the field of education. This expansion has led U.S. Secretary of Education Richard Riley, to proclaim, "The Information Age must also be the Education Age" (1995, p. 1). In the most recent national survey of the use of information technology in higher education, Green (1996) reported rising levels of computer ownership by college students (now at about 33 percent, but approaching 80 percent or more at some institutions) and faculty (over 50 percent across all of academe, but close to 100 percent on some campuses). The majority of entering college freshmen reported a half-year or more of some kind of computer training in high school. The proportion of college courses using some form of information technology rose significantly between 1994 and 1995, increasing by at least one-half, and in some cases doubling. In this annual survey, Green (1996) discovered that "the use of information technology resources is often greater in community colleges than in other sectors" (p. 4). In 1995, 28 percent of community colleges used commercial courseware in their courses compared to only 17 percent of public universities. Thirty-one percent of community colleges used computer labs for teaching and instruction compared to 23 percent of public universities. Education in general, and community colleges in particular, are rapidly expanding their use of information technology resources; in some cases that use is doubling annually. The ubiquity of information technology in American society, in education in general, and increasingly in community colleges is building a firm foundation for the creation of the learning college.

Technology is a time- and place-free medium and usually an ism-free medium. Technology is the cornerstone of the learning college in that it frees learning from time and place constrictions. "The real strength of technology is its flexibility. It frees us from such constraints as time, place, institution, and perhaps most significantly, teacher" (Oblinger and Maruyama, 1995, p. 1). Correspondence courses, as the earliest forms of distance education, set the pattern for breaking the bonds of time and place. In the last several decades, distance education through telecourses has extended and greatly increased opportunities for students beyond the campus and beyond scheduled courses. The Internet provides a dramatic shift in technological opportunities for learners to engage in learning experiences totally free of the time and place bonds associated with traditional educational structures. Learning will become more useful and more meaningful when it can be scheduled at the learner's convenience, and when it can be individualized for the learner's time and the learner's place.

The 18 governors holding membership in the Western Governors' Association (WGA) have plans for bringing education directly to the learner through their *Virtual University*. Planned as a joint project between the Educational Management Group, a unit of Simon and Schuster, and the WGA, the project is scheduled for release in 1997. Jonathan Newcomb, president and CEO of Simon and Schuster, said of the new venture "The use of interactive technology is causing a fundamental shift away from the physical classroom to focus on the learner. Multimedia instruction makes 'anytime, anywhere learning' realistic today and a model for postsecondary education as we move into the twenty-first century" (Media Advisory, 1996, p.2).

An additional value that technology brings to the learning college model is that, for the most part, technology is ism-free. Unless it is designed into the system on purpose or unintentionally, technology is free of racism, sexism, and ageism. A computer cannot tell if a student is black or white, male or female, young or old, fat or thin, ugly or pretty, tall or short, dirty or clean, passive or aggressive, or funny or somber. Teachers, on the other hand, are sometimes strongly influenced by these characteristics in their interactions with students, sometimes to the detriment of the learners. If a computer program is not ism-free, it is open for review and correction by numerous students and teachers who use the program. The isms of individual teachers, on the other hand, may go undetected for years and even when identified may go uncorrected because of the nature of academic culture that protects teachers in the name of academic freedom.

Technology can assess differences, individualize instruction, test for progress, record achievement, and transfer results to other sources. Educators place great value on "individualizing instruction" as the hallmark of their best efforts. "Mark Hopkins on one end of the log and a student on the other" has been an ideal of individualized instruction for decades. This ideal guides the limits placed on the number of students in a class and the number of courses taught in a term—not too many of either so that the teacher can "individualize instruction."

Individualized instruction has been one of the most enduring myths in all of education, and faculty members have struggled valiantly to live up to expectations that are impossible to meet. In no human way can a teacher assess the differences and teach to those differences in a class of 30 students, even if that one class were to be scheduled with the same teacher six hours a day, five days a week. If this "idealized" setting can't provide individualized instruction, the current context in community colleges where one teacher meets 30 students three times a week for 16 weeks and repeats this schedule four or five times each term makes such a goal completely unachievable.

> Researchers have studied in classrooms with stopwatches and tracked what actually happens during a school day, and they have found that generally speaking, students can only have 10 seconds of individual instruction for every hour spent in class. This means that in a 6-hour school day, the average student in an elementary school in the U.S. has approximately one minute of individual instruction. In a 180-day school year, this means that each student has approximately 1/2 a day of individual instruction per year, and when this statistic is extrapolated to the entire elementary and secondary school, this student will graduate from school with slightly less than one full week of individual instruction for the previous 13 years of school attendance. The mathematical reality is that 1/360th of the time spent in school is apt to be in individual instruction. The best teachers who concentrate very hard can sometimes double this statistic, but even two weeks of individual instruction over 13 years is not enough for many students. (Heuston, 1986, pp. 10-11)

Technology, on the other hand, can greatly assist in achieving the goal of assessing differences and providing "individualized instruction" for those differences in a variety of learning options. Gates (1995) said, "Technology can humanize the education environment . . . will bring mass customization to learning. . . and will fine-tune the product to allow students to follow somewhat divergent paths and learn at their own rates" (p. 66).

For the last three decades, the major use of computers in teaching and learning has been in the application of individualized computer-assisted instruction. In this mode, instruction is presented and students are asked questions and provided feedback. Based on the students' answers, new material is then presented. Students generally move through the material in a different way and at their own rates. James Kulik (1991) and his colleagues at the University of Michigan have summarized a large number of studies on computer-assisted instruction and have concluded that this approach results in about 20 percent improvement in learning outcomes and speed over traditional methods.

With technology, learning can be individualized. Computerized placement tests from the Educational Testing Service and American College Testing can assess student differences; hundreds of self-paced, computer-assisted programs are readily available for individualized instruction; programs to assess progress, record achievement, and make the results easily available are in place in hundreds of community colleges. In the learning college, technology to provide these services will be the norm for *all* courses as one of the major options available to learners. Such an arrangement will free faculty from a great deal of their current workload, providing opportunities to apply faculty talent and expertise to other learner needs.

Technology can provide access to great amounts of information including the most recently discovered knowledge. Storing and easily retrieving information is, of course, the original great value of computers. This characteristic is now so obvious that it is taken for granted and seldom mentioned directly in the current literature on information technology. Through Gopher and World Wide Web resources, a fifth-grade student in Pecan Gap, Texas, can access the White House, the Library of Congress, the National Library of Medicine, the Vatican Museum, and the Elvis museum at Graceland. "The rich array of periodicals, databases, scholarly literature, image libraries, federal and state documents and scientific research coming online on a daily (or even hourly) basis is stunning—and fundamentally changes the traditional definition of the library as the primary campus archive or information repository" (Green and Gilbert, 1995, p. 15).

One stunning example of the power of technology to access information is The Visible Human Project coordinated by the National Library of Medicine. The project to date includes an extensive service of anatomical images taken from real cadavers, stored in computers, and distributed over the Internet. With a grant of $1.4 million from the National Library of Medicine, scientists at the University of Colorado froze, sliced, and photographed a male and female cadaver—four months of slicing and filming 1,871 cross sections of the male and more than a year of slicing and filming more than 5,000 cross sections of the female. The tiniest details of the human body are now displayed on computer monitors around the world, portrayed in commercial CD-ROMs, and manipulated by artists, medical students, and radiologists. The male cadaver is contained in 15 gigabytes of data and his images have already been hung in a gallery in Japan alongside sketches that Leonardo da Vinci made of the human body. The U.S. Army is using the data to simulate damage caused by shrapnel. Engineers are using the digital cadaver to simulate what happens in car crashes. Scientists at the State University of New York at Stony Brook have created an "interactive fly-through" of the colon. (Wheeler, 1996, p. A6). The Visible Human Project will serve as a major resource of stored but accessible information for science students, art students, and many others and will radically change the content of current textbooks in anatomy and physiology.

Other stunning examples of the use of information technology include the use of pictures from the Hubble spacecraft by Paula Knoeller, a faculty member in astronomy at Catonsville Community College in Maryland. Just a day or two after the Hubble captured movies of what was interpreted as star formation in October 1995, Knoeller downloaded these video clips from the NASA website. Only days later, she was sharing these experiences with her students. A week later, her students were having asynchronous conversations with NASA scientists, and three weeks later she was sharing these experiences with a national audience of peers at the League for Innovation's annual conference on information technology in community colleges. Leo Hirner, a physics instructor at Longview Community College, is able to access a telescope on Mt. Wilson outside of Los Angeles over the Internet from his Lee's Summit, Missouri, office. He and his students download the photographic images that had been taken the night before for analysis and discussion in class the next day. Technology not only provides access to nearly limitless resources, but it also provides immediate access, a powerful tool with which to support learner-centered education.

The vast array of accessible resources also fundamentally changes the role of the teacher in the education enterprise. In the learning college, the instructor no longer has to be the sole knowledge expert trying to keep up to date with an exploding field of information. Information is simply there. It is readily available to everyone, immediately accessible, easily compiled, and creatively presented. The instructor in the learning college is now free to become a learning facilitator, assisting learners in accessing and organizing information, and, more importantly, assisting them in analyzing and using that information for their personal meaning. Learners no longer have to store information in their heads; they are free to analyze, integrate, create, solve, apply—in other words, *to learn by doing* something with information. In this way, knowledge that is meaningful and relevant is gained and learners become educated.

Technology can manage and coordinate complex arrangements and activities. Information technology has been widely adopted in colleges and universities for administrative functions. "As in the corporate domain, computers have improved productivity related to a wide range of data management and transaction processing activities: personnel files, course schedules, library catalogs, budgets and accounts receivable, student transcripts, and admissions information" (Green and Gilbert, 1995, p. 10). Few educational institutions these days fail to use information technology for these basic administrative functions.

At the instructional level, a number of new systems are being designed to coordinate a variety of instructional activities, freeing the instructor to facilitate learning for students. CONNECT, a software system produced by W.W. Norton and Company, provides teachers with the tools they need to manage a class. Teachers can use the system to distribute assignments, with or without worksheets; to place students into work groups or to dissolve work groups; to join any group's discussion and move easily from group to group; to comment on papers and return them for revision at any point in the writing process; and to collect, comment on, grade, and return papers over the network. Depending on how the teacher prefers to have students work, CONNECT allows students to discuss assignments electronically; to use pre-writing comments in drafting; to share drafts for review and comments; to post papers to the teacher for comment and grading; and to read graded papers. At any time, students and teachers may print out comments or papers. Basically, CONNECT merges the utility of multiple software packages (word processing, e-mail, collaborative projects) into a tidy, easy-to-use bundle (Hoge, 1995, pp. 41-42).

With support of over $5 million from IBM and the U.S. Office of Education, the Miami-Dade Community College District and the League for Innovation in the Community College have created Project SYNERGY Integrator (PSI), a system to manage learning in reading, writing, mathematics, ESL, and study skills/critical thinking. Project SYNERGY Integrator is an adaptive management system for local area networks (LANs). It provides, on the one hand, a system that has standard faculty and student interfaces and, on the other hand, a platform of neutrality that accommodates multivendor software without affecting the standard user interfaces. It incorporates Project SYNERGY learning objectives and mastery test questions from a selected group of vendors and provides installation options that will run the multivendor software used for assessment and instruction. It provides links among diagnostic tests, learning objectives, instructional software, and mastery tests in order for the student to have smooth transitions from one learning objective to another and from one software package to another. It allows departments and faculty to indicate how PSI should manage their courses and gives them a more efficient handle on how their students are progressing. More than 400 faculty and administrators at two- and four-year institutions have been involved in specifying the necessary features and functions of PSI (Project SYNERGY, May 1995).

CONNECT and Project SYNERGY Integrator are only two examples of early experiments with instructional management systems. They hold great promise for coordinating a vast array of content and for providing learners individual access to that content as well as individual coaching and monitoring. In these early models, the teacher still plays a primary role; in subsequent developments these systems should also be designed so that students have the option to navigate their own learning. Increasingly, the systems will need to take over repetitive roles and functions of "teaching" so that the teachers have more time to coordinate and facilitate learning experiences. These instructional management systems will play a key role in developing the learning college for they make it possible to manage the numerous options required for the diverse needs of learners, freeing up teachers to become learning facilitators.

Technology can extend and expand a sense of community and connectedness. When computers were first beginning to be used on a wide-scale basis in education, there was a great deal of concern about their dehumanizing effect, as if they would create barriers to human interaction. More recently, now that computers have been used to create new and unique connections among human beings, the criticism is focused on the quality of the interaction, as if the quality of interaction via technology could never measure up to the quality of face-to-face interaction. In part, the resistance of educators to using technology to build personal connections reflects their continuing allegiance to the myth of individualized instruction.

It is a moot point. Regardless of the findings of future researchers on the quality of interaction through technology, humane and fulfilling interactions through technology are already firmly established in the culture, first by the U.S. mail, then by the telephone, and now by the Internet. It only remains to be seen how educators will creatively apply the technology to extend and expand opportunities for connectedness, community, and collaboration. In the learning college such use of technology will be an everyday reality. Technology allows learners and learning facilitators to create collaborative projects, to connect with resources, and to form communities *as needed.* Freed from the time- and place-bound architecture of the traditional school, learning can begin to occur anyway, anyplace, anytime.

"The emerging uses of the Internet by faculty and students may provide ways to change the structure of the fundamental 'business' of education" (Green and Gilbert, 1995, p. 15). Who knows what will emerge from an opportunity for human beings to be connected to and communicating with other human beings anywhere in the world in the immediate moment. Current faculty are beginning to use the technology for communication and collaboration in ways that will become commonplace in the next few years. A professor at Temple University, describing her first use of the Internet for conducting a class, reported, "I was also pleased to observe that students who did not normally talk in class participated in this online discussion. My personal favorite was the one student who intermittently chimed in with, 'Group hug!' I also noted afterwards that there were students talking to each other in person who previously hadn't talked to one another" (Stewart, 1995, p. 52).

These enhanced opportunities for communication—for learners who do not talk in regular class and for learners who will meet face-to-face only after the technological interaction—are widely reported in the Maricopa Community Colleges. Through the *Electronic Journal*, initially piloted by

Karen Schwalm at Maricopa's Glendale campus, students interact with each other and with the instructor in greatly increased quantity, and some say quality, that is not possible in the face-to-face traditional classes. The *Electronic Journal* has been so successful in classes that it has evolved into a collegewide *Electronic Forum*, providing unlimited opportunities for students on a commuter campus to connect, communicate, and collaborate. This kind of application of current technologies will assist greatly in building a solid foundation for the learning college.

Technology can challenge, stimulate, simulate, and even create new forms and connections. Paul Privateer, a professor at Arizona State University, predicts that technology will create a brave new world for education. In "The Future of Academic Computing" (1993), he described a world in which new marriages between technologies will create entirely new technologies; learners will develop symbiotic relationships with computers; and new relationships among institutions of learning, technology vendors, government, and the marketplace will create new structures and opportunities. Technological advances will be used to build smaller and more powerful machines that will incorporate video, phone, fax, paging, mail, and interactivity in one portable unit. A new kind of interface between user and machine will evolve that will make the traditional architecture of education obsolete. Advances in artificial intelligence will create personal companions that can be "trained" to remember learners' personal preferences and styles. Instead of going to a lab for self-paced computerized instruction or accessing such instruction through the Internet, a learner will carry his or her own personalized teaching machine/learning facilitator unit in a wallet.

Privateer (1993) also noted that technology can create new ways of thinking and quoted from Heinz Pagels' *Dreams of Reason*, "The computer, with its ability to manage enormous amounts of data and to simulate reality, provides a new window on . . . nature. We may begin to see reality differently simply because the computer produces knowledge differently from the traditional analytic instruments. It provides a different angle on reality" (p. 13).

Privateer (1993) went on to say:

> Given the speed and capability of future technology, our little hand-held machines will empower learners with the capacity to build sophisticated knowledge relationships, sophisticated models of complex phenomena, in which to explore them and to also, in a meta-critical manner, understand the nature of model building itself as a mode of inquiry. New technology will allow us to manipulate how we interface with both our subject areas and our machines. These new manipulations have already begun with the advent of hypertextuality, low-level virtual reality constructs, cyberspace, multidimensional databases, and

4GL object-oriented programming. The future of technology will make it clearer that the sole purpose of technology is not simply to solve problems. New technology will create new philosophies and new concepts and new ideologies. The goal of learners in this new space is to explore these inventions and to know them if they are to understand and choose what they will become as a result of what they have made. (p. 13)

CONCLUSION

When these advances and applications in technology become commonplace, the learning college will have to evolve into a new form. The principles and examples in this book will appear ancient; the learning college now envisioned will become obsolete. In the future, if advances in technology continue at the current pace, learning will become commonplace—everyday, just-in-time experiences provided by technology anyway, anyplace, anytime. These sweeping changes will happen because of the unique nature of technology to build on itself. "All the technological knowledge we work with today will represent only one percent of the knowledge that will be available in 2050" (Cetron, 1994, p. 5). Even if this prediction is only half realized, the world will never be the same, and learning and school will never be the same. The new tools and opportunities created by technology provide a firm foundation on which to build a learning college for the twenty-first century.

REFERENCES

Baker, Warren. Quoted in "Cal Poly: Actual or Virtual University Campus?" *Columns: IBM's Newsletter for Higher Education*, Fall 1994.

Blumenstyk, Goldie. "Faculty Group Calls for Caution and Curbs on Distance Education," *The Chronicle of Higher Education*, January 26, 1996.

Cetron, Marvin. *An American Renaissance in the Year 2000*. Bethesda, MD: World Future Society, 1994.

CommerceNet and Nielsen. *The CommerceNet/Nielsen Internet Demographics Survey: Executive Summary*. Online. Available HTTP: http//:www.commerce.net. November 1, 1995.

Committee for Economic Development. *CED News Release*, September 19, 1995.

Doucette, Don. "Transforming Teaching and Learning through Technology." In *Teaching and Learning in the Community College* by Terry O'Banion and Associates. Washington, D.C.: American Association of Community Colleges, 1994a.

———. "Transforming Teaching and Learning Using Information Technology," *Community College Journal*, October/November 1994b.

Ehrmann, Stephen C. "Asking the Right Questions: What Does Research Tell Us about Technology and Higher Learning?" *Change*, March/April 1995.

Gates, Bill. "The Road Ahead," *Newsweek*, November 27, 1995.

Geoghegan, William H. "A Revolution Gone Awry: Getting Instructional Technology Back on Track." Speech presented at League for Innovation in the Community College's Annual Conference on Information Technology, Kansas City, Missouri, November 8, 1995.

————. "Stuck at the Barricades: Can Information Technology Really Enter the Mainstream of Teaching and Learning?" *AAHE Bulletin*, September 1994.

Gilbert, Steven W. "Teaching, Learning, and Technology: The Need for Campuswide Planning and Faculty Support Services," *Change*, March/April 1995.

Green, Kenneth C. "The Coming Ubiquity of Information Technology," *Change*, March/April 1996.

Green, Kenneth C. and Gilbert, Steven W. "Great Expectations: Content, Communications, Productivity, and the Role of Information Technology in Higher Education," *Change*, March/April 1995.

Heterick, Robert C. Quoted in "EDUCOM's New Leader Expected to Play a Key Role in Promoting Technology" by Thomas J. Deloughry, *The Chronicle of Higher Education*, October 7, 1992.

Heuston, Dustin H. "The Future of Education: A Time of Hope and New Delivery Systems." Unpublished paper. 1986.

Hoge, Steve. "Early Adapters in the Mainstream: A Note from W.W. Norton," *Change*, March/April 1995.

The Institute for Future Studies. *Critical Issues Facing America's Community Colleges.* Warren, MI: Macomb Community College, 1992.

Institute for Research on Higher Education. "The Academy in a Changing World: Restructuring in Higher Education," *Change*, July/August 1995.

Jobe, Holly M. "The Global Teenager," *interface*, April 1995.

Kozma, Robert B. and Johnston, Jerome. "The Technological Revolution Comes to the Classroom, " *Change*, 1991, 23.

Kulik, Chen-Lin C. and Kulik, James A. "Effectiveness of Computer-Based Instruction: An Updated Analysis," *Computers in Human Behavior*, 1991.

Levy, Steven. "The Year of the Internet," *Newsweek*, December 25, 1995/January 1, 1996.

Media Advisory. "Western Governors Announce Plans, Funding for Western Virtual University." Denver, CO: Western Governors' Association, February 6, 1996.

Monaghan, Peter. "Technology and the Unions," *Chronicle of Higher Education*, section A, February 10, 1995.

National Education Commission on Time and Learning. *Prisoners of Time.* Washington, D.C.: U.S. Government Printing Office, April 1994.

Oblinger, Diana and Maruyama, Mark. "Transforming Instruction in Preparation for a High Bandwidth NII." Proceedings of the National Infrastructure Conference, Monterey, CA, September 26-29, 1995.

Privateer, Paul. "The Future of Academic Computing: A World of New Interfacings," *Computing News*, Dec/Jan/Feb 1993.

Project SYNERGY. *Project SYNERGY Software Report for Underprepared Students: Year Four Report.* Miami, FL: Miami-Dade Community College, May 1995.

Riley, Richard. W. "Statement on the Release of *Connecting Students to a Changing World* from the Committee on Economic Development." News release September 19, 1995.

Stewart, Concetta M. "Going On the Net," *Change*, March/April 1995.

Wheeler, David L. "Creating a Body of Knowledge," *Chronicle of Higher Education*, February 2, 1996.

CHAPTER 5

How Firm a Foundation

Learning Research, Outcome Measures, and Learning Organizations

T echnology is one of the keys to building a solid foundation for the creation of the learning college. Without current and anticipated advances in technology, the model of the learning college suggested in this book would not be possible. Technology will continue to play a major role in evolving concepts of the learning college, but technology, though necessary, is an insufficient condition by itself.

The solid foundation required for a learning college is greatly strengthened by an emerging body of research on learning which affirms that learners learn best by doing, by working on real problems in real environments; that human ability is much more complex and diverse than is suggested by one-dimensional measures of intelligence; that there are significant differences in learning styles of individuals; and that the natural functioning of the brain provides the best road map for the learning enterprise.

The foundation becomes firmer still when new concepts of assessment and outcome measures are added. When assessment is viewed as a continuing process for understanding and improving student learning, when competencies required for advancement and exit are agreed upon and made visible to all, and when the learner is a respected partner in the deliberations about how to define and apply assessments and outcomes, the foundation for a learning college begins to take shape.

The timing for educational institutions to experiment with the learning college could not be better. Many colleges are applying the concepts of Total Quality Management (TQM) and "learning organizations," and the use of these concepts can prepare the way for the learning college. As colleges flatten their organizations, empower individuals, develop collaborative processes, commit to quality, and make learners of the stakeholders, they are taking some of the first steps in building the learning college foundation. The learning college, in fact, can provide the transcendent vision and purpose for employing these organizational concepts borrowed from the business world. Thus the foundation for creating a learning college is significantly strengthened when colleges are already engaged in complementary processes found in TQM and learning organizations.

NEW RESEARCH ON OLD LEARNING

"For technology to 'work' in the classroom, there has to be a convincing pedagogy and rationale behind it" (Common, 1994, p.33). Common argued that pedagogy is the "essence of schooling" and must undergird the entire educational enterprise:

> I contend that the reform of schooling must begin with and be subsequently defined by democratic pedagogical practice. The new organizational design must emerge from pedagogy, the essence of schooling, and be shaped by it. It must not be the way it has been throughout the century, pedagogy accommodating to organization. Rather, pedagogy must create organization's structure; pedagogy must shape organizational culture. From democratic pedagogy will rise democratic organization. (p. 245)

Pedagogy is the science and art of education. If pedagogy is stretched to mean "how learners learn," then applying what is known about learning becomes the underlying rationale for organizational culture. How learners learn dictates how the learning college is organized, and it also dictates the roles of learning facilitators.

Educators know a great deal about how learners learn, a great deal more than is actually applied in practice. In 1986, in response to increasing dissatisfaction with the state of education, a group of the leading educational researchers in the United States gathered at Wingspread in Racine, Wisconsin. Convened by the American Association for Higher Education and the Education Commission of the States, with support from The Johnson Foundation, the group's purpose was to review all the literature on learning in college and reduce that information to a set of guiding principles. "Seven Principles for Good Practice in Undergraduate Education" was the outcome and the principles included:

1. Good practice encourages student-faculty contact.
2. Good practice encourages cooperation among students.
3. Good practice encourages active learning.

4. Good practice gives prompt feedback.
5. Good practice emphasizes time on task.
6. Good practice communicates high expectations.
7. Good practice respects diverse talents and ways of learning. (Chickering and Gamson, 1987, p. 1)

These seven practices distill what was known at the time about learning in college. They are powerful principles and were widely disseminated to provide guidance for the reform of higher education. Their impact has been minimal, however, because as sound as these principles are, they were created and have been applied in the context of the time-bound, place-bound, role-bound, and efficiency-bound model characteristic of most institutions of higher education. Now that this constrictive architecture of education is opening up to concepts of the learning college, these seven principles could form a solid pedagogical foundation for the learning college. They can be expanded and enhanced in coming years as educators begin to apply new understandings about learning that are emerging from advances in brain research, cognitive science, and psychology. These new understandings are reflected in theories of constructivism, multiple intelligences theory, research on learning styles, and brain-based research.

Constructivism vs. Objectivism

A number of recent theorists have made a case for a constructivist view of education in contrast to the more traditional objectivist view. In the objectivist view, knowledge is objective and exists outside the individual, waiting there to be learned. The goal of education for the objectivist is to ensure that the learner knows the external world, which is interpreted primarily by the teacher. In this model, learners demonstrate their mastery of this external knowledge, and the school tests and credentials their performance.

A basic premise of the constructivist view is that "Construction does not cause learning. At best it can support and nurture it" (Cunningham, 1991, p. 16). Constructivists create real problems for real environments (contextual learning), and learners examine, analyze, and create to solve these problems and make meaning for themselves. Knowledge is "constructed" by each learner in terms of his or her own perceptions of the world, the learner's mental models. Understanding comes from working with and experience in problems and issues rather than from memorizing information about problems and issues. Two goals of pedagogy in the constructivist's view are to facilitate the learner's in-depth examination of knowledge and to develop multiple perspectives.

Contextual learning reflects the constructivist view. Dale Parnell (1995) said, "The term 'contextual learning' marks an educational philosophy and an educational strategy that centers on enabling students to find *meaningfulness* in their education" (p. 2). It "endeavors to help students make the connection between learning and doing" (Parnell, 1995, p. 2). The deeply embedded wisdom that "learning by doing" is best—evident in the collective unconscious and championed by Aristotle, Dewey, and the humanistic educators—percolates to the top once again in concepts of "contextual learning" and constructivism.

John Cleveland (1994) described ideals of the constructivist view:

> Constructivism is a philosophy of learning founded on the premise that we construct our own understanding of the world we live in, through active reflection on our experience. Through this process, we develop "rules" and "mental models" for making sense of the world and guiding our behavior. Learning occurs when we have to adjust our mental constructions to take into account new information in our environment that doesn't fit those constructions. "Knowledge" is created through the relationship between the student and the world. It is inherently subjective and provisional. Knowledge is valued because it improves the "map" between our mental constructions and actual experience not because it matches what the "teacher" already knows. (p. 6)

In great part, the constructivist view is the most recent reincarnation of the ancient stream-of-consciousness referred to in chapter 3 and epitomized in the fundamental "learn by doing" principle. The philosophy and pedagogy of Progressive Education and of Humanistic Education are the precursors of constructivism. This connection is abundantly clear in the seminal work of Arthur Combs' and Donald Snygg's *Individual Behavior* (1959). Combs and Snygg created a framework for phenomenological psychology that profoundly influenced educational practice in the 1960s and 1970s. For Combs and Snygg, perception is key. Each individual perceives the world in his or her own special way, primarily based on one's self-concept, or the way one perceives one's self. If a person holds himself or herself in high regard, that is, has high self-esteem, one is not limited by the confused images that accompany low self-esteem, and thus more authentic perceptions are allowed to enter the views of the perceiver. A primary goal of education then was to increase self-esteem (still a goal of some segments of education) for, it was posited by the phenomenologists, increased self-esteem leads to increased self-concept, which in turn leads to increased ability to perceive and understand the world and others in it. Maslow's goal for human beings was "self-actualization." Privette suggested "transcendent functioning" as the goal for human development; Jourard preferred "transparent selves." The constructivists have avoided this poetic language of the humanistic educators, but their basic beliefs are the same.

The views of constructivists provide additional building blocks for creating a foundation for the learning college. In the learning college the student is responsible for constructing his or her own learning by active involvement in creating learning opportunities and by direct participation in the opportunities created. Learners learn best by doing.

Multiple Intelligences

The concept of the intelligence quotient (IQ), in which the mental age is divided by the actual age in younger children to achieve a score of mental development and ability, has been a great curse on education. As adapted by practicing teachers, IQ has come to mean a fixed kind of general ability that one is born with and subsequently stuck with throughout life. Consequently, for decades, students have been perceived by teachers as "dumb," "average," or "smart," and they have been dealt with accordingly. IQ has even influenced the architecture of education; in certain periods of educational practice students have been grouped by their scores and the curriculum arranged to accommodate these group differences.

Many educators have long known that human ability and performance are far more diverse and complex than is suggested by the one-dimensional concept of IQ. For over two decades, Howard Gardner at Harvard University has been studying human intelligence based on his early medical school research on victims of brain damage. Six books and numerous articles later, Gardner has helped dispel the idea of intelligence as a single and simple measure of competence, and he has identified seven kinds of "intelligence" or seven ways of knowing in human beings that act independently of each other. These "multiple intelligences" combine differently in different people, and each individual has generally developed some of the intelligences more than others. The seven "multiple intelligences" are illustrated in Figure 5-1 (Gardner, 1983).

1. Verbal/Linguistic Intelligence
2. Logical/Mathematical Intelligence
3. Visual/Spatial Intelligence
4. Body/Kinesthetic Intelligence
5. Musical/Rhythmic Intelligence
6. Interpersonal Intelligence
7. Intrapersonal Intelligence

GARDNER'S SEVEN WAYS OF KNOWING

FIGURE 5-1

René Díaz-Lefebvre, a psychology teacher at Glendale Community College in Arizona, has studied Gardner's work extensively and has begun to implement his theories in teaching an introductory psychology course. Díaz-Lefebvre first assesses students to determine their dominant or preferred intelligences and then provides a variety of learning options from which students may select those most complementary to their preferred intelligences. To date, 15 different learning options, reflecting various intelligences, have been created, and each is worth a number of points to be accumulated into a final grade. Students are encouraged to earn extra points by experimenting with learning options that do not complement their preferred intelligences. In a pilot study of 130 students, Díaz-Lefebvre (1996) reported that students want choices and options in proving "how they are smart," will take risks in looking at different ways of learning when encouraged to do so, and are highly motivated to spend extra time learning course material (p.1).

Daniel Goleman, a Harvard-trained psychologist, has recently elaborated on Gardner's interpersonal and intrapersonal intelligences in his book, *Emotional Intelligence* (1995). Goleman hopes to raise the level of social and emotional competence of learners by teaching "life skills" as a key part of the curriculum. A National Collaborative for the Advancement of Social and Emotional Learning has been established at Yale University to promote courses in emotional literacy. Topics include self-awareness, decision making, alternative choices, managing emotions, taking responsibility, empathy, and assertiveness. Emotional intelligence is another reincarnation of the Humanistic Education theories of the 1960s that placed great value on affective education. John Dewey and Arthur Combs would be pleased with this latest attempt to educate the whole person.

In the learning college, options will be created so that learners can explore and expand each and any of these various intelligences. Complex problems will provide opportunities for exploring combinations of the various ways of knowing. Learners will navigate the Internet and will collaborate with other learners and with experts to plumb the parameters of a broader and deeper view of their rich and complex talents. Learning facilitators will use pedagogies and resources representative of the various intelligences to provide different learning options; or at least they will recognize and value the variety of intelligences in learners. Their roles will be, in part, defined by this emerging, more comprehensive view of human nature.

Learning Styles

If human beings have "multiple intelligences," it automatically follows that they have multiple learning styles that reflect those various intelligences.

Some individuals learn best intuitively, while others find logical analysis to work best. Some learners must touch objects to really "know" them. These different learning styles are sometimes cast as "preferences" for using one side of the brain over another. Right-brained individuals have a propensity for processing information in intuitive ways; left-brained individuals "prefer" logical and analytical thinking. Different systems for distinguishing between these various learning styles have been developed by David Kolb—who has created the Kolb Learning Style Inventory—Joseph Hill, Bernice McCarthy, researchers at Educational Testing Service, and others.

In the classic *Women's Ways of Knowing* (1986), it was firmly established that there are significant differences in learning styles between women and men. A more recent study (cited in *Women in Higher Education*, 1995, p. 7) confirmed the gender differences and suggested that "traditional educational settings may not be the best learning environments for females." The authors of this study noted that traditional education favors analyzing abstract information and testing hypotheses as the preferred learning styles, a style much preferred by men. "Traditional education is directed toward and appeals more to males since it is primarily abstract and reflective. Females learn better in hands-on and practical settings, emphasizing the realm of the affective and doing" (cited in *Women in Higher Education*, 1995, p. 7).

It has also been firmly established that there are significant differences in learning styles among cultural groups. "There is very little disagreement that a relationship does exist between the culture in which children live (or from which they are descended) and their preferred ways of learning" (Guild, 1994, p. 17). Guild (1994) has summarized the literature on the learning styles of various cultural groups as follows:

- Mexican Americans regard family and personal relationships as important and are comfortable with cognitive generalizations and patterns. They often seek personal relationships with teachers and are more comfortable with broad concepts than more specific facts and components.
- African Americans tend to value oral experiences, physical activity, and loyalty in interpersonal relationships. They prefer classroom activities such as discussion, active projects, and collaborative work.
- Native Americans generally value and develop acute visual discrimination and skills in the use of imagery, perceive globally, and have reflective thinking patterns. Thus, schooling should establish a context for new information, provide quiet times for thinking, and emphasize visual stimuli.

- White Americans tend to value independence, analytic thinking, objectivity, and accuracy. These values translate into learning experiences that focus on competition, information, tests and grades, and linear logic—patterns most prevalent in American schools. (pp. 17-18)

Even though these differences exist among cultural groups, Guild (1994) cautioned against stereotyping all learners within a specific cultural group. "In both observational and data-based research on cultures, one consistent finding is that within a group, the variations among individuals are as great as their commonalities" (p. 19). Recognizing differences in learning styles between men and women and among cultural groups may be helpful to learning facilitators as they assist in the creation of collaborative networks, but the emphasis should always be on the learning style and needs of a specific learner.

In the learning college, these differences in learning styles will be assessed at the point of initial engagement and will provide a map for the learners in navigating the many learning options provided. All learning styles will be valued (and represented among learning facilitators), and a rich variety of kinds of learning will be available through a rich variety of means. Most learners will begin their activities using learning styles they prefer and with which they have been most successful, but in the learning college, they will also be challenged to explore learning styles that do not fit so comfortably as a way of broadening their understanding of themselves and the complexities of knowledge.

Brain-Based Research

The human brain is where learning occurs. It follows logically (for those who "prefer" a learning style based on logic) that educators are great consumers of the latest brain research so they can implement sound educational practices to expand and increase learning in their students. But such is not the case; most educators are completely unaware of the vast amount of knowledge that has accumulated in the past 30 years on how the brain works. In fact, it is becoming increasingly clear that the school is organized in ways that are completely antagonistic to how learning occurs in the brain.

Caine and Caine (1990) observed that "the greatest challenge of brain research for educators does not lie in understanding the anatomical intricacies in brain functioning but in comprehending the vastness, complexity, and potential of the human brain" (p. 66). Based on an extensive analysis of brain research, Caine and Caine proposed 12 principles as a basic foundation for brain-based learning.

- The brain is a parallel processor.
- Learning engages the entire physiology.
- The search for meaning is innate.
- The search for meaning occurs through "patterning."
- Emotions are critical to patterning.
- Every brain simultaneously perceives and creates parts and wholes.
- Learning involves both focused attention and peripheral perception.
- Learning always involves conscious and unconscious process.
- We have two types of memory: a spatial memory system and a set of systems for rote learning.
- The brain understands and remembers best when facts and skills are embedded in natural spatial memory.
- Learning is enhanced by challenge and inhibited by threat.
- Each brain is unique.

These 12 basic principles confirm and extend concepts noted earlier in constructivist theories, learning styles, and multiple intelligences. These concepts form a complementary pattern that frames the foundation for the learning college. This framework is described in Figure 5-2 (Cleveland, 1995, p.5).

The old view of learning is mechanical; it is the factory model in which learners move through the line at the same rate imprinted with the knowledge the school deems important. The new learning views learning as organic and natural; learning is unique for each person, and it is related to personal meaning and real life. The new learning, supported by creative applications and use of new technology, builds a solid foundation for the learning college of the future.

ASSESSMENT OF STUDENT LEARNING

Historically, the individual teacher, alone in the classroom, has been the sole judge and jury of a learner's needs and abilities and of a learner's progress. In this role-bound model, the teacher functions independently of the system, making key decisions about a learner's life. A kind of sloppy assumption undergirds this assessment process: 1) based on previous grades, scores on the teacher's self-designed instruments, standardized test scores, and the teacher's "objective" judgment, the student is "sized-up" for this course; 2) the teacher provides clear directions for success in this course and provides "individualized instruction" for students in need of it; 3) the teacher is flexible and provides a variety of methods and options to accommodate the student's "learning style"; 4) during the progress of the course the teacher provides formative evaluations to reinforce success or to

Old Learning	New Learning
Closed: Inputs are carefully controlled.	**Open:** We are provided a rich variety of inputs ("immersion").
Serial-Processed: All learners are expected to follow the same learning sequence; learners only learn one thing at a time.	**Parallel-Processed:** Different learners simultaneously follow different learning paths; many types of learning happen at the same time for individual learners.
Designed: Both knowledge and the learning process are predetermined by others.	**Emergent:** Knowledge is created through the relationship between the knower and the known. The outcome cannot be known in advance.
Controlled: The "teacher" determines what, when, and how we learn.	**Self-Organized:** We are active in the design of curriculum, activities, and assessment; teacher is a facilitator and designer of learning.
Discrete, Separated: Disciplines are separate and independent; roles of teacher and student clearly differentiated.	**Messy, Webbed:** Disciplines are integrated; roles are flexible.
Static: Same material and method applied to all students.	**Adaptive:** Material and teaching methods varied based on our interest and learning styles.
Linear: Material is taught in predictable, controlled sequences, from simple "parts" to complex "wholes."	**Nonlinear:** We learn nonsequentially, with rapid and frequent iteration between parts and wholes.
Competing: We learn alone and compete with others for rewards.	**Co-Evolving:** We learn together; our "intelligence" is based on our learning community.

NEW VIEWS OF LEARNING

FIGURE 5-2

correct directions; and 5) at the end of the course the teacher calculates measures that are translated into a grade—a permanent record of achievement that influences the life of the student ever after. The teacher in the community college performs these key functions for over 100 students every term with no training whatsoever in assessment and measurement theories and practice. Once again, the system has failed the teacher. This sloppy assumption is allowed to stand, and teachers themselves accede to the myth that as "professionals" they are entirely capable of performing these assessment functions—indeed, it is their "right" to do so.

Student Assessment

Even in the best of circumstances—the best-trained staff using the best instruments in the most controlled situation—assessment is far from being an exact science, especially when applied to individuals. For assessment to "work" for the individual learner, the teacher must be freed from the expected role of sole judge and jury, and the process must be framed around the needs of the learner.

The ultimate goal of education is to help the student develop satisfactory answers to the questions: Who am I? Where am I going? What difference does it make? A complementary goal of a workable assessment process for the learning college is based on securing the best possible answers to two key questions: What does this student know? What can this student do? The process will begin, as noted in chapter 3, by engaging the learner as a full partner in creating a personal profile of the learner's abilities, achievements, values, needs, goals, expectations, learning styles, resources, and environmental/situational limitations. The learning college will provide a qualified specialist in assessment to assist the student in creating this personal profile, which also includes a personal learning plan. The personal learning plan will include the learning options to be pursued immediately and will project future learning options for exploration later.

For each learning option—a discrete module or learning package that may be a unit in a program or a complete program—competencies required for entry will have been determined by a group of experts, often based on emerging national standards. Each learning option will also include a set of competencies required for exit, and these will also be determined by a group of experts, and again, will often be based on emerging national standards. These competencies will reflect the learning college's attempt to provide a framework for the questions: What does this student know? What can this student do?

The competencies will also provide a framework for the content of the learning option, but they will not limit how or when this content is to be learned or applied. Ideally, each learner, armed with information about his or her personal learning style, will be able to select from a variety of approaches or methodologies to successfully navigate each learning option. For example, to learn skills in analyzing, understanding, and appreciating the sonnet form of poetry, a learner may join a seven-member tutor-led group of other learners as the primary approach. In addition, the learner may also review a series of videotapes in which celebrated orators read selected sonnets followed by a taped discussion of the sonnets' meaning conducted by leading critics. The learner may team up with a colleague from the seven-member group to participate in a weekly forum on the Internet that features a selection of Shakespeare's sonnets. If the group-based approach is not helping the learner achieve the competencies designed for the learning option—determined by computerized "progress feedback" assessments initiated by the student or a learning facilitator— the student may switch options, perhaps to a computerized instructional package that individualizes the pace and the level of content to the needs of the learner.

The competencies will provide the framework for the learning activities. They are external standards, visible and agreed upon by experts. Competencies will also be flexible, subject to change as new knowledge emerges or as increasing complexities or new social and economic values become apparent. Since the competencies will be highly visible, everyone can be aware of the goals; the "game" of trying to guess what the teacher wants or what comprises an A grade will be eliminated. Furthermore, the teacher— where teachers are still participating as direct players in some of the learning options—will be freed from having to be an expert on determining what is to be learned and whether or not anything has been learned. The role of the learning facilitator will be to assist the learner in discovering a pathway among the learning options that leads to success, and to achieve the competencies in the learning options.

The Boy Scouts of America have embedded a system of competencies in their culture that could serve as a model for the learning college. To advance through levels of scouts such as tenderfoot, second class, first class, star, life, eagle with palms, and explorer, scouts must demonstrate mastery of specific competencies, which have been established for each level. The competencies have been developed by experts, and they are visible to all those engaged in the process. The role of boy scout leaders is to facilitate successful experiences for those who wish to achieve the competencies.

Fortunately, community colleges have considerable experience in competency-based education. Entry/exit competencies have been established in many community college occupational programs, and there is some experimentation in transfer and liberal arts programs. This experience helps to build the foundation for the learning college.

In the learning college, however, more than entry/exit competencies will be needed. Assessment must become a continuing pedagogical process in which the learner begins to make assessments, i.e., check progress and make corrections all along the way. The learner will learn to "think critically" in real-life time about his or her own real life: How am I doing? Am I learning enough, fast enough for me? Is there a better way for me to learn about this topic or learn this skill? What does this learning mean for me? Mean for the way I feel about life, mean for the job I have in mind, or mean for my goal to complete an advanced degree at another institution?

What do I know and what can I do? For the learner, continuing self-assessment needs to become an internalized process so that a self-reliant learner can make real the goal of lifelong learning. Learners will learn the process of self-assessment by doing it, by being expected to do it, and by being given responsibility for doing it.

While one of the goals of the learning college is to assist the learner to gain skills and confidence in self-assessment, the learner will not be alone in the process. The extent to which a learner achieves competency will be based on a "community of judgment" in which the learner is one of the responsible participants. Other key players who make up the "community of judgment" will include learning facilitators, assessment specialists, learner peers, supervisors of applied and experiential learning, and employers. While assessment scores and data on levels achieved will provide important information regarding competency, the overall quality and quantity of a competency or of competencies will be best judged by the collective observations of all key players working from the same scoreboard.

Institutional Assessment

Educational enterprises are not just interested, however, in the assessment of individual learners at the course level, especially as faculty grading practices have come under severe criticism due to grade inflation. Rather, beginning in the 1980s, colleges and universities and the regional associations that accredit them began responding to calls from external constituents (primarily state legislators) for increased accountability by developing measures and procedures to assess programs, departments and divisions, and entire institutions. In this application of assessment, broad goals or indicators are usually established by a consensus of the key constituents on the basis of narrative or loosely quantifiable information.

In its original incarnation in the mid-to-late 1980s, assessment in response to accountability focused on institutional effectiveness as demonstrated by measurements of the outcomes produced by colleges and universities that were consistent with their institutional missions. For instance, community colleges might be appropriately measured by the number of transfers who achieved subsequent academic success at four-year colleges and universities, by the number of students placed in jobs directly related to their career program preparation, and by the number or percent of students who complete developmental course sequences and then succeed in college-level programs.

The Southern Association of Colleges and Schools, a regional accrediting agency, pioneered such institutional assessment by its early requirement that institutions under its jurisdiction demonstrate they had in place processes to assess institutional effectiveness by outcome measures such as these. In one of the first major documents on institutional effectiveness in community colleges, the authors said "assessment of institutional effectiveness has become more rational, more public, more systematic, and more consistently based upon data and other objective measures. Recently, the focus of such assessments has been on student outcomes, which is a significant departure from process measures historically used by all regional educational accrediting agencies" (Doucette and Hughes, 1990, p. 1).

In recent years, partly in response to the general reform movement, the focus has shifted, and increased attention has been placed on the assessment of student learning as the principal means by which to demonstrate overall institutional effectiveness. In this regard, the North Central Association of Colleges and Schools (NCA), the regional accrediting agency for colleges and universities from Arizona to Ohio, has led the charge. Although the NCA has been careful not to deny the importance of outcome and productivity measures in the form of degree completion, or in the form of transfer and job placement rates, it has evolved a conceptual framework that insists on assessing what students learn as a direct outcome of their educational programs and experiences. By 1993, NCA had revised and published its guidelines for implementing the expectations it had established four years earlier. Every college and university under NCA's jurisdiction was required by the threat of loss of accreditation to submit a formal institutional plan for assessing student academic achievement no later than June 20, 1995, which must specify formal processes for using the results of the assessment to improve learning processes. (North Central Association of Colleges and Schools, 1994).

NCA has been fairly thorough regarding the characteristics it requires of effective assessment plans. An important feature of plans to assess student academic achievement is that both faculty and students are actively involved in determining what students should know, how they learn, and how learning outcomes should be measured. Students become actively engaged in assessing their own academic achievement because the learning process invariably necessitates their interaction with faculty. NCA is far along in laying the groundwork for the kind of assessment required in the learning college.

While the focus of much of NCA's assessment initiatives concern the outcomes of general education, the plans also address a complete range of cognitive and noncognitive outcomes for a range of programs and disciplines. Needless to say, NCA's strong stand on the importance of student learning and outcome measures has caused considerable ferment among faculties and administrations of the colleges and universities in the North Central region—institutions which only ten years ago were being evaluated for accreditation primarily on such criteria as the number of books in their libraries.

State legislatures and higher education coordination boards have also gotten into the act. The idea that public colleges and universities should be funded, at least in part, upon their demonstrated performance in achieving student learning has circulated among state officials throughout the country, and a few have put funding where their mouths are. One state, Missouri, is in its fifth year of performance-based funding. Its "Funding for Results" model is a hybrid that combines funding rewards for the production of specific state-level performance indicators—including degrees and certificates, job placements, and results on general education assessments—with funding for campus-designed projects that are aimed at improving learning. In 1996-97, a full 1 percent of the instructional budgets of all of Missouri's public state universities and community colleges has been set aside to fund rewards for faculty-designed projects to improve student outcomes. This funding is scheduled to increase to 2 percent by 1998-99, with funding contingent upon demonstrated improvements in student learning.

This institutionwide concern about student learning and its assessment has helped create a solid foundation for the new learning college. With learning a clear priority of educational institutions, the new focus on how and how much learning occurs, and under what circumstances, creates a mind-set that encourages the examination and change of the time-bound, place-bound, efficiency-bound, and role-bound architecture that has restricted learning for decades. Agreed-upon standards, more sophisticated and sensitive assessment instruments, and computer-adapted assessment are new developments that will make it possible for the learning college to function efficiently and effectively.

A definition of assessment has now emerged from the Assessment Forum of the American Association for Higher Education that reflects the basic goals and principles of the learning college:

> Assessment is an ongoing process aimed at understanding and improving student learning. It involves making our expectations explicit and public; setting appropriate criteria and high standards for learning quality; systematically gathering, analyzing, and interpreting evidence to determine how well performance matches those expectations and standards; and using the resulting information to document, explain, and improve performance. When it is embedded effectively within larger institutional systems assessment can help us focus our collective attention, examine our assumptions, and create a shared academic culture dedicated to assuring and improving the quality of higher education. (Angelo, 1995, p. 7)

TOTAL QUALITY MANAGEMENT AND LEARNING ORGANIZATIONS

The foundation of the learning college is also greatly strengthened by applying the principles of Total Quality Management and "learning organizations." These principles have only begun to be applied in education since 1990, but where they are being considered for the long-haul, they promise substantive change in educational policy and practice complementary to the basic philosophy of the learning college.

Total Quality Management

The term "Total Quality Management" was first suggested by a behavioral scientist in the U.S. Navy in the summer of 1985 (Schmidt and Finnigan, 1992, p. 12), but as a concept, it has been emerging for decades in American business. TQM has roots in Frederick Taylor's "scientific management" that emerged in the early 1900s; in the group dynamics movement that surfaced in the 1940s in the form of "T-groups" and their later offspring "organizational development"; in McGregor's "Theory Y" and "Theory X"; in Quality Circles created in the 1940s to improve labor and management communication; in Likert's linking-pin concept that led to cross-functional teams; and in a number of other developments designed to increase productivity and empower and connect the people who work in organizations. TQM has become a set of organized principles leading to improved quality in business, and increasingly in government and education, because of the work of the quality gurus, W. Edwards Deming, Joseph M. Juran, and Philip B. Crosby. Deming is often cited as the father of the quality movement, but he was virtually unknown in the United States prior to 1980. The story of his and others' contributions, noted here briefly, is well known in U.S. business circles.

Following World War II, the United States was the undisputed leading economic force in the world. The country controlled a third of the total world economy and made half of all manufactured goods sold around the world. Consumers wanted products, and they could afford them. Quantity was more important than quality, and American business met the demand. With Japan's defeat and devastation, the U.S. government asked General Douglas MacArthur to help rebuild Japan. MacArthur needed well-built radios, the only way to reach Japanese citizens who were to begin the rebuilding process. Japanese manufacturing, however, had been wiped out in the war. MacArthur brought in Homer N. Sarasohn, a 29-year-old systems and electronic engineer, and Charles Protzman, an engineer from Western Electric, who started teaching the Japanese how to manage manufacturing firms. Sarasohn and Protzman wrote an instruction manual and on the first page quoted an American industrialist, who in the late 1800s built the Newport News Shipbuilding and Drydock Company in Virginia. His motto captured the philosophy that would become Total Quality Management: "We shall build good ships here; at a profit if we can, at a loss if we must, but always good ships" (Dobyns and Crawford-Mason, 1991, p. 11).

In 1950, Edwards Deming was also brought to Japan to teach "Elementary Principles of the Statistical Control of Quality." Japan's senior industrialists, managers, and engineers began to learn the basics of TQM and soon began to apply these concepts with great zeal. As a result of Deming's work and that of many others, Japan began to produce the *quality* of products the world wanted while the United States remained devoted to producing the *quantity* the world had needed. In 1979, the Japanese priced their copiers at almost half of what it cost Xerox to manufacture the same product, and the Japanese got their products to the market in half the time (Schmidt and Finnigan, 1992, p. 7). In 1985, the United States shifted from being a creditor nation to a debtor nation for the first time in this century. In 1989, Japan passed the United States as the principal donor of foreign aid to underdeveloped nations.

TQM transformed the Japanese economy and made Japan an international competitor of the United States. An NBC documentary, *If Japan Can, Why Can't We?* aired in 1980 and galvanized American business into action. Total Quality Management is rapidly changing the basic philosophy of American business, and along with the complementary concepts of "learning organizations" and "reengineering" that have emerged in its wake, is having considerable impact on many American institutions, including education.

In the early 1900s, educators embraced the "cult of efficiency" from the business world that turned schools into factories. In the 1990s, educators are turning to the world of business once again, trying to adapt practices designed to develop quality products to the culture of academe. "Total Quality Management has proven to be very effective in the business setting; Deming called it the 'Third Industrial Revolution.' . . . TQM is not just another technique; it is a new way of organizational life. It is not just an approach to be tested in a limited way; it is a new paradigm of management" (Schmidt and Finnigan, 1992, p. 5).

Oberle (1990) summarized the core concepts of TQM, suggesting that the fundamental message of the quality gurus—Deming, Juran, and Crosby—is the same.

> Commit to quality improvement throughout your entire organization. Attack the system rather than the employee. Strip down the work process—whether it be the manufacturing of a product or customer

service—to find and eliminate problems that prevent quality. Identify your customer, internal or external, and satisfy that customer's requirement in the work process or the finished product. Eliminate waste, instill pride in teamwork, and create an atmosphere of innovation for continued and permanent quality improvement. (p. 48)

Hundreds of educational institutions are applying these core concepts. The Continuous Quality Improvement Network is a group of leading community colleges especially committed to TQM, and leaders in these institutions indicate that substantive changes are occurring in their colleges. The experimentation, however, at this early point in its educational application, appears to work best in changing management processes and structures rather than improving and expanding learning. An assessment of quality improvement activities coordinated by the American Association for Higher Education reports that success in education to date includes "reducing the graduate admissions processes from 26 days to three; restructuring and dramatically improving library services; significantly increasing student retention; streamlining a business school by replacing departments with interdisciplinary faculty teams; and at one institution, saving hundreds of thousands of dollars in physical plant" (Brigham, 1994, p. vii).

These are hardly the indicators of a revolution in learning called for by education reformers. A leading TQM consultant in education has observed, "The application of TQM principles and concepts to teaching and learning is a difficult issue for higher education" (Seymour, 1993, p. 49). K. Patricia Cross (1994) noted that "Today, TQM's application in higher education is far from the dramatic reforms that seem called for in the language of TQM and in view of the challenges faced by higher education" (p. 147). A number of colleges and universities claim that they have applied TQM to teaching and learning, but close examination reveals that most of these institutions have included TQM concepts as content only in courses such as business and engineering; the basic teaching and learning approaches of traditional education have remained fairly impervious to TQM.

Learning Organizations

Perhaps the concepts emerging from the theories and practices of learning organizations will prove to be more useful in education. As noted before, the basic ideas of TQM and learning organizations are very compatible. Peter Senge (1994) has said, "One of the most powerful discoveries for us during the past several years has been seeing how closely our work on learning organizations dovetails with the 'Total Quality' movement" (p. 10).

The learning organization is the antithesis of the hierarchical and authoritative models that have guided American institutions for decades, a model described by Jack Welch, chairman and CEO of General Electric, as "an organization with its face towards the CEO and its ass toward the customer" (Ghoshal and Bartlett, 1995, p. 87). Even the U.S. Army, the epitome of the hierarchical and authoritative model, has been influenced by the ideas behind the learning organization. "The Army is striving to become everything the modern organization is supposed to be—adaptive, flexible, a learning enterprise, even getting closer to the needs of the customer" (Smith, 1994, p. 203).

David Garvin (1993) suggested a definition: "A learning organization is an organization skilled at creating, acquiring, and transferring knowledge, and at modifying its behavior to reflect new knowledge and insights" (p. 80). The goal is to create a "community of commitment" among the members of an organization, so that they can function more fully and more openly to achieve the goals of the organization. This is a page taken directly from the Humanistic Education Movement of the 1960s and is another example of the old stream of consciousness noted in chapter 3 surfacing once again.

Senge, who charted this territory in his 1990 book, *The Fifth Discipline: The Art and Practice of the Learning Organization,* is perhaps the leading spokesperson for the concept of the learning organization. Senge described the learning organization as one in which "people continually expand their capacity to create the results they truly desire, where new and expansive patterns of thinking are nurtured, where collective aspiration is set free, and where people are continually learning how to learn together" (1990, p. 3). According to Senge, a learning organization depends upon five disciplines: systems thinking, personal mastery, mental models, building shared vision, and team learning.

> *Building shared vision* fosters a commitment to the long term. *Mental models* focuses on the openness needed to unearth shortcomings in our present ways of seeing the world. *Team learning* develops the skills of groups of people to look for the larger picture that lies beyond individual perspectives. And *personal mastery* fosters the personal motivation to continually learn how our actions affect our world. (Senge, 1990, p. 3)

Senge said that *systems thinking* is the fifth discipline. "It is the discipline that integrates the disciplines, fusing them into a coherent body of theory and practice. It keeps them from being separate gimmicks or the latest organization change fads" (1990, p. 12).

John Cleveland and Peter Plastrick (1995) linked the learning organization to the new paradigm on learning: "[B]oth the 'new' learning and the 'new' organization emphasize a reduction in hierarchy; open information flow; a focus on the whole system; working together in teams; and flexible, versatile structures of knowledge and organization" (p. 237). Furthermore, Cleveland and Plastrick linked the learning organization and TQM to the new learning paradigm and expressed the hope these concepts have for reforming education. "If approached in the spirit of organizational learning, Total Quality Management can be a powerful tool to help educational institutions make the journey from the learning of the past to the learning of the future, and from the organization of the past to the organization of the future" (p. 242).

Leaders in education must be careful, however, not to assume that "a learning organization" is automatically "a learning college." A learning organization can apply all of the processes and principles developed by Senge and others and still not become a learning college. It is possible for a college to flatten its organization, develop models of collaboration for faculty and administrators, develop processes for evaluating and reviewing its goals, and involve all stakeholders in learning how to do their job better and still retain all the same models of classrooms, lecturing, and teacher-as-sage as have been employed in past practice. In some ways, a learning organization is designed for the staff of the institution, while a learning college is designed for the students. There is no guarantee that a learning organization will become a learning college.

The basic concepts of TQM and learning organizations, however, do provide a powerful foundation on which to build a learning college. The concepts are philosophically compatible with the concepts of the learning college; the processes are compatible with the processes of the learning college. Senge said, "Guiding ideas to learning organizations start with vision, values, and purpose; what the organization stands for and what its members seek to create" (Senge et al., 1994, p. 23). When educational institutions express the vision, values, and purpose of their learning organization in learning college terms—*The learning college places learning first and provides educational experiences for learners anyway, anyplace, anytime*—then they can claim that their learning organization is becoming a learning college.

CONCLUSION

The timing could not be better for the creation of a learning college. Serendipitously, a number of key developments have converged in the last decade of this century to provide an excellent opportunity for the construction of a new kind of educational enterprise—a learning college for the twenty-first century.

First, there is a widespread recognition that the first wave of educational reform initiated by A *Nation at Risk* was a failure. We learned in this decade-long effort how *not* to bring about substantive change in education. The second wave of educational reform that emerged in the early 1990s pointed the way to real change by making learning and the learner the central focus for all reform efforts.

Second, it has become increasingly clear that if learning is to become the central focus for educational institutions, the traditional architecture of education will need to be demolished and a new system constructed. Currently, learning is constricted in an educational architecture that is time-bound, place-bound, efficiency-bound, and role-bound.

Third, a new system that places learning first will be built on a firm foundation, the building blocks of which are still emerging. Foremost among the building blocks is information technology with its potential to expand and support learning in ways not previously imagined. An additional key building block is the developing body of research on learning: learners learn best by doing, all human beings have multi-intelligences, human beings learn differently from each other, and learning activities should be keyed to the natural functioning of the brain.

Fourth, the assessment movement, which has flourished for almost two decades, is now positioned to provide the tools to determine what kinds of and how much learning has occurred. Formerly associated with selection, placement, and credentialing, assessment is now viewed as a continuing process for understanding and improving student learning.

Fifth, the quality movement has influenced educational leaders to be more analytical of the processes they use to create and manage the educational enterprise. TQM's focus on the customer parallels the increased focus on the learner encouraged by the second wave of educational reform. Moreover, the values inherent in the concept of the "learning organization" are highly complementary to the values inherent in the learning college. Thus, when colleges are engaged in quality movement practices, they are taking the initial steps toward creating a learning college.

Finally, the convergence of these various developments and opportunities have taken root in the community college, an ideal crucible for substantive educational change. Long committed to teaching as a strategy to help students make passionate connections to learning, the community college is strategically positioned to lead the way in creating a learning college for the twenty-first century.

In the next six chapters, six pioneering colleges describe their initial journeys toward becoming a more learner-centered institution. Some of the colleges prefer to call such an institution a "learner-centered college"; others are comfortable using the author's term of a "learning college." All of the colleges, however, are moving toward placing the learner and learning as their central concern and focus. The journeys are different because some of the colleges have been engaged in the transformation for almost a decade and have evidence of their progress. The other colleges have only recently launched their efforts, and they are still in the early stages of forming their purposes and strategies. For the hundreds of community colleges contemplating making the journey, each of the stories will be relevant and will provide guideposts and encouragement for a venture worth all the effort and all the risk.

REFERENCES

Angelo, Thomas A. "Reassessing (and Defining) Assessment," *AAHE Bulletin*, November 1995.

Brigham, Steve. "Introduction," *CQI 101: A First Reader for Higher Education*. Washington, D.C.: American Association for Higher Education, 1994.

Caine, R.N. and Caine, G. "Understanding a Brain-Based Approach to Learning and Teaching," *Educational Leadership*, October 1990.

Chandhok, Rob. "An 'Online' Experience: Discussion Group Debates Why Faculty Use or Resist Technology," *Change*, March/April 1995.

Chickering, Arthur W. and Gamson, Zelda F. "Seven Principles of Good Practice in Undergraduate Education" *The Wingspread Journal*, June 1987.

Cleveland, John. "The Changing Nature of Learning." Background Information for the Community Learning Enterprise Design Workshop, March 22-24, 1995.

————. "Learning at the Edge of Chaos," *The Chaos Network Newsletter*, August 1994.

Cleveland, John and Plastrick, Peter. "Learning, Learning Organizations, and TQM." In *Total Quality Management: Implications for Higher Education* edited by Allan M. Hoffman and Daniel J. Julius. Maryville, MO: Prescott Publishing Company, 1995.

Combs, Arthur W. and Snygg, Donald. *Individual Behavior: A Perceptual Approach to Behavior*. New York: Harper and Row, 1959.

Common, Dianne L. "Conversation as a Pedagogy of Reform for Public Education," *The Journal of General Education*, 1994.

Cross, Patricia K. "Involving Faculty in TQM through Classroom Assessment." In *Teaching and Learning in the Community College* edited by Terry O'Banion. Washington, D.C.: American Association of Community Colleges, 1994.

Cunningham, D.J. "Assessing Constructions and Constructing Assessments," *Educational Technology*, May 1991.

Díaz-Lefebvre, René. "It's Not How Smart They Are; It's How They Are Smart." Presentation at International Conference on Teaching and Leadership Excellence, Austin, TX, May 26, 1996.

Dobyns, Lloyd and Crawford-Mason, Clare. *Quality or Else: The Revolution in World Business*. Boston: Houghton Mifflin Company, 1991.

Doucette, Don and Hughes, Billie. *Assessing Institutional Effectiveness in Community Colleges*. Mission Viejo, CA: League for Innovation in the Community College, 1990.

Gardner, Howard. *Frames of Mind: The Theory for Multiple Intelligences*. New York: Basic Books, 1983.

Garvin, David A. "Building a Learning Organization," *Harvard Business Review*, July/ August 1993.

"Gender Affects Educational Learning Styles, Researchers Confirm," *Women in Higher Education*, October 1995.

Ghoshal, Sumantra and Bartlett, Christopher A. "Changing the Role of Top Management," *Harvard Business Review*, January/February 1995.

Goleman, Daniel. *Emotional Intelligence: Why It Can Matter More Than IQ*. New York: Bantam Books, 1995.

Guild, Pat. "The Culture/Learning Style Connection," *Educational Leadership*, April/May 1994.

North Central Association of Colleges and Schools. *Handbook of Accreditation 1994-96*. Chicago, IL: First Edition, September 1994.

Oberle, Joseph. "Quality Gurus: The Men and Their Message." *Training Magazine*, January 1990.

Parnell, Dale. *Why Do I Have to Learn This? Teaching the Way People Learn Best*. Waco, TX: Center for Occupational Research and Development, Inc. 1995.

Schmidt, Warren H. and Finnigan, Jerome P. *The Race without a Finish Line*. San Francisco: Jossey-Bass Inc. Publishing, 1992.

Senge, Peter M. *The Fifth Discipline: The Art and Practice of the Learning Organization*. New York: Doubleday, 1990.

Senge, Peter M. et al. *The Fifth Discipline Fieldbook: Strategies and Tools for Building a Learning Organization*. New York: Doubleday, 1994.

Seymour, Daniel. *The IBM-TQM Partnership with Colleges and Universities: A Report*. Washington, D.C.: American Association for Higher Education, 1993.

Smith, Lee. "New Ideas from the Army," *Fortune*, September 19, 1994.

CHAPTER 6

The Journey of Transformation for Sinclair Community College

*David H. Ponitz**

S inclair's initial steps in its ongoing journey of transformation into a learning college began in the mid-1970s, when the college began to emphasize and encourage self-directed learning on the part of students. Teachers became facilitators who, as part of the instructional team, helped students become major participants in managing their own learning through alternatives to traditional classroom instruction.

Among these alternatives were a College Without Walls (CWW) and a Credit for Lifelong Learning Program (CLLP). The CWW is a degree program that offers students the opportunity to pursue directed, self-paced learning within a flexible time frame. The CLLP allows students to have their experiences evaluated for credit through the development of "portfolios" of prior learning experiences acquired through work, volunteer services, conferences and workshops, in-service training, special interests, and independent research. The CWW and CLLP were developed primarily as a result of partnerships with businesses. Companies needed not only greater access to education, but also employees who could assume greater responsibilities for their own work and learning. The CWW and CLLP focused on student-managed learning and expanded access to individualized, self-paced instruction.

---

*The following members of a cross-functional team from Sinclair Community College contributed to this chapter: David Ponitz, president; Bonnie Johnson, dean of extended learning and human services; Stephen Jonas, vice president for administration; Kathyrn Neff, director of the Center for Interactive Learning Laboratory; Ned Sifferlen, provost; Karen Wells, vice president for instruction.

In the early 1980s, public demand for the reform of higher education increased. The publication of A *Nation at Risk* (1983) called for new standards to assess learning in colleges and universities. Other national reports, all calling for attention to teaching and learning with an emphasis on measuring outcomes, followed—including *To Reclaim A Legacy* (1984) and the report of the National Governors' Task Force on College Quality, *Time For Results* (1986). The focus was clearly shifting to an emphasis on student performance and learning as measures of institutional effectiveness.

Throughout the 1980s, legislators and governors in many states mandated colleges and universities to develop assessment plans and withheld subsidies until plans were completed. Regional accrediting associations adopted guidelines that made assessment of student academic achievement an integral part of accreditation.

In the early 1990s, the North Central Association of Colleges and Schools (NCA) required evidence of assessment plans as part of the next accreditation review for each of its member institutions. In 1992, a decade after A *Nation at Risk* was published, the Ohio Board of Regents (OBOR) cited growing concerns about the academic enterprise and indicated that Ohio's colleges and universities were being challenged as never before to change the ways in which they were operating.

THE BEGINNING OF THE JOURNEY—ASSESSMENT OF STUDENT LEARNING

As early as 1985, serious discussions were underway at Sinclair Community College (SCC) about developing learning outcomes for each of the college's programs. The learning outcomes discussions were fueled in part by SCC's president who introduced the idea of offering a "guarantee" for Sinclair graduates. The concept was to "guarantee" each graduate's level of performance in the workplace as well as the transferability of courses for those students who planned to pursue baccalaureate degrees. There was consensus that before SCC could "guarantee" its graduates' competencies, the college needed to focus on the development of learning outcomes, the methodologies for assessing student learning, and a process to ensure continuous improvement. In 1988, Sinclair began a major assessment initiative toward this goal. The president's call for a "guarantee" propelled SCC toward further development as a learning-centered college. SCC's conscious commitment to becoming an innovator by using a formal assessment program as one means for shifting the paradigm from teaching to learning was another important step toward the development of the learning college.

It was clear that a long-term, coordinated, institutional effort would be needed to assist in continuing the shift. An Assessment Steering Committee, formed in 1988 and chaired by a full-time faculty member, was charged with reviewing the status of assessment practices at Sinclair and making appropriate recommendations for improving assessment of student academic achievement.

The goal for an institutionwide assessment effort was to improve student learning and the processes that contribute to effective and efficient learning. The issues of assessment and student learning are not ones that can be studied and resolved in a short period of time. With strong grassroots faculty involvement, these issues have been reviewed and acted on at SCC since the mid-1980s. Studies of assessment practices nationwide consistently demonstrate that resources invested in assessment activities yield tangible payoffs in terms of student learning, faculty re-invigoration, and program excellence (Banta et al., 1996).

The Assessment Steering Committee defined assessment as a process that asks important questions about student learning, that gathers meaningful information related to those questions, and that uses the information for academic improvement. The committee adopted 12 principles of assessment that provided guidance for subsequent assessment initiatives. (See Figure 6-1.)

The committee then developed three assessment policies, focused on student learning, that were adopted by Sinclair's board of trustees—The Entry Level Assessment and Placement Policy, the Learning Outcomes Assessment Policy, and the General Education Assessment Policy. These policies, effective in the fall of 1990, became the cornerstone for subsequent assessment initiatives. The policies clearly define involvement for students, faculty, and academic departments and require the cooperation of many areas throughout the college. The major focus of the policies is student learning.

The Entry Level Assessment and Placement Policy addresses the need to assess entering students' basic skills in writing, reading, and mathematics and provides benchmarks for the placement of students into appropriate courses. Sinclair views entry level assessment as essential for ensuring that students have the opportunity to succeed. Research has shown that students who are assessed and enroll in courses appropriate to their skill levels are three to four times as likely to succeed academically as students who are not assessed or who ignore placement requirements (Colorado Assessment and Basic Skills Committee, 1990).

1. The primary reason for assessment is to improve student learning and development.
2. The development of an effective, valid assessment program is a long-term dynamic process.
3. Top priorities of the assessment program should be founded in the core goals of Sinclair's mission statement.
4. Assessment must involve a multimethod approach.
5. Assessment of student learning and development is a process that is separate from faculty evaluation.
6. The assessment program is most beneficial when used primarily for making internal decisions that seek to improve programs, instruction, and related services.
7. Assessment program initiatives must include training and related support for faculty and staff who are responsible for assessment activities.
8. Assessment results are not intended to be used punitively against students.
9. The assessment program will seek to use the most reliable, valid methods and instruments of assessment.
10. Assessment objectives/goals should be stated in terms of observable student outcomes and are generally categorized into one of the following areas:
    • Basic College Readiness
    • General Education
    • Major Areas of Study
    • Career Preparation
    • Personal Growth and Development
11. Assessment is never an end in itself, but only a means to an end. In education, the end is to benefit the student, and assessment is but one of many possible bases on which to make decisions regarding admissions, grades, remediation, intervention programs, policies, etc.
12. A comprehensive assessment program is an effective and efficient way to provide the database on which to build better instructional effectiveness for all concerned.

PRINCIPLES OF SINCLAIR'S ASSESSMENT PROGRAM

FIGURE 6-1

The Learning Outcomes Assessment Policy and the General Education Assessment Policy address the assessment of graduates' learning and performance in their majors as well as in general education. The policies stipulate mandatory summative assessment of learning outcomes for all degree programs as well as the assessment of students' general education skills. As a result, all degree programs have clearly defined learning outcomes that demonstrate levels of competence. The learning outcomes for each program are published, and these published outcomes identify specific courses related to preparing students to achieve each learning outcome in each program.

An additional policy, The Sinclair Guarantee of Graduate Quality, adopted by the board of trustees in 1992, was a direct result of the prior focus on learning outcomes and the adoption of the other assessment policies. The "Guarantee for Job Competency" gives graduates of the college's associate of applied science (AAS) programs the opportunity to be awarded up to nine tuition-free credit hours of additional education if they are judged by their employers to be lacking in technical job skills identified by the program outcomes for their specific degree programs. The "Guarantee of Transfer Credit" provides associate of arts (AA) and associate of science (AS) degree graduates with tuition-free alternative courses for those courses that do not transfer to other institutions of higher education with which Sinclair has articulation agreements. Recently, the Ohio Board of Regents pointed out that Sinclair is at the leading edge in its commitment to accountability and outcomes assessment. The Sinclair "guarantee" for career and transfer programs was cited as one element of a broader and well-conceived assessment plan.

Many factors have contributed to Sinclair's success in assessment: strong leadership, grassroots faculty involvement, top-level administrative support, resources for development and training, funds for faculty projects, and expert advice from external sources. Key decisions have been influenced by input from nationally known consultants who visited Sinclair to review the college's progress in making the shift to a learning college. Theodore Marchese, Patricia Hutchings, Peter T. Ewell, Trudy Banta, and James O. Nichols are some of the consultants who have provided assistance. A local expert, Peg Leahy from the University of Dayton, has provided ongoing consultation to departments and individual faculty members to help shape Sinclair's assessment initiatives—focusing in particular on learning outcomes and the development of appropriate assessment methodologies. In 1991, Sinclair was awarded one of the American Association of Community College's Beacon College projects. A national conference on assessment, held at the college in 1993, further heightened SCC's leadership role in accountability and measurement.

Another major component of Sinclair's assessment initiative was the design of a long-term plan for the assessment of student academic achievement. The plan is based on the Shewhart Cycle (Plan-Do-Study-Act Model—PDSA Model) for continuous quality improvement (Dobyns and Crawford-Mason, 1994). The PDSA Model, which provides a process for measuring the implementation of the assessment program and identifying strengths and areas needing improvement, is used to ensure that assessment results are used to make improvements. An annual review of the model gives the steering committee an ongoing opportunity to evaluate the assessment plan.

Sinclair's 15-year history of assessment initiatives is helping to transform the institution. The assessment program continues to focus on learning outcomes and ongoing improvements as the college moves further toward becoming a total learning college.

FURTHER PROGRESS TOWARD BECOMING A LEARNING COLLEGE

Sinclair's Quality Initiative–a Total Quality Management effort designed as *the primary strategy for making further progress toward becoming a learning college*–began in December 1991, when the president, provost, and vice presidents participated in a two-day awareness training session. Forty-seven deans, directors, and leaders from the faculty and staff senates participated in similar three-day sessions, held in May and June 1992. In the fall of 1992, these participants met with the president and provost to determine the future direction of SCC's Quality Initiative. In January 1993, the president appointed the members of the Sinclair Quality Council. The provost chairs the 17-member council which has broad representation from all campus constituencies, including, faculty, administrative/professional staff, support staff, and students.

In February 1993, the Quality Council agreed that the college needed a statement of its vision for the future—a statement that would describe a realistic, credible, attractive future for SCC. With the assistance of consultant Robert Schuetz, the council adopted the following modified 7-S model (Waterman et al., 1980). See Figures 6-2 and 6-3 as the basis for the development of the Vision Statement.

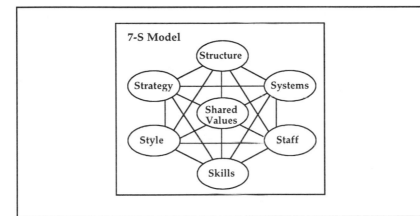

DEVELOPMENT OF THE SINCLAIR VISION: THE 7-S MODEL

FIGURE 6-2

Productive organizational change is not simply a matter of structure, although structure is important. It is not so simple as the interaction between strategy and structure, although strategy is critical too. Effective organizational change is really the relationship between structure, strategy, systems, style, skills, staff, and something called shared values.

Structure: Structure refers to what the organization "looks" like with respect to executing the strategy.

Strategy: Strategy consists of those actions that an organization plans and executes in response to realizing or anticipating changes in the external environment–its customers, its competitors.

Systems: Systems are the procedures, formal and informal, that make the organization go, day by day, year by year, or, in other words, how work gets done.

Style: An organization's style is a reflection of its culture(s) and a vehicle through which philosophy is realized.

Staff: Staff describes the process through which the college recruits, hires, trains, and develops its employees.

Skills: Skills are the dominating attributes, or capabilities, within an organization.
Shared Values: Shared values are the guiding concepts—a set of values and aspirations, often unwritten, that go beyond the conventional formal statement of Sinclair's objectives.

STRUCTURE IS NOT ORGANIZATION. . . THE 7-S MODEL

FIGURE 6-3

DEVELOPMENT OF THE SINCLAIR VISION: THE 7-S MODEL

Using the 7-S model as a guide, the Quality Council developed the following lists to illustrate the characteristics of each of the seven key elements.

Structure

- Facilitates/coordinates/communicates
- Creates cross-functional teams
- Recognizes need for informality/user friendly
- Evolves
- Provides bridges
- Decentralizes
- Empowers/encourages
- Encourages collective process ownership/ours vs. mine

Skills

- Cross-functional teams
- Community leadership

- Understanding and promotion of change
- Determination of what is really important
- Problem solvers
- Listening/team/facilitation skills
- Interpersonal skills
- Coaching vs. managing
- Self-development, including students' self-responsibility
- Constituency relations
- Opportunity makers
- Leveraging technology
- Training of faculty and staff to encourage/support students' growth
- Interactive learning

Systems

- Foster empowerment
- Integrate information linkages
- Foster creativity
- Celebrate success
- Re-invent processes
- Make communications effective
- Minimize bureaucracy
- Provide work semester
- Utilize team support/approach
- Solve problems
- Emphasize from individual to team
- Recognize/reward/reinforce 7-S

Style

- Community centered
- Customer centered
- Fact-based decision making
- Connections/impact driven
- Measurement driven
- Mutual respect
- Quality focused
- Proactive/ask customer/feedback
- Informal/creative
- Learning organization
- Participative
- Flexible/approachable
- Caring/personal attention
- Open-minded/"can do"
- Risk-taking

- Innovative
- Balance of intuitive/fact-based
- Sinclair leadership

Staff

- Values diversity
- Provides challenges/opportunity
- Employs Kaizen/continuous improvement
- Recruits quality staff consistent with the "vision"
- Rewards quality/excellence
- Acts responsibly
- Reaches self-actualized potential
- Motivates
- Instills positive attitude
- Enables lifelong learning
- Feels proud of SCC
- Welcomes training as critical

Strategy

- Dedication to quality/excellence
- Caring approach
- Bridge across functions/forge partnerships
- Global/community
- Quality communication—sharing of information
- Learning organization
- Dynamic curriculum
- Risk-taking
- Willingness to explore
- Commitment to growth
- Anticipation of changes in environment
- Student-centered
- Achievement beyond customer expectations
- Value-added driven
- Promotion of diversity
- Individual access

Shared Values

- Realize unlimited human potential/personal attention/dedication/ respect
- Provide fun/excitement
- Value education
- Promote community harmony

- Provide open accessibility/opportunities for all
- Instill pride of accomplishment
- Fulfill dreams/lifelong learning
- Strive for continuous improvement
- Reward leading edge/future-looking ideas and innovations
- Go the "extra" mile beyond job description
- Instill self-worth
- Focus on customer
- Make SCC a "family"
- Manage resources wisely

Sinclair . . . Bridge to the Future—A Vision Statement

As a result of the 7-S process, the Quality Council drafted a Vision Statement for the college. Focus group sessions, providing the opportunity for input from all college employees, were held in the fall of 1993. On March 8, 1994, the Sinclair Board of Trustees adopted the Vision Statement shown in Figure 6-4, reflecting further movement toward a learning college. At the fall conference in 1994, the Vision Statement was read together by all employees and a 16" x 20" copy of the Vision Statement was given to each individual.

Sinclair. . . Bridge to the Future

Before us lie uncharted worlds of opportunity. Sinclair will be the bridge into that future, giving open access to opportunity, intellectual challenge, and self-discovery for students with diverse needs.

- With Sinclair, people will pursue their quests for lifelong learning through affordable, high-quality education.
- At Sinclair, people will benefit from a caring approach to teaching and learning that provides personal attention and encourages individual growth.
- Through Sinclair, people will be empowered with knowledge and skills for their journeys into tomorrow.

Our success shall hinge on turning these values into action:

- dedication to quality and excellence;
- reliance on anticipation, imagination, and innovation;
- commitment to responsible citizenship within our community;
- adherence to the Sinclair credo—"find the need and endeavor to meet it";
- confidence in the courage, determination, and diversity of our students, employees, and supporters; and,
- belief in unlimited human potential.

SINCLAIR COMMUNITY COLLEGE VISION STATEMENT   ©SINCLAIR COMMUNITY COLLEGE

FIGURE 6-4

The Learning Mission Model

The 7-S Model also played an important role in the institutionwide effort to develop mission models for divisions and departments that began in the summer of 1994. A mission model is a tool that allows staff (with the assistance of a facilitator) to portray, in a single image, the relationships between individual tasks carried out in a department and the central mission of the college. The mission model helps ensure that all activities support the central mission of the institution. Sinclair's central mission is "learning." The mission model initially developed for SCC's Instruction Division is shown in Figure 6-5. It is typical of the mission models that were also initially developed for each of the other major divisions at SCC, i.e., Student Services, Administration, and Business Operations.

As part of the process for developing mission models, every SCC employee was asked individually about his or her role in creating a learning environment. Departmental discussions were then held to help departments focus on their roles in contributing to learning as the central mission of the college.

Core Indicators of Institutional Effectiveness

After the mission models were completed, core indicators of institutional effectiveness were developed. The core indicators are the primary values or overall goals the college wishes to achieve. Input included information from focus group sessions and reviews by department and division personnel of their mission models to determine how success would be measured. Six core indicators that align closely with the vision, mission, and concept of the learning college were identified: Access to Success, Lifelong Learning, Student Development, Community Focus, Quality Workplace, and Stewardship. SCC then developed critical success factors (CSF's) for each of the core indicators. CSF's are actions and/or outcomes that support the core indicators. Meaningful CSF's are essential to the accomplishment of the mission model, are practical to measure and/or document, and provide useful information for improving performance. The CSF's identified show strong support for further movement toward a learning college. As part of the evolutionary process, Sinclair refined the mission models developed by the divisions into an overall mission model for the institution. SCC's mission model, the core indicators, and CSF's are shown in Figure 6-6.

Since the beginning of Sinclair's Quality Initiative—the primary strategy for making further progress toward becoming a learning college—in December 1991, the college's commitment has been demonstrated by the number, variety, and quality of conferences, workshops, and training sessions that have been held; by the broad-based participation by SCC

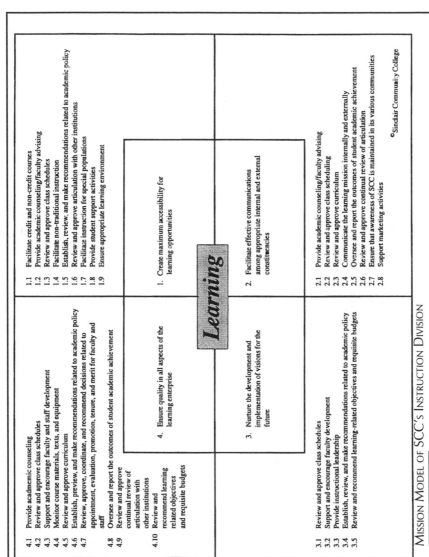

MISSION MODEL OF SCC's INSTRUCTION DIVISION

FIGURE 6–5

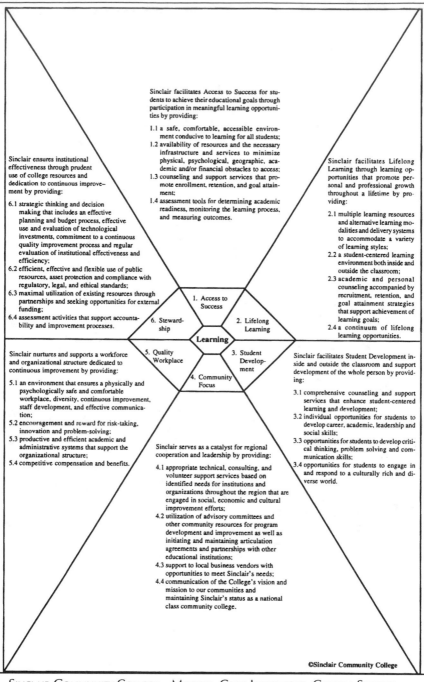

Sinclair facilitates Access to Success for students to achieve their educational goals through participation in meaningful learning opportunities by providing:

1.1 a safe, comfortable, accessible environment conducive to learning for all students;
1.2 availability of resources and the necessary infrastructure and services to minimize physical, psychological, geographic, academic and/or financial obstacles to access;
1.3 counseling and support services that promote enrollment, retention, and goal attainment;
1.4 assessment tools for determining academic readiness, monitoring the learning process, and measuring outcomes.

Sinclair ensures institutional effectiveness through prudent use of college resources and dedication to continuous improvement by providing:

6.1 strategic thinking and decision making that includes an effective planning and budget process, effective use and evaluation of technological investments, commitment to a continuous quality improvement process and regular evaluation of institutional effectiveness and efficiency;
6.2 efficient, effective and flexible use of public resources, asset protection and compliance with regulatory, legal, and ethical standards;
6.3 maximal utilization of existing resources through partnerships and seeking opportunities for external funding;
6.4 assessment activities that support accountability and improvement processes.

Sinclair facilitates Lifelong Learning through learning opportunities that promote personal and professional growth throughout a lifetime by providing:

2.1 multiple learning resources and alternative learning modalities and delivery systems to accommodate a variety of learning styles;
2.2 a student-centered learning environment both inside and outside the classroom;
2.3 academic and personal counseling accompanied by recruitment, retention, and goal attainment strategies that support achievement of learning goals;
2.4 a continuum of lifelong learning opportunities.

1. Access to Success
6. Steward-ship
2. Lifelong Learning
Learning
5. Quality Workplace
3. Student Development
4. Community Focus

Sinclair nurtures and supports a workforce and organizational structure dedicated to continuous improvement by providing:

5.1 an environment that ensures a physically and psychologically safe and comfortable workplace, diversity, continuous improvement, staff development, and effective communication;
5.2 encouragement and reward for risk-taking, innovation and problem-solving;
5.3 productive and efficient academic and administrative systems that support the organizational structure;
5.4 competitive compensation and benefits.

Sinclair facilitates Student Development inside and outside the classroom and support development of the whole person by providing:

3.1 comprehensive counseling and support services that enhance student-centered learning and development;
3.2 individual opportunities for students to develop career, academic, leadership and social skills;
3.3 opportunities for students to develop critical thinking, problem solving and communication skills;
3.4 opportunities for students to engage in and respond to a culturally rich and diverse world.

Sinclair serves as a catalyst for regional cooperation and leadership by providing:

4.1 appropriate technical, consulting, and volunteer support services based on identified needs for institutions and organizations throughout the region that are engaged in social, economic and cultural improvement efforts;
4.2 utilization of advisory committees and other community resources for program development and improvement as well as initiating and maintaining articulation agreements and partnerships with other educational institutions;
4.3 support to local business vendors with opportunities to meet Sinclair's needs;
4.4 communication of the College's vision and mission to our communities and maintaining Sinclair's status as a national class community college.

©Sinclair Community College

SINCLAIR COMMUNITY COLLEGE—MISSION, CORE INDICATORS, CRITICAL SUCCESS FACTORS

FIGURE 6-6

employees; and by the projects that have been undertaken, such as the development of benchmarks, process improvement teams, and Quality in Daily Work processes. The latter project is intended to enable employees to identify and act on opportunities for improving the workplace processes that enhance customer satisfaction. The college is committed to training all employees in the use of principles and practices that improve organizational processes, such as the use of cross-functional teams empowered to provide solutions at operating levels closest to the problem.

LESSONS LEARNED

It is one thing for a college to say that it is going to explore as yet undefined new ways of learning and that it is going to work diligently to adapt new technologies, to incorporate collaborative learning models, to implement assessment and outcome measures, and to realign organizational structures to adapt to a new paradigm that places a greater value on learning than on teaching. It is an entirely different matter to make the commitment—to provide the energy, administrative and staff resources, financial support, and other means necessary to accomplish meaningful change.

A number of factors have been essential to Sinclair's success in continuing to evolve into a learning college. Broad-based involvement has occurred, and many sources of expertise have been tapped to develop an eclectic approach that is unique to and appropriate for Sinclair. But these steps alone won't build the learning college. Many observers believe colleges will not make significant progress toward the transformation from teaching institutions to learning institutions without the vision, direction, and formal encouragement of those who have the responsibility for moving a general vision to a specific reality.

The Role of the President

To encourage positive change, the college president needs to be a scholar of the process, read widely about the issues, develop an internal and external network of experts on the topic of learning, and be a part of the college's learning team—only then will the project move forward. This is not a "jump in, jump out" exercise for the president. Rather she or he must understand that this process is a long-range effort to radically change not only the ways students receive and process data, but also the ways they develop critical thinking skills essential to top quality performance.

Elements of a continuing, professional involvement by the president include the need to

- Encourage interested faculty members to enter the dialogue. Many faculty will wish to become involved early on. Those who do, need to be encouraged to exchange ideas, research the information superhighway, find the best possible thinking on the issues in books and magazines, and review reasons for successes and failures of different learning hypotheses.
- Provide opportunities for special study of the issues through mini-sabbaticals, networks for exchange, and specialized conferences. Many of these opportunities for study will be outside traditional college network systems and will be cross-functional.
- Drive the concept not only throughout the organization among those who are willing to study the issues at the college level, but also throughout the community and the state among those at local and state levels who make decisions.
- Insist that progress be measured. This provision is essential because society is not willing to support a "bells and whistles" approach to new ideas that have no long-term value.
- Determine vision and goals and identify who can help. This involves developing new partnerships within the institution with individuals who have varying academic backgrounds, continuing dialogue with traditional partners, and searching for emerging partnerships that go beyond most college/university initiatives with business and industry.

A *Caution:* When substantial progress has been made, other organizations may ask to participate. They may want partnerships solely for prestige and may not have the necessary work ethic. Partnerships should be beneficial experiences for *every* partner. Collaboration requires *each* partner to bring hard work, expertise, and progress with students to the table. At the risk of being too abrasive, institutions that are moving forward must recognize that many colleges have not been willing to put the time or energy into systemic change. Involvement with those nonparticipants will slow down the process. Accomplishing elements of the vision will require unique relationships with other energized colleges, outside entrepreneurs, and emerging high technology learning organizations that enable faculty to work beyond the traditions of academe.

Moving from a teaching to a learning environment is not easily accomplished. It is a team effort and, at times, rough going. The president must be persistent about the issues, while at the same time personally and organizationally gentle with the pioneers who are forging the future. They deserve praise and recognition for their efforts, their skills, and their willingness to step beyond "the comfort zone."

The Role of the Board of Trustees

The president is also responsible for keeping the board informed about important policy issues. Moving from a teaching to a learning institution is a long-term transition for the board, as it is with faculty and staff.

A "reciprocal nudging" approach is appropriate since so many sequential steps are a part of the process both for board members and college employees. Opportunities for growth and decision-making by the board depend upon

- Providing information to the board that will assist in the definition of the issues and the formulation of policies;
- Sharing ideas under consideration and identifying guiding principles for action; and,
- Suggesting the vision and a strategic plan for accomplishing the vision.

It then becomes the board's responsibility to develop policies to determine how the college will proceed and at what risk, to identify and develop funding sources, and to adopt procedures for oversight and measurement. The board and the president have the responsibility for sharing information with a variety of publics that are interested in the reform process and that need to know what opportunities are available for helping a wide variety of students achieve new goals.

The Role of External Consultants

External consultants can be extremely helpful in assisting all parties in moving an organization forward. Their role includes helping define issues, suggesting approaches for implementing complex equations, and providing third-party analyses of work in progress. Consultants also help by accomplishing tasks for college staff who may not have the time or requisite expertise. The dialogue among consultants, college personnel, and other external partners is a key ingredient for expediting action.

Delineating specific responsibilities and selecting the right consultant are essential actions for success. It is important to take time to define responsibilities first and then determine which consultant to select, rather than choosing a consultant first and defining responsibilities afterward.

Sinclair has made a serious commitment to bringing in outside expertise, the "best of the best." A number of expert consultants on quality in higher education have provided advice to Sinclair. And a considerable amount of time was spent on a national search to find a primary consultant who could understand the college's culture and relate to the various constituencies involved in transforming Sinclair. The selected consultant's experience and knowledge have been valuable; however, it is his ability to *guide* and *facilitate* but not *direct* the process of change that has made him a key asset.

The Importance of Publications

It is vital to stay abreast of cutting-edge theory and research published in areas such as education, reengineering, environmental scanning, organizational impact, and change processes. Sinclair has found the following publications to be particularly helpful in stimulating discussion and forging change at the college:

- *The Fifth Discipline—The Art & Practice of the Learning Organization* by Peter M. Senge
- *Flight of the Buffalo—Soaring to Excellence, Learning to Let Employees Lead* by James A. Belasco and Ralph C. Strayer
- *Once Upon a Campus—Lessons for Improving Quality and Productivity in Higher Education* by Daniel Seymour
- *Safer Than a Known Way—The Deming Approach to Management* by John McConnell

Human and Financial Resource Commitments

The considerable financial investment that is necessary to transform an institution includes a substantial commitment to the professional development of people. This commitment runs the gamut from hiring consultants to sponsoring workshops and seminars. About 2.5 percent of Sinclair's budget is devoted to professional development activities. That percentage is likely to increase in the future to ensure continued progress toward becoming a learning college.

The Learning Challenge Awards program is one concrete example of how Sinclair is allocating significant resources to support the transformation into a learning college. The program supports projects designed to strengthen the efficiency and effectiveness of academic programs and instructional services at Sinclair. Funding is granted to support the transformation from teaching to learning. Each year, approximately $200,000 is allocated to support this initiative.

The criteria for the Challenge Awards include demonstrating how a proposed project will reach new audiences (e.g., retraining professionals, distance learning, etc.), describing how the success of the project will be measured, and addressing the project's contribution to institutional efficiency and effectiveness. A faculty-administrative committee administers the awards.

Some of the projects funded by the Learning Challenge Awards Committee include:

- Can Faculty Productivity Be Increased in the Restructured Classroom?
- Interactive Multimedia—"The Business of Art: A Historical Perspective"
- Interpreter Training Interactive Teleclass
- Meta-Morphing: Transforming Faculty and Instruction
- Multimedia Based Course on Electrical Distribution Safety Practices in Compliance with OSHA Regulations
- Multimedia Interactive Learning for Managers

Summary

It is important that faculty be involved and assume leadership from the beginning, because they are the key for promoting the change in focus from teaching to learning. Sinclair has made a conscious effort to accommodate all levels of acceptance among faculty—from innovators and early adopters, who are able to find or develop resources on their own and operate more horizontally in the organization, to "mainstreamers" who require increased instructional support.

Implementing restructured workloads for faculty, helping them transform teaching and learning, and facilitating their roles as lifelong learners require working through faculty governance processes. For example, faculty members are well represented on Sinclair's Vision for Learning Excellence Task Force, which has, among its charges, the responsibility for determining strategies for using technology to enhance learning opportunities; for shifting faculty responsibilities to student-centered activities; and for improving effectiveness as well as efficiency.

Working with consultants, reading articles and books by a range of experts, and talking with key players in organizations undergoing change have provided an eclectic approach to shaping models and strategies that fit the unique circumstances at Sinclair. When it comes to quality, Sinclair is neither following Deming nor emulating Juran; it is devising models appropriate for Sinclair's unique circumstances and culture.

Change, especially the kind of significant change that is involved in moving from a teaching to a learning college, is evolutionary. It is important to remember that transforming a culture and managing the people, processes, and technology associated with change is time-intensive and a long-range effort.

THE FUTURE

In the November/December 1995 issue of *Change*, Robert Barr and John Tagg wrote "For many of us, the Learning Paradigm has always lived in our hearts. As teachers, we want above all else for our students to learn and succeed. But the heart's feeling has not lived clearly and powerfully in our heads. Now, as the elements of the Learning Paradigm permeate the air, our heads are beginning to understand what our hearts have known. However, none of us has yet put all the elements of the Learning Paradigm together in a conscious, integrated whole"(p.14). After drafting the vision, developing the mission models, creating the core indicators of success, and identifying the critical success factors at Sinclair, it was clear that a framework for synthesizing the elements of a learning college was needed. The vice president for Instruction drafted a Vision for Learning Excellence for Sinclair. Excerpts from the most recent draft follow:

Excerpts from a Vision for Learning Excellence

Sinclair Community College is a national class community college, but like other institutions of higher education, it will undergo significant changes during the next five years as it transforms teaching and learning in the face of increasingly unacceptable levels of student costs, rising institutional expenses, decreasing state subsidies, local levy campaigns that will focus on doing more with less, and new electronic technologies that enhance student learning. When projections of increasing faculty retirements, as well as increasing numbers of nontraditional students seeking higher education, are considered against the backdrop of a transformation of teaching and learning, the need for defining the duties of the faculty of the future becomes especially critical. The following provides a conceptual framework for the college's evolution and a description of the faculty of the future.

The New Paradigm for Sinclair. Significant competition will enter the higher education marketplace. Higher education will continue to strive for lifelong learning and not solely the preparation of youth. Retraining the current workforce will continue to be a principal task of higher education with an increasing focus on process skills rather than content applications. Current employees/students at Sinclair will become more interested in personal, customized learning strategies than in careers and the requisite career ladders.

Learning will become more outcome-based. Knowledge will become our most important resource. The ability to locate and incorporate knowledge will be a required basic skill as businesses and industries demand knowledgeable workers.

Distance education at Sinclair will become a more pervasive mode of delivery as an alternative to classroom-based instruction. Distance learning will expand beyond telecourses so that the learner is freed from constraints of place and time and has multiple opportunities for interactivity with faculty, other students, and information (*anyway, anytime, anyplace education*).

Information technology will provide the major infrastructure to support learning—including campuswide networks to share instructional resources and student and college information; remote access to worldwide, digitized resources from classrooms, offices, businesses, and homes; individually tailored instruction packages providing learner-centered interaction with information; outcomes-based, open-entry/open-exit courses supported by new assessment tools; and routine electronic communications among students and faculty, students and other students, and students and the campus.

Differences between credit and noncredit instruction will continue to blur. Learning providers will continue to find different ways to serve more diverse students. Curricula and services will continue to be adapted to multicultural perspectives.

Sinclair as an Organization. Sinclair has traditionally been a teaching organization; it will continue to become a learning organization. The distinctions that define academic divisions and the departments within those divisions are already becoming blurred. Hiring practices and the composition of search committees will change. The college will be looking for learning facilitators whose educational credentials and experience cross existing boundaries and demonstrate technological expertise. Faculty will no longer be clustered according to the subjects they teach. Cross-functional teams of employees from across the college will address issues that were once the purview of discrete groups of employees.

The Sinclair Student. Global economic competition will intensify—putting greater pressure on the members of the workforce to be critical thinkers, problem solvers, and independent learners. Sinclair students will become active learners and will be expected to be more accountable for learning outcomes. The Internet and the World Wide Web will continue to demonstrate the possibilities for student-directed, teacher-facilitated, global learning opportunities. Faculty will facilitate student learning by becoming more knowledgeable about their students and their students' learning styles. They will provide students access to tools that help them learn.

The Sinclair Full-Time Faculty Member. The core responsibilities of Sinclair faculty will change from the presentation of content (lecturing) to the design, development, and delivery of knowledge-seeking and thinking skills. Job descriptions will change to reflect role differentiation, new classifications, and recertification. Sinclair's faculty evaluation process (the Faculty Performance Review) will be revised to reflect the college's core indicators of success as demonstrated through SCC's Plan for Student Academic Achievement (focusing on assessment), student learning outcomes, and the Sinclair Quality Initiative for continuous improvement. Policies, procedures, and criteria for promotion and tenure will reflect the values of the new paradigm and the new structure of the organization. Merit will be awarded to teams as well as to individuals. Faculty workloads will be restructured, and faculty may not have the same control over their schedules as they have had in the past. For example, a faculty member might be assigned 150 students as her workload. Freed from traditional lecturing and other current teaching practices, she will then be able to create learning environments for those students while using facilities and technologies in new, unique formats to move students toward achieving core competencies.

Faculty Development. Just as the population at large must become lifelong learners, members of the Sinclair community must also become lifelong learners—especially those who facilitate lifelong learning abilities in students. The opportunities for Sinclair faculty development will be more clearly redefined and differentiated. These opportunities will possess the same qualities of easy access and convenience that the new learning environment will provide for students, e.g., opportunities for development through interactive distance education will increase. Faculty will begin to transform learning, and they will achieve and maintain technological literacy by designing and following a faculty technology development plan that focuses on using technology to enhance personal productivity, lecture presentation, interactivity, and student-centered learning.

Student Services. The distinctions that separate student services, e.g., admissions, registration, counseling, and financial aid, from instruction are breaking down as Sinclair applies technology throughout the college. Student success and learning are everyone's responsibility. Faculty and staff are exploring new ways of looking at how students develop, including students who are participating in distance learning. Faculty, as they increase their use of technology, will provide access to student services in new and unaccustomed ways. They will experience new ways of communicating with and assisting students. All faculty and staff will be concerned with the activities of students as one of their primary institutional roles.

Stewardship. Increasing economic constraints and public demand for efficiency and accountability will continue to require the college to find ways to meet the needs of more students at ever higher levels of quality and reduced cost. SCC's administrators must provide leadership, support, and services to ensure that Sinclair continues to be a national class community college within the new paradigm. And they have to communicate the new paradigm to Sinclair's customers. Administrators will continue to ensure that the learning environment fosters change and continuous improvement.

The Center for Interactive Learning

One of the highlights of the future of learning at Sinclair is an exciting technology/learning initiative that is an outgrowth of recommendations developed in 1992 by the college's Alternative Learning Strategies Committee. The Center for Interactive Learning Laboratory (CILL) was established in 1994 to help Sinclair faculty adopt interactive learning methods, including the use of electronic information resources and instructional technologies. The goal of the CILL is to transform the educational process from passive, lecture-based instruction to an environment in which students are intensely engaged and absorbed in the learning process. To facilitate this goal, the CILL sponsors faculty workshops, offers internal grants for innovative projects, and provides a laboratory with multimedia resources for use by faculty.

The CILL is preparing the Sinclair academic community for learning and teaching in the twenty-first century. Sinclair's Center for Interactive Learning (CIL), a new facility planned for completion in 1997, will house the CILL and will serve as a hub of activity for the transformation of teaching and learning. Faculty have met with architects and consultants, have been involved in on-site visits and teleconferences, and have participated in a summer institute as part of the planning for the CIL building.

Sinclair's vision for the CIL is as follows:

> The Center for Interactive Learning (CIL) will be a place where people of diverse backgrounds can see and experience the future of learning and work. In the CIL, students, faculty, and staff will connect with global communities of learners to share knowledge and ideas, to invent the future, and to construct personal paths into that future. The Center for Interactive Learning will be a place that delights in the empowerment of people through technology and a place that honors scholarship.
>
> The Center for Interactive Learning will be, above all, a place where everyone is a student. In the CIL, everyone can fearlessly try out new ways of learning and teaching, evaluate experiments, and ponder their implications. In the CIL, we will work to assimilate our best ideas into the fabric of Sinclair's academic programs and culture and to disseminate our innovations to a regional, national, and worldwide audience.

The CIL is another strategy that will help Sinclair continue its transformation from a teaching to a learning organization. The CIL facility will provide a unique environment for

- faculty, administrative, and technical staff training and development
- instructional design and pilot projects
- technological investigation and evaluation
- exhibitions and demonstrations
- instructional media production involving teams

- community outreach to K-12, other colleges, and the business community

CONCLUSION

Sinclair's vision of the future is based on the assumption that learning will remain a social activity requiring the highest level of cognition and complex human interaction. The college's faculty members will not be replaced by robo-teachers, and, in fact, the demands on their thinking skills will only increase. SCC will need to call on the creativity and ingenuity of its faculty to develop new learning formats for students that will remove barriers to access so that everyone will have the opportunity to discover the satisfaction and rewards of learning. Sinclair's vision of the future is extremely optimistic. The college will use its strengths, critical thinking, open discussion and debate, and creativity to continue the journey toward the kind of future it envisions for America's current and future generations of learners.

REFERENCES

Banta, Trudy W. et al. *Assessment in Practice: Putting Principles to Work on College Campuses.* San Francisco: Jossey-Bass, Inc., Publishers, 1996.

Barr, Robert B. and Tagg, John. "From Teaching to Learning—A New Paradigm for Undergraduate Education," *Change,* November/December, 1995

Bennett, William John. *To Reclaim A Legacy—A Report on the Humanities in Higher Education.* Washington, D.C.: National Endowment for the Humanities, November, 1984.

Colorado Assessment and Basic Skills Committee. *Colorado Assessment and Basic Skills Study.* Denver, CO: University of Colorado, 1990.

Dobyns, Lloyd and Crawford-Mason, Clare. *Thinking about Quality: Progress, Wisdom, and the Deming Philosophy.* New York: Times Books, 1994.

The National Commission on Excellence in Education. *A Nation at Risk: The Imperative for Education Reform.* Washington, D.C.: U.S. Government Printing Office, April 1983.

National Governor's Association. *Time for Results—The Governors' Report on Education.* Washington, D.C.: Center for Policy Research, 1986.

Ohio Board of Regents. *Securing the Future of Higher Education in Ohio.* Columbus, OH, December, 1992.

Waterman, Robert H., Jr. , et al. "Structure Is Not Organization," *Business Horizons,* June, 1980.

CHAPTER

Emerging Models
of the New Paradigm at Jackson
Community College

Lee Howser and Carole Schwinn

A CASE OF THE BOILING FROG

Most community college presidents have probably experienced the "Boiling Frog Syndrome," even if the old story has not reached their ears. As Clyde E. LeTarte, former president at Jackson Community College in Michigan, relates the story, a frog dropped in a pot of boiling water will immediately jump out, saving its own life. However, a frog placed in a pot of cool water that is brought to a boil slowly will joyfully paddle around until its demise. These days a lot of college presidents are "in the pot," and the water is hot—or at least it's heating up pretty rapidly. A reasonable person might ask what a boiling frog or a boiling president has to do with a "learning college," but that, as Paul Harvey would say, "is the rest of the story."

Origins of Reform at Jackson

Jackson Community College (JCC) personnel did not deliberately set out to design a "learning college." In many ways, it already was one. The college had a long record of service dating back to 1928, when the first class of students enrolled. When the current transformation began at JCC, the intent was simply to expand "Continuous Quality Improvement" efforts undertaken in 1990, but a learning experience intended as a staff development exercise in systems design turned into a transformation process that touched everyone on campus. It is a process that reaches into the community and holds promise for providing new services and generating new revenues, nationally and internationally.

Even before the transformation to a learning college began, politics was changing the lives of the Jackson Community College family in a big way. After 12 years of outstanding service to the college and the community, President Clyde LeTarte chose to run for Michigan's House of Representatives. Elected in a tough battle in 1993, LeTarte resigned his position at JCC. The board of trustees named Lee Howser to the presidency later that same year. Not many days passed before he began to understand Clyde's story of the boiling frog.

The new president's first order of business was to confirm that the members of the administrative cabinet were still committed to the continuous improvement philosophy. The answer was affirmative and unanimous. Cabinet members recognized that the practice of Continuous Quality Improvement had significantly improved numerous individual operations as well as several larger systems of the college. Staff members had developed a great deal of expertise in systems thinking using an analytical approach: taking a system apart, understanding the behavior of the parts, making corrections, and putting the system back together with the expectation that it would operate better than before. In general, the old saw "If it ain't broke, don't fix it" sounded just right, and there was a commitment to staying the course. The water temperature went up just slightly.

Concerns Despite a Rich Tradition

Jackson Community College deserved its fine reputation as an institution offering quality instruction, responding to community needs, operating efficiently, and playing a leadership role in the continuous improvement movement at the national level. The community consistently rated the college as a major asset, providing a home for the cultural arts and for the faculty and staff who were community leaders in every walk of life. Most people were enjoying the "warm" water, comfortable in thinking there was little to worry about.

The president began to worry anyway. After 24 years of service to the college, the last 12 as vice president for Administration and Business, the new president's first analytical look at the total institution was a new and sobering experience. Realities constantly surfaced that forced him to look to concerns about the future, rather than the successes of the past. The situation heated up further when a staff development program was initiated to help design new systems where none previously existed. Given the staff's experience and knowledge in improving small and large system operations, this new learning experience held great promise.

Working with Jamshid Gharajedaghi, president and CEO of INTER-ACT, The Institute for Interactive Management in Philadelphia, several small teams set out to learn and apply an interactive-design methodology to the design of selected college subsystems. Participants learned that syn-thetic thinking (vs. analytic thinking) begins with understanding the larger system of which the system to be designed is a part. In this case, the larger system was the whole college. Consequently, the teams set out to design the whole college, both as a practice exercise and as a way to understand the context for designing subsystems and their interactions. The work of these teams raised some serious concerns and potential opportunities for the institution and its future viability. The water temperature was really heating up.

A Look at the Future Contained in the Present

Interactive design begins with "formulation of the mess," or an understand-ing of the set of interacting problems faced by the system. Those problems are usually the unintended consequences of past successes carried to their extreme. The "formulation of the mess" exercise serves as an early warning system by exaggerating the system's vulnerability if it does not change with the changing environment. The story of JCC's mess showed that

- Faculty and staff were aging and very concerned about the future with a new president and uncertainty of funding.
- Equipment was aging, much of it 30 years old. Even the newer computers were now facing obsolescence.
- Fewer and fewer curriculum updates were being made.
- There was a perception that the college was becoming more traditional than it was in the 1960s and 1970s, when growth was dramatic and new and exciting projects were common.
- Enrollment was dropping on campus, although increasing a bit at extension centers. Competition was everywhere.
- The district had lost hundreds of base manufacturing jobs over the last few years, and the perception was that any growth would be in lower paid service industry jobs.
- There was a perception that the employee collective bargaining agreements were restrictive and not conducive to flexibility and change.
- College employees expressed frustration at a lack of a shared vision, disconnected systems, fragmented sources of information, and a lack of understanding about where decisions were made and the criteria on which decisions were based.

As these concerns surfaced, others could begin to feel the hot water. It became more and more obvious that the best individual efforts of the board of trustees, and of the faculty, support staff, and administration could not change these conditions. It had to be done together, and a new way to do it was needed. But two huge obstacles were in the way.

First, funding was a real and worsening problem. With state appropriations and local property taxes expected to increase at inflation rates only (JCC lost 12 tax elections in a row), and huge tuition increases no longer a viable option, over 93 percent of revenues were stagnant. Finding new revenues was imperative. Second, while continuous improvement had improved the efficiency and effectiveness of *independent* systems, it was obvious that the system had reached a point at which it was necessary to deal with the *interdependencies* of increasingly complex systems.

The Commitment to Design

During a college design team meeting on March 16, 1994, Carole Schwinn, then assistant to the president for special projects, leaned over and asked the president, "Wouldn't it be great if we could design the college for real, rather than as an exercise?" With that question, the floodgates opened and the boiling water rushed in. Designing a new college became the order of the day, and even the most insensitive frog could no longer paddle around oblivious to the magnitude of change about to occur at JCC. After a few weeks of thinking about the possibility of completely redesigning the college; gaining commitments from cabinet; and forming a new, seven-member college design team; it became apparent that need and opportunity for change had arrived simultaneously at Jackson Community College.

THE DESIGN OF THE "LEARNING" COLLEGE

One of Jamshid Gharajedaghi's pearls of wisdom is, "The world is not won by those who are right. It is won by those who can convince others they are right." Thus, an obvious task for the president and the new design team was to convince the board of trustees and approximately 650 full- and part-time employees of the college that the decision to completely design a new college, rather than "fix" the one that was known and loved, was the right decision. In assessing the environmental and system conditions that needed to be addressed, four compelling issues emerged:

- quality and financial conditions
- fear and uncertainty about the future
- empowerment and information dissemination
- trust and confidence

From these issues, three major design goals became the central thrust of the reform process. The major goals became creating a college that

- is capable of self-renewal
- generates new capacity for revenue generation
- presents an opportunity for all stakeholders to provide input into organization and operation

A significant commitment was made to build capacity for revenue generation through redesign rather than to reduce cost by downsizing, an approach taken by many organizations undergoing major change. Employees would be maintained whenever possible, moving them to positions where their skills could contribute to success. Within the constraints of personnel and money, the college would increase flexibility and create new opportunities in roles and job responsibilities.

Destruction of the Old

Once "mess formulation" is completed and the story is told about the need to redesign, interactive design calls for assuming that the system "blew up last night," and that only the environment remains intact. Designers, however, can remember what they loved about the system and keep the best practices and systems. The rest of the system is designed from a clean sheet of paper, leaving the "mess" behind.

JCC's design team worked on the whole college design for several months, gathering information from the environment and from staff, students, and community members. Then, in an all-college meeting on Tuesday, September 6, 1994, the president announced that "the college had been blown up last night." He shared with those in attendance the first iteration of the new college architecture (Figure 7-1), along with the values and goals underlying the design.

In his address, the president made the following commitments:

- All employees would have a chance to participate and contribute to further iterations of the design.
- The college would continue to operate within the principles of continuous improvement and quality of program and service.
- The college would work toward creating capacity rather than automatically downsizing. People would be the top priority.
- A campuswide visioning process would occur to inform and guide decisions, actions, and relationships.

At this all-college meeting, the faculty was asked to design the Core Knowledge Component from a clean sheet of paper. Core Knowledge is the faculty's unit, responsible for articulating learning theory, designing methodologies, delivering learning experiences, and conducting evaluation and faculty development. The president's address concluded with these words,

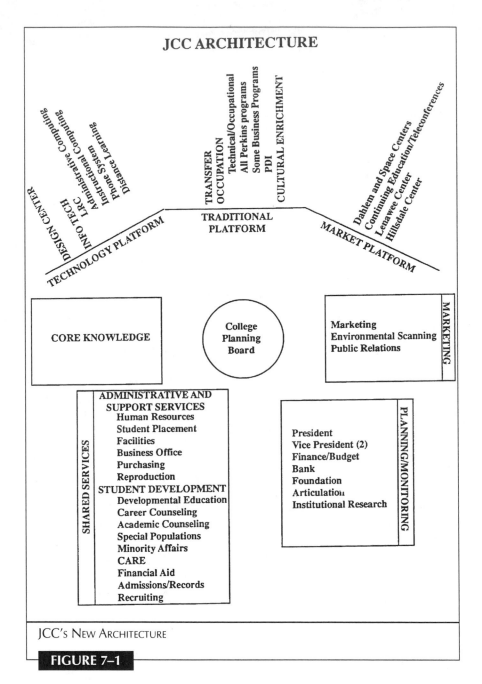

JCC's New Architecture

FIGURE 7-1

"For 25 years, I have heard you say to the JCC administration, 'Give us leadership, but don't tell us what to do.' Here is your chance to design your world and realize your dreams."

Design of Platforms, Components, and Their Interactions

As promised, opportunities were provided for all faculty and staff to comment on, suggest changes, complain about, and otherwise discuss the first iteration of the JCC architecture. Members of the seven-person design team spent a great deal of time in staff and departmental meetings explaining and listening. Primary responsibility for coordinating these sessions was assigned to Bonnie John-Murray, vice president for Institutional Services. Based on feedback, further iterations of the college architecture were completed. Simultaneously, staff members in the new Center for Design and Continuous Improvement were designing their own component and preparing to help others learn and apply the interactive-design methodology.

Once the architecture was finalized, system managers were named for the major components, and new component design teams set out to design all platforms, components, and their interactions. The following list outlines some of their design decisions:

- *Traditional Platform.* Includes Transfer programs, Occupational Education/Workforce Development (OEWD) programs, and Cultural Enrichment programs. Programs are subsidized and headed by deans. Transfer co-deans are on three-year assignments from faculty, while OEWD's dean and associate dean are administrators. Cultural Enrichment is directed by an administrative system manager.
- *Technology Platform.* Consists of two components. The Information Technology Component provides computing and communication services inside the college and sells services externally. The Center for Design and Continuous Improvement also provides services internally and sells consulting services nationwide. Both components are directed by system managers.
- *Market Platform.* Generates programs that are entrepreneurial and self-supporting. Each program is directed by a system manager.
- *Core Knowledge.* Home of the faculty regardless of the platform or component from which they deliver services. Headed by the dean of faculty on three-year assignment from faculty.
- *Shared Services.* Contains services that are used by all components. Shared Services are subsidized. The component's primary services are Student Development and Administrative Services, and are directed by system managers.
- *Marketing.* The window to the environment, interpreting JCC to stakeholders and, in turn, communicating stakeholders' needs and

desires to the college community. Marketing is subsidized and directed by a system manager.

- *Planning/Monitoring.* The executive function is located here, with the overall responsibility of managing the interaction of the components rather than managing the components themselves.
- *College Planning Board.* Includes system managers of all major college components and college support staff. Responsible for integrating the designs and plans of all components. Provides information and recommendations to the board of trustees, as well as a shared decision-making role with the executive unit. Presidents of the Faculty and Support Staff Bargaining Units are ex-officio members.
- *Component Planning Boards.* All components have planning boards made up of component personnel and other institutional representatives with interest or stake in operations of the component. Responsible for planning and monitoring for the component.

Vision Statement—A Community of Learners

As promised, a one and one-half day, large-scale event designed by a team of employees to create a vision statement was held in February 1995. Three draft vision statements were developed by the nearly 250 student and employee participants, and project task force teams were appointed to work toward resolution of several major issues. Over the next months, several iterations of the Vision Statement were completed under the direction of faculty member Mark Harris. On October 24, 1995, the college planning board adopted the following new college vision:

> A Community of Learners: *Jackson Community College is a community of learners. The Trustees and College employees are committed to the intellectual, physical, emotional, and cultural development of students, ourselves, and our community. We are dedicated to academic excellence, open communication, respect for differing viewpoints, mutual trust, and lifelong self-improvement.*

The new college vision now appears in all the college's major publications and is now a part of JCC's culture.

The process of participative design is not an easy one. It prompts all the difficulties and anxieties that one might expect from a change of this magnitude. But the involvement and empowerment of all involved has marvelous payoffs when faculty and staff have the information on which to base decisions and the freedom to create their own future.

THE VISION OF A COMMUNITY OF LEARNERS

In chapter 1 of this book, Terry O'Banion references the Wingspread Group on Higher Education's publication, *An American Imperative*, which spells out the implications of viewing a college as a "community of learners." "Putting learning at the heart of the academic enterprise," the Wingspread group suggests, "will mean overhauling the conceptual, procedural, curricular, and other architecture of postsecondary education on most campuses" (1993, p. 14). Overhauling JCC and realizing its vision has dramatic implications for the students, the faculty, the cross-functional teams, the new governing planning boards, the board of trustees, the community of Jackson, and beyond.

A Community of Learners for Students

Currently students at JCC have the opportunity to join a "learning community" in which they enroll in "linked" courses taught by teams of faculty members. In the future, they can expect to encounter learning communities well in advance of entering JCC. In fact, their first point of contact with the college might well be with members of one of many learning communities of JCC students organized around student interests and aspirations. Those communities, with assistance from faculty "guides" or "mentors," will be responsible for determining their own learning goals, for actively participating in the design of their own learning experiences, for sustaining the community, and for recruiting and supporting new members. Members of communities will be engaged in research, in peer learning experiences, and in service learning in the community. Learning communities will document their learning plans and projects for the use of future members. It is anticipated that some learning communities will actually produce products and services to be distributed in the community and beyond. Students pursuing careers in education or human development, for instance, might produce thematic learning modules for use in the public schools.

The Core Knowledge design document below attests to the desired future expectations for students.

> We assert that all students will be self-determined, self-directed, responsible, technologically literate, and willing to suspend their disbelief as they enter the academic environment. Students will, as a result of their contact with our faculty, develop lifelong learning strategies and problem-solving skills which extend beyond the classroom. All of these skills are vital for their success and for ours.

A Community of Learners for Faculty

When faculty were charged with the responsibility of designing the Core Knowledge component, they were asked to articulate a theory of learning and to provide for the continuous development and evaluation of their members. The learning theory espoused in the design document below rejects old paradigms of learning and builds on an emerging, new paradigm.

> In the future, teachers will no longer ask the question, "What is the best way to teach mathematics or English?" But in order to get to that point, we will need to develop new metaphors and new learning theories. Behaviorism and cognitive learning theories have been our guides for the last half century. We accepted the classroom-as-workplace metaphor and the "cult of efficiency" that had moved from business to industry into schools early in this century. In this old world, lecture and the transmission model (or "banking model," to use Paulo Freire's terminology) controlled what happened in the classroom.
>
> Social constructionists see education as reacculturative; that is, switching membership from one community or culture to another. Viewed this way, classrooms and the role of teachers take on a different look. Teachers must allow students to try on various roles previously reserved for the teacher—teacher, expert, leader, scholar—as they socially construct and justify knowledge. Students in this environment will no longer be expected to simply "know," but instead will be expected to "understand." Teachers will act as facilitators, guides, coaches, and full members of the discourse community or culture that the student is attempting to enter, but they will no longer be the "sage on the stage." The classroom-as-factory metaphor will be replaced by the classroom as a community-of-scholars metaphor.

In designing a development model for themselves, the faculty are experimenting with a three-phase process in which faculty

1. Create an annual development plan by identifying goals, activities, and accomplishments in teaching, professional development, and service to the institution and the community.
2. Demonstrate teaching effectiveness, professional growth, service, and student learning (annual formative evaluation).
3. Organize portfolios representing their work, their accomplishments, and the learning of their students (summative evaluation, every sixth year).

This development model assists the faculty member in targeting areas for improvement and utilizes professional development as the "mechanism by which the targeted areas are changed for the better."

The redesign of JCC's Core Knowledge unit has dramatically accelerated faculty professional development activities, reformed faculty evaluation, and changed the college calendar to reflect an emphasis on continual learning. Orientations and forums for conversation have been instituted for part-time faculty; workshops covering active learning, classroom assessment techniques, interactive classrooms, early semester formative feedback from students, problem-centered education, and other topics have been held; and numerous professional development grants have been awarded. Information about the alternative faculty evaluation system based on teaching and learning portfolios has been disseminated, training in the new system has been provided, learning materials on reflective and active teaching have been made available, and 20 out of 46 faculty undergoing evaluation have chosen the new process. The renegotiated calendar increased nonteaching days from 4 to 19, with the benefits of additional professional development, increased departmental collaboration, departmentwide participation in course review and assessment plans, inclusion of part-time faculty, and ongoing discussions of academic issues.

Linked courses with an interdisciplinary perspective and team teaching are now offered across eight disciplines, and a Freshman Year Experience for new students in which three or more courses will be linked is being piloted. A faculty/staff learning community has been formed to learn how to develop and deliver online courses, and a faculty/staff and student learning community is compiling data to make strategy recommendations about a potential millage campaign. A "travel and learn" learning community of interested faculty/staff, students, and community members will study a particular country and then travel to that country in the summer of 1998.

Work is continuing in the redesign of the Core Knowledge unit. Departments are being realigned into "schools" to match the educational/occupational career paths of incoming high school students, and occupational and transfer programs are being blended into schools so that courses include both workplace applications and theory. The schools will become profit centers responsible for their own revenues and costs, resulting in new revenues for the college.

A Community of Learners for Departments

Putting learning "at the heart of the academic enterprise" is also evidenced in the design of a completely new curriculum in JCC's Nursing Department. The design team, made up of the entire nursing faculty, began their design with an understanding of the larger whole of which their curriculum is a part. They studied emerging trends in health care and the implications of government changes and funding models. They researched trends in the nursing profession, health concerns and status of the community, and changes occurring in the traditional clinical settings.

The members of the design team studied emerging learning theories and developed their own conception of learning to guide their design. They also researched nursing theories and adopted a self-care model and conceptual framework that fit with their own mental models and their understanding of how industry and community needs are evolving. Significantly, they sought to understand the new JCC architecture, the role of the nursing program in it, and how the program would interact with other components of the architecture. They met with other faculty to discuss the implications of change for other departments, and how collaborative, win/win solutions to conflict might be achieved.

Because they were seeking accreditation by the National League for Nursing for the first time, they also studied that agency's requirements and made contacts with "state of the art" accredited programs. The depth of learning and commitment from their synthetic/design approach resulted in newly designed ADN and LPN nursing curricula that have received over-whelmingly positive early reviews.

During the past year the Mathematics Department has formulated a new governance model that has two major goals: 1) to share the responsibility of day-to-day operations of the department, and 2) to share the information and knowledge obtained as a result of these operations.

In the past, the department chair individually assumed the responsibility of carrying out all departmental operations, including scheduling of classes, establishing the budget, revising curriculum, and selecting textbooks. Under the current architecture, many additional responsibilities have become part of the operations of the department. A multifunctional computer laboratory, course review, and assessment and placement exams have made it necessary for all department members to become involved and to share responsibility. Among other responsibilities, individuals and small groups now conduct placement exams, assemble assessment data, conduct formal course reviews, select course software, and prescreen textbooks. The re-sults of these efforts are analyzed at regular meetings of the whole member-ship, facilitating shared learning and uniform output from the department.

A Community of Learners for Cross-Functional Teams

The fact that learning occurs in cross-functional teams can be illustrated by a simple story that had a profound effect on those who heard it and acted on it. Early in the college's experience with Continuous Quality Improvement, JCC's former president and several deans and directors were participating in a Quality in Daily Work workshop. In the workshop, they were learning and applying a seven-step process for documenting and standardizing routine work processes. The team was reviewing the process for canceling low enrollment courses, and its members were diligently constructing a flow chart. In the midst of enormous frustration about their inability to reach consensus on how the process really worked, and how they could possibly make sure the process resulted in enrolled students' ability to make alternate choices, they started asking themselves a different set of questions. They began to ask, "Why do we cancel low enrollment courses?" and began to answer, "[B]ecause we don't know what courses our students need and want to take, or in which time slots or locations they prefer to take them."

By asking these more essential questions, the cross-functional team reframed the issue to look at the broader picture. Using this wider focus, JCC determined that a student-focused course schedule would offer courses at convenient times for students and in a sequence that allowed for program completion in a timely manner. Student needs and preferences were determined by a survey and scheduling hot-line. Information obtained from the hot-line, interviews with faculty, and a second student survey were used to develop schedules. The schedule development process now in place involves ongoing input, involvement, and feedback from all stakeholders. The cross-functional team's ability to look beyond the narrow problem, how to cancel low enrollment classes, allowed JCC to make substantive improvements in its scheduling process and in its service to students. Their *operational learning* of working on a routine process gave way to a level of *conceptual learning* or reframing of the problem, which has opened up new possibilities in the way learning experiences are scheduled at JCC.

A Community of Learners for Planning Boards

The new architecture and its new planning board structures have created new communities of employees who have never worked together before. The College Planning Board, for example, is made up of system managers from all major components, representing a cross-section of the entire campus. Members are struggling to learn and develop new habits and patterns of interacting that replace old adversarial relationships with cooperation and shared responsibility for the whole. Most members slip less and less frequently into the old "default" methods of acting and interacting, as the new design becomes a reality.

A Community of Learners for the Board of Trustees

The JCC Board of Trustees adopted a Policy Governance Structure in November 1994. The premise of the model, as developed by John Carver, is that the board acts as purchasing agent for the community by prescribing "Ends," relating primarily to what programs will be offered for which people, at what price. The board sets certain limitations on the president and then accepts any action, within the limitations, to achieve the "Ends." Thus, the board reserves the prerogative of goal setting and monitoring while leaving design, implementation, and assessment to the professional staff.

The first "Ends Statement" considered by the board was Associate Degree Outcomes—designating the skills, knowledge, and abilities that associate degree recipients are expected to demonstrate. Four monthly meetings of the board were devoted to testimony and dialogue with employers from the community, current and former students, and college faculty, administrators, and support staff. On the strength of that exchange, the board's paradigm of instruction shifted to learning and teaching from teaching and learning. That shift makes all the difference in thinking about the process.

A Community of Learners for Jackson County and Beyond

The Core Knowledge design document suggests that "it is not only for their individual good that students must achieve."

> We must create an environment in which students succeed and in which they develop, along with a healthy self-interest, an understanding of the sociological and cultural necessities for preserving the community.

If the promise of the Jackson Community Transformation Project (JCTP), recently funded by the W.K. Kellogg Foundation, bears fruit, that understanding will become a reality. The purpose of the project, which is a partnership with the Jackson Area Quality Initiative, is to create a community in which citizens develop the skills required to increase their desire and ability to meet their own needs, the needs of others, and the needs of the larger society. Over a four-year period, the interactive-design approach will be used to engage citizens in the design of the community's desired future, to implement that design, and to sustain an ongoing process of design and continuous improvement in the community.

The project has already provided opportunities for JCC faculty, staff, and students to engage in their own development and the development of the whole community. Many attended the initial event of the project, a teleconference called "From TQM to a Learning Community." Broadcast to over 130 sites around the world, the teleconference featured a dialogue among Peter Senge, author of *The Fifth Discipline*; Margaret Wheatley, author of *Leadership and the New Science*; and Thomas Berry, coauthor of *The Universe Story*. The dialogue, facilitated by Clare Crawford-Mason and Lloyd Dobyns, introduced attendees to the concepts of systems thinking;

transformations of large-scale, complex adaptive systems; and chaos theory. Following the teleconference, a meeting between JCC staff and members of the community provided an opportunity for many JCC employees to interact with community members from all walks of life.

Several nationally recognized consultants to the JCTP have engaged faculty and staff in conversations related to a "community of learners," including Ira Shor, author of *Empowering Education,* and Peter Block, author of the *Empowered Manager* and *Stewardship,* as well as Jamshid Gharajedaghi, author of *A Prologue to National Development Planning* and other works.

NEW RESEARCH ABOUT LEARNING

Perhaps the most exciting adventure in JCC's transformation process is the ongoing engagement of the college community in learning about learning itself. When one of the authors of this chapter (Schwinn) was an adult student at JCC in the early 1970s, she used to walk by the boardroom where cabinet meetings were taking place and imagine the intellectual exhilaration of the kinds of conversations that must be going on at that level in an institution of higher education. Once she was employed at the college, she could hardly wait to become part of those conversations. It is only now, 19 years later, that the conversations all around JCC have the intellectual exhilaration she once imagined. While the conversations will continue and the meaning of a "Community of Learners" will evolve over time, several distinctions in JCC's current theory and definition can be made.

Distinctions Among Data, Information, Knowledge, Understanding, and Wisdom

When the distinctions between these concepts were made explicit in early design team work with Jamshid Gharajedaghi, it marked the beginning of reconceptualizing JCC's future. The following is paraphrased from Russell L. Ackoff:

> Data are symbols that represent the properties of objects and events. Information is contained in descriptions, answers to questions that begin with such words as who, what, when, where, and how many. Knowledge is conveyed by instructions, answers to the how-to questions. Understanding is conveyed by explanations, answers to why questions. Wisdom deals with values. It involves the exercise of judgment through dialogue.

During design conversations, the team began to recognize that community colleges have historically been in the business of dispensing data and information, packaged as degrees. Some have even been good at generating and disseminating knowledge and understanding. The team realized that with the advances in technology, the introduction of distance learning, the opportunity to earn a degree via the Internet, and the competition from PBS and others in packaging data and information, JCC needed to completely reconceptualize how it adds value for learners. Ackoff has suggested that wisdom is the characteristic that differentiates humans from machines and that the educational process should allocate as much time to the development and exercise of wisdom as it does to the development and exercise of intelligence.

The challenge of reconceptualizing how JCC can even begin to develop and exercise wisdom remains a most significant challenge, but the fact that conversations about learning and how JCC adds value are occurring everywhere on campus nearly every day is a crucial step in building the foundation of the learning college.

Distinction Between Operational Learning and Conceptual Learning

This distinction, made by Daniel Kim, parallels Chris Argyris's distinction between single-loop and double-loop learning. Kim (1993) writes, "*Operational learning* represents learning at the procedural level, where one learns the steps in order to complete a particular task. This *know-how* is captured as routines, such as filling out entry forms, operating a piece of machinery, handling a switchboard, and retooling a machine" (p. 38).

At JCC, examples of operational learning abound. The routine approach to standardizing existing systems and the early, standard approach to Strategic Quality Planning represent learning at the procedural level and are essential for smooth day-to-day operations. By contrast, Kim defines conceptual learning as follows:

> Conceptual learning has to do with thinking about why things are done in the first place, sometimes challenging the very nature or existence of prevailing conditions, procedures, or conceptions and leading to new frameworks in the mental model. The new frameworks, in turn, can open up opportunities for discontinuous steps of improvement by reframing a problem in radically different ways. (p. 38).

Examples of conceptual learning are much more recent and primarily involve learning that came about while designing the new JCC. In fact, engaging in the interactive-design process challenged and changed our mental models about most every concept, and every structure, function, output, and process in the institution.

Distinction Between Analytic and Synthetic Approaches to Learning

JCC's applications of Continuous Quality Improvement—including Break-through projects, Quality-in-Daily-Work (QIDW) activities, and Strategic Quality Planning—were based on the Plan-Do-Study-Act Cycle (the Deming Cycle or Shewhart Cycle for Learning). These applications represent analytic thinking, a method of breaking the organization down into its component parts and improving them independently, or identifying critical problems and focusing on the prioritized few. Analysis, for example, treats enrollment, student satisfaction, retention and graduation rates as independent variables.

Synthetic thinking, on the other hand, begins with an understanding of the largest whole of which the system being studied is a part, and derives the part's purpose from the roles and functions it serves in the whole. In this approach, the variables listed in the previous paragraph are treated as interdependent, and solutions are sought by reconceptualization and redesign. This distinction became clear when JCC became involved in interactive design principles and methodology. Designing the whole college meant that a shared understanding of the larger systems of which it is a part—the community and higher education, for example—was critical. Designing highly interdependent components of the college that would interact to achieve a set of desired results substantially replaced the more analytic approaches during the design process. Understanding the ongoing interaction of design (synthesis) and continuous improvement (analysis) has been a powerful learning experience for many JCC employees.

A system of Learning and Continuous Improvement was introduced to the college in July 1996. This system supports four critical arenas: Process Management, Performance Development, System Alignment, and System Interaction.

Operational learning is the basis of Process Management where standardization and improvement initiatives are expanding throughout JCC. From internal processes for student services, to external processes in grant funding, teams and individuals are learning more about their key processes and how they impact each other in their daily work. Starting with a pilot group of 8 employees in the Registrar's Office, JCC now has more than 35 employees from 19 work units actively participating in Quality-In-Daily-Work (QIDW) projects.

Performance Development at JCC is expanding to the conceptual level of learning. The traditional annual performance evaluation was ineffective in improving performance for staff and supervisors. JCC's new Performance Development Plan, however, focuses on improved communication, data-driven decision making, and objective criteria-based performance expectations. Each employee involved in process management activities is building a portfolio that effectively represents his or her job responsibilities and his or her performance of key processes. This new way of thinking goes beyond the procedural level (traditional evaluation) to the systemic level (performance development). There is also a new sense of ownership for employees and a comfort level for managers that encourages shared decision making.

JCC is also learning the benefits of System Alignment. Employees commented that they did not see a clear connection between their daily work and the mission and goals of the college. They became lost in their work and lost sight of their overall importance to the new design of the college. Those involved with Process Management and Performance Development are encouraged to write their own mission and goals relative to those of the institution. In turn, their key processes are identified as supporting these goals to align their work within the college. Once again, a sense of ownership develops and grows.

Although overlapping planning boards support System Interaction throughout the college, individual learning and participation are also important. Employees are learning to model expected behaviors in team environments by using team meetings as learning laboratories. Roles are defined in each meeting as individuals act as facilitator, leader, recorder, or team participant. Verbal and nonverbal behaviors are discussed and ground rules established to develop the habits necessary for effective teamwork. Another example of improved interaction is the newly developed Face-To-Face Feedback Network, which consists of a number of one-on-one question-and-answer feedback sessions for JCC employees. The network acts as a "controlled grapevine" for anonymous, candid input on critical issues. The pilot project began with 5 listeners and 25 participants voicing their opinions on a topic of interest. The network will expand quickly as the 25 participants are recruited as listeners and each one is asked to find 5 people to meet face-to-face on critical issues throughout the year.

Distinction Between Social (Group, Organization, or Community) and Individual Learning

Social learning is not simply a matter of adding up all the learning of individuals. While individual learning is a change in the individual's know-how (routines or habits) and know-why (beliefs, assumptions, mental models), social learning is the change in collective routines or mental models of groups, organizations, or communities.

Through its own learning and transformation process, for example, JCC has come to play a significantly different role in the community's "social" learning. Through the college's CommUnity Transformation Project, citizens are creating new and shared mental models, beliefs, and behaviors.

Issues of learning, health and economic well-being, for example, are understood as emergent properties of a community whose citizens, organizations, and institutions work together to create a better future, rather than isolated problems to be solved independently. Out of new collective thinking, building new relationships, and dissolving conflict through reconceptualization will come new forms and structures for ongoing learning, participation, and mutual responsibility for the community.

Social learning, then, is cultural transformation: a change in the beliefs, assumptions, and mental models of a group of purposeful individuals in a purposeful group, organization, or community. A group, organization, or community builds its capability for social learning when its members collectively and systematically

1) Come to a common understanding of their history, their current condition, the set of interacting problems they face, and the environmental events and trends impacting their future

2) Bring up, examine, and make explicit their shared beliefs, assumptions, and mental models regarding their stakeholders' needs and expectations; and the conceptual frameworks for organizing themselves

3) Design the system's structure, functions/outputs, and processes for learning and adaptation in changing conditions

4) Establish shared expectations for the system's performance and methods for monitoring

5) Identify gaps between expected and actual performance of the system

6) Examine and improve the information system, decision-making systems, and implementation capabilities (first order learning or improving know-how)

7) Periodically reexamine fundamental beliefs, assumptions, and mental models and redesign the system (second order learning or improving know-why)

These distinctions about types of learning are not drawn to determine which is the most important or which should be the focus of JCC's practice. They are drawn to create new conversations about learning with new groups of people to rethink and redesign JCC's role as a learning college committed to a vision of a "community" of learners.

LEARNING NEVER ENDS

In "The Rules for Being Human" from *Chicken Soup for the Soul* (1993), an anonymous author wrote, "learning lessons does not end. There is no part of life that does not contain its lessons. If you are alive, there are lessons to be learned" (Canfield and Hansen, p. 81).

Many lessons have been learned in JCC's design process, and many more remain to be learned. But by far the most important is that fundamental change in an institution of higher education is like no other. Some corporations may have a cultural history of 30 to 50 years, most far fewer. And although there may be larger numbers of employees in business and industry, few will have had the freedoms that faculty and some educators have enjoyed since the early days of Greek history. Some cultural practices in higher education were established in the Middle Ages. Such deeply rooted traditions are resistant to change and may be far less amenable to cookbook approaches than those of business and industry. Some guiding principles and philosophies for educators planning to move toward the new paradigm of learning include the following:

1. *Keep the focus.* The sharper the focus of the effort, the more successful it will be. Asking such questions as, "Is it good for the students?" and "Will it contribute to learning?" is helpful in maintaining focus. A set of principles and underlying assumptions provides a touchstone for guidance.

2. *Expect conflict, unhappiness, and pain.* Human beings like and seek stability. When stability is upset, they try to return to the original state or as close to the original state as possible. *Leadership and the New Science* author, Margaret J. Wheatley, was helpful in understanding the nature of chaos in understanding organizations.

3. *Be open to honest criticism.* The CEO, in particular, must see that the environment is one which permits, not actively promotes, change. People must be free to speak their minds and to be heard. Punitive action against opposition will doom any effort.

4. *Involve everyone.* Involvement of all the primary stakeholder groups (students, faculty, board of trustees, support staff, administrators, and community residents) is extremely important. Not all have to be involved at the same time or at every step, but there is a time and place for everyone.

5. *Promote constant communication.* Provision of a communication process and a forum for discussion is important. While many people will choose to participate, it is essential to continue to reach out to the more reluctant ones with the invitation and the opportunity to participate. Modification of the form and flexibility in specific details of communication methods are mandatory.

6. *Double your time estimates.* Making cultural changes in an organization takes an extraordinary amount of time. Whatever the original timeline, double it! While there are many "Nike's" or changes of the

"Just do it!" variety, fundamental change requires conflict resolution and substitution of old behaviors. The process just takes time.

7. *Provide coping strategies.* Many people experience profound change as a grieving process. The old ways are going or gone and the new ways have not yet emerged. Expect denial, resistance, and the other human reactions to loss. Providing coping strategies will help people move through the grieving stages more smoothly and rapidly.

8. *Provide for "new" learning.* Expecting new behavior from people without "new learning" is not realistic. People must have new information with which to challenge old assumptions and expectations. Given a successful challenge to the old assumptions and expectations, the decision rules can be changed and followed by new implementation methods and strategies.

9. *Use specialized language sparingly.* Language specific to the effort may create a problem as people try to understand what is happening and learn the new language at the same time. Even the president found words in the interactive-design process that caused him much concern. The specificity of the terms' meanings, however, required his acquiescence.

10. *People will react differently.* Many people within the organization will rise to the challenges and expectations that are placed before them. Others will be uncomfortable and will leave. Others will resist change and hope to survive this latest fad.

11. *Control rumors.* Rumor control is as important as anything that will be planned. It is important that people get frequent, accurate information and that there is a trustworthy clearinghouse.

TRANSFORMATION OF THE CULTURE

Another "Rule for Being Human" reads, "A lesson is repeated until learned. A lesson is presented to you in various forms until you have learned it. When you have learned it, you can go on to the next lesson" (Canfield and Hansen, 1993). One can only imagine what the future will hold, but here are a few fairly safe assumptions about the promise of the future.

The college community will continue to learn how to live in change, maybe even to welcome it with open arms. Thus far, the process has been exciting for some, frustrating for many, and deeply painful for a few.

The college community will also continue to work on realizing the vision of becoming a "Community of Learners." For such a vision to manifest itself in real change, it has to be more than a statement and more than an event.

Ask Peter Senge what fish talk about, and he will tell you that he's not sure, but he does know they don't talk about water. Fish are so close to water, just as we are to our culture, that they, and we, don't give it a second thought. Yet, our beliefs, moral code, values, and patterns of behavior are part of our culture and how we interact with our environment. Without examining the current culture and how it works, colleges won't be able to make the changes so desperately needed.

The task of changing organizational culture is a huge one, though. Certainly, adoption of a student/employee Vision Statement to support the board-adopted Mission Statement and Values is important. Adoption of the Policy Governance Model at the board level and the participative model of the College Planning Board is also important. From the president's point of view, however, the most important cultural change has been the willingness and readiness of faculty and staff to accept responsibility for their own behavior and future as they assume authority and control over their own actions.

There is ample evidence that change is occurring. The faculty has printed 19 iterations of their Core Knowledge design in 16 months. Each iteration is a learning experience and improves on the last one. The Student Development Component's design team is designing methods of assuring that each student has a personal plan for success and that progress is assessed just as it is in the classroom. The Occupational Education and Workforce Development Component is exploring a learning model that provides for individual as well as enterprise and community development. They are designing processes for establishing excellence guidelines, for self-assessing learning needs, and for creating learning experiences at all stages of individual, enterprise, and community development. These are but a few examples of how thinking within the college is changing. The lapsed time is much too short to properly assess the extent of cultural transformation, but change agents, early adapters in the college, and other observers indicate that they are beginning to see changes that promise a real difference in the future.

A DIFFERENT ROAD

Shortly after the all-college presentation in September 1994, a senior faculty member advised the president that the success of the new architecture would depend on concrete results, and the sooner something changed, the better. His concern was shared by a lot of people, including the president.

Reflecting on that conversation, the story about a Chinese village is illustrative. The streets of the village were very narrow and crowded. One day, a horse drawing a cart became unruly and stubborn. The animal kicked and charged people as they attempted to move past the horse and cart. No one could get past, and the business of the town slowed. Suddenly, one young man suggested that the wise old man of the village be summoned.

Surely, if anyone would know how to get around the horse or stop the disruption, the old man would. So a contingency went to get him. They explained their need to get by the horse so the town's business could continue. As they returned to the street entrance, the old man took one look at the horse, still kicking and charging toward people, and then promptly turned away and went down a different street.

The moral of the story is that sometimes it makes more sense to follow a new path than to keep fighting the obstacles in the way. While the senior faculty member and the president both sought concrete examples of better results for the college, one saw only the desired results and the obstacles in the way. The other saw the endless possibilities for unexpected results that open up when a new path is chosen and followed. On the latter premise JCC is committed to continually re-creating itself for the next generation.

REFERENCES

Ackoff, Russell L. *Ackoff's Fables*. New York: John Wiley and Sons, Inc., 1991.

———. *Creating the Corporate Future*. New York: John Wiley and Sons, Inc., 1981.

———. *The Democratic Corporation*. New York: Oxford University Press, 1994.

Canfield, Jack and Hansen, Mark Victor, eds. "Chicken Soup for the Soul," *Health Communications, Inc.* Deerfield Beach, FL: 1993.

DiBella, Anthony J., Gould, Janet M., and Nevis, Edwin C. "Understanding Organizations as Learning Systems," *Sloan Management Review*, Winter 1995.

Gharajedaghi, Jamshid. *A Prologue to National Development Planning*. New York: Greenwood Press, 1986.

Kim, Daniel H. "The Link Between Individual and Organizational Learning," *Sloan Management Review*, Fall 1993.

Schon, Donald A. "The Theory of Inquiry: Dewey's Legacy to Education." The Ontario Institute for Studies in Education, 1992.

Wingspread Group on Higher Education. *An American Imperative: Higher Expectations for Higher Education*. Racine, WI: The Johnson Foundation, Inc. 1993.

CHAPTER

Lane Changes

Transformation at Lane Community College

Jerry Moskus

The year 1987 was, in one way at least, the best of times for Lane Community College: a national panel of experts selected Lane as one of the five community colleges most often cited for teaching excellence (Roueche and Baker, 1987). In many other ways, however, 1987 was the worst of times. The college was facing financial and administrative turmoil. The long, successful presidency of Eldon Schafer had ended with his death in 1985, and his successor, encountering resistance to change and budget cuts, resigned in 1988. By 1989, the college was searching for a new president—what one board member termed a "healer."

When the new president arrived in March 1990, his first challenge was to shore up the budget, and in November 1990 the college won voter approval of a new, larger tax base. But jubilation was muted. At that same election, the voters of Oregon passed a sweeping tax reduction measure. Although the new measure validated tax increases passed prior to November 1990, it did not mention increases passed at that same election. It was not clear whether Lane's much needed new tax base would stand. Oregon Community College Commissioner Mike Holland characterized Lane's plight as a "cosmic joke."

The cosmic joke helped bring into focus what college leaders had known for some time: Lane was in a period of fundamental change. The source and amount of its funding were in jeopardy, enrollments were increasing at a record pace, and the local economy was shifting from timber to service and high-tech jobs. The college could be tossed about by these changes or it could chart its own course.

Thus began a new chapter in the history of Lane Community College as it set out to shape itself for the future. The vision that arose from this shaping process was one of a flexible, responsive college where everyone is focused on learning.

A CLOSER LOOK AT CHANGE

November 1990 marked a turning point in the history not only of Lane Community College but also of education in Oregon. Prior to that date, education funding was largely a local responsibility. After 1990, funding became primarily an obligation of the state. Required to replace local revenues lost through the tax-reduction measure, the state entered a fiscal crisis that decimated public schools and universities—but not, for a time, Lane Community College. The college was able to lobby successfully for recognition of its new tax base, and college personnel envisioned a return to a better time. But there were signs that neither Lane nor Oregon would ever be the same.

First, there were indications that the community colleges would be "equalized"—relatively well-funded colleges like Lane would suffer revenue freezes while lower-funded colleges caught up. Awaiting equalization, Lane leaders were reluctant to use the new tax base for recurring expenditures that probably could not be sustained long term. This strategy created tensions in a college that associated higher quality with more full-time staff and expansion of programs.

Second, between 1990 and 1994, the college was experiencing dramatic increases in enrollment. Much of the growth resulted from students unable to get jobs in a sluggish economy; some of the increase was overflow from the state universities, which were downsizing because of budget shortfalls. Rapid growth created pressure on existing Lane staff, since permanent staff could not be added to serve the new students. Instead, in an effort to help overburdened workers, the college made a one-time purchase of new operations software. Unfortunately, the transition from the old to the new software provided yet another source of stress.

Third, timber-rich Lane County was in the midst of severe workforce dislocations. The spotted-owl crisis had resulted in the laying off of thousands of timber and wood products workers. At the same time, several large high-tech companies were moving into the county. Workers needed the help of the college to make the difficult transition from a resource-based economy to a technology- and service-based economy, but the college's traditional two-year technical programs did not always meet the needs of an impatient workforce.

At the state level, two important new policy initiatives had implications for community colleges. The legislature passed an education reform act that promised to transform K-12 education in Oregon from a traditional model to a workforce-based, outcomes model. To make the transition, local schools were seeking help from community colleges. In addition, the state formed local workforce quality committees to eliminate duplication in training programs and coordinate workforce development. Community colleges were expected to make important contributions to this initiative.

Besides these changes in its environment, the college was challenged by issues affecting community colleges generally, such as changes in technology, and by other problems unique to Lane: changes in board membership, a complete turnover at the vice president level, and projections that the college could lose nearly half its faculty to retirement by the year 2000. College leaders began to realize that Lane was entering a future for which its past had not prepared it. What was needed was a leaner, more flexible Lane—a college that could change to address the challenges.

REVISIONING

One of the first steps in the development of a "new" Lane was taken by the College Council, a representative group of faculty, managers, classified staff, students, and the president. Over a series of meetings the council discussed the need for change and the direction that change should take, and decided to develop a vision statement. The statement captures Lane's historical strengths—a concern for quality and a caring attitude toward students—and adds a new element—a focus on *learning*. It was determined that the new Lane should be learner-centered, that all staff should think of themselves as educators, and that everyone at Lane, including support staff, should be engaged in learning. The vision that emerged recast Lane as an organization that *"provides quality learning experiences in a caring environment."*

Council members agreed that a major barrier to realizing this vision was fragmentation. In the language of organizational science, Lane was highly differentiated but not highly integrated. The council envisioned the new Lane as a *caring community*, where isolation and divisions between people are actively resisted and where board members, faculty, managers, staff, and students care about each other and work in teams to strengthen learning.

Armed with this new vision, the president and his assistant set about writing a paper that would *restructure* Lane. The restructuring paper was to involve more than reorganizing the administrative units; it was to explain the new Vision Statement and begin the process of rethinking nearly everything the college did. The paper went through a number of drafts as College Council members and many others submitted responses and ideas. In the end, a copy was sent to each member of the college staff. The following are excerpts from the final version:

- Above all, Lane must put the learner first by shifting more and more to a learner-focused organization. This means that our structure should help customers and clients accomplish their goals as easily as possible. In some cases, this means organizing around whole processes; in others, this means that our structure must be transparent to those who use our services and must not cause obstacles.
- Change must be built into our organization; we must become a learning organization. Bureaucracies are not amenable to change. Organizations that move routine decision making and problem solving to work teams are better able to adapt to continual change. We must break down the walls between departments by designing our processes and services around work teams that cut across artificial organizational lines.
- Our ideas of management and supervision must change. As employee groups are empowered to problem-solve and make decisions in their work areas, managers must learn to be coaches, advisors and consultants rather than "bosses" and day-to-day decision makers.
- We must put more emphasis on training and socialization of Lane employees. The new Lane described here will require intensive training for many, if not all, current employees.
- Finally, it is clear that we must rely more and more on technology to help us do our jobs. In order to do that, our organization must facilitate cooperation and collaboration among the various units that provide and support the use of technology.

RESTRUCTURING

In traditional bureaucracies, organizational structure is paramount. In the kind of organization that Lane hoped to become, human resources and infrastructure are more important. It is ironic, but understandable, that in early efforts to implement the new vision, the president and others devoted much of their time to revising the organizational structure. Before May 1994, when the final version of the restructuring paper appeared, Lane had been organized around four "branches," or separate administrative entities.

Because the tree metaphor suggested a bureaucracy with secondary parts growing from a main "trunk," the term "branches" was rejected in favor of the term *groups*, or dynamic assemblages of similar teams: Executive Services, College Operations, Student Services, and Instructional Services. Executive Services and College Operations retained a departmental substructure, but departments in Student Services and Instructional Services were blended into subgroups of two or more departments with common elements. For example, the Physical Education Department and Family and Health Careers Department were blended into "Health Services." Initially, these subgroups were humorously called "clumps." Later the term *cluster* was applied because it suggested that the original departments would be joined but would retain their identities. The groups and subgroups were displayed in a circle on the organizational chart to indicate that Lane was no longer to be a hierarchial, bureaucratic organization.

Formerly, instructional personnel had been separated into a credit and a noncredit branch, each with its own vice president. The new Instructional Services group combined all instructional personnel under two vice presidents who work together as a team, dividing their responsibilities along no particular bureaucratic lines. The instructional vice presidents were charged with working toward developing values and rewards for collaboration and common goals among disciplines, departments, and support functions.

Instructional Services was organized into ten clusters, six of which were based on the "endorsement" or career areas contained in Oregon's new education reform act. The six are Arts and Communications, Business and Computer Information Technology, Industrial and Engineering Technology, Health Services, Social Sciences, and Science and Mathematics. The other clusters within instruction are Adult Basic and Secondary Education, Learning Resources, Outreach Services, and Instructional Systems. For each cluster, faculty leaders were appointed to coordinate important initiatives such as education reform and outcomes assessment.

In addition to the restructuring of administrative units, Lane made a concerted effort to form new strategic planning units. All four of the main administrative groups were to contribute members to *strategic teams*, defined as "cross-functional, vertically integrated assemblages to pursue ongoing institutional objectives." Also to be developed were vertically integrated *project teams* to address shorter-term, limited objectives. Strategic teams address topics like marketing and diversity, whereas project teams are formed and disbanded to address, for example, a specific construction project.

The college's existing governance system—its councils and committees—was left intact, except that the roles of existing groups in governance began to change. The leaders of the faculty union had expressed early and strong support for the new vision and structure, and it became clear that they wanted to play a greater role in governance in the future. While the support of the union was welcomed, and its influence in governance did indeed increase, the more aggressive stance of union leaders created tensions that remain unresolved at Lane to this day. For instance, managers have been reluctant to accede to union requests to take over such traditional management prerogatives as choosing faculty for committee memberships or having the final word on textbook selections. Eventually, these and many other role conflicts between management and the union were addressed in a formal process of role clarification that helped to alleviate some, but not all, of the tension. Still, the support of the union for many of the goals of restructuring has been an important impetus to implementing Lane's new vision.

If staff are to be empowered to make decisions, they need to know more about the issues facing the college and they need opportunities to become involved. To open two-way communication, the president and vice presidents met for several hours with each of the clusters on campus to present planning information and to discuss challenges the college was facing. The cluster meetings reinforced the idea that most Lane staff—including those in the least skilled jobs—can contribute to solving college problems.

Restructuring alone, however, is not a cure-all, as can be seen from the developments at Lane since the reorganization. Even though Lane's new organizational structure remains basically intact, the cluster concept has never really caught on. With a few exceptions, departmental identities have remained stronger than cluster identities. Nevertheless, the goal that clusters were developed to address—overcoming fragmentation and divisions between departments—is being slowly realized. Lane's experience suggests that changes in attitudes are more powerful than changes in structure as a means of producing change.

An important part of changing attitudes is avoiding the temptation to ridicule the past. Although "old Lane" is occasionally used as a pejorative phrase on campus, a conscious effort has been made to preserve in the "new Lane" the traditional strengths of the old Lane. These strengths are listed in the restructuring paper as an innovative spirit, a commitment to student success, a tradition of quality teaching, and a sense of pride in the institution. Whenever possible, Lane leaders reinforce the continuing importance or presence of these strengths, or as in the case of "quality teaching," describe the strength in terms of the new emphasis on learning. Lane's unifying principles, developed in 1988 and still displayed prominently on posters throughout the college, are important ties to the past:

- Respect the individual
- Provide quality learning experiences
- Commit to excellence
- Promote a sense of achievement
- Ensure a participatory environment
- Communicate openly
- Manage with goals
- Connect with our community
- Develop a sense of community ownership

College leaders learned that one of the most difficult challenges in making this kind of change is to explain to people what is ending and what is not. As William Bridges (1993) notes

> Never denigrate the past. Many managers, in their enthusiasm for a future that is going to be better than the past, ridicule or talk slightingly of the old way of doing things. In doing so they consolidate the resistance against the transition because people identify with the way things used to be and thus feel their self-worth is at stake when the past is attacked. (p. 30)

Bridges suggests that symbolic actions or ceremonies are a useful way of marking new beginnings. Accordingly, to kick off the new vision, Lane held a restructuring ceremony, complete with refreshments—which helped attendance dramatically. The two vice presidents of Instruction came dressed as the Blues Brothers, the Research and Planning choir performed, and the president and others spoke about why change was needed and what changes were envisioned. A good time was had by all.

One of the activities considered for the restructuring ceremony, and rejected, was the symbolic burning of the college's large procedure manuals. This act, intended to represent the end of unnecessary bureaucracy, would have been viewed by many who have developed or who use the manuals as an attack on their departments. In fact, the group that leaders expected to have the least affinity for the new vision at Lane was the managers, and especially managers of departments with an abundance of rules and regulations. It turns out, however, that given an opportunity to eliminate or simplify rules in their departments, many apparently bureaucratic managers have proven to be very adept at "reinventing" policies and procedures that at once serve students better and make the work of their department more manageable.

A 1995 survey of a sample of 141 Lane staff revealed that 85 percent agreed or strongly agreed that "change is needed." Ninety-two percent agreed or strongly agreed that "a better way of doing things *is* possible." And 82 percent believed that "improved work processes would bring greater satisfaction." These results indicate that many Lane staff are ready for change.

TOWARD A NEW LANE

With the Vision Statement and restructuring paper in hand, the first impulse was to tackle the curriculum, but, in fact, the college found other arenas equally pressing. Work to date falls into the following areas: human resources, technology, instruction, and process redesign.

Human Resources

One of the most ambitious initiatives was undertaken by a project team made up entirely of faculty. The team was formed to address the high faculty turnover expected from retirement. After nearly two years of deliberations, the team published the *Future Faculty Task Force Report,* which contains 18 recommendations on faculty hiring, orientation, and staff development. As part of its work, the project team recommended a revised faculty hiring process and developed an annual hiring calendar. They envisioned a future faculty that would form a learning community, play a more active role in college governance, better reflect the diversity of society, and be substantially full-time.

One of the recommendations of the project team is that the college devote 2 percent of its operating budget to organizational development. Several years ago Lane added to its program of *staff development*—or staff training programs based on individuals' perceived needs—a new program of *organizational development*—the training of groups in support of collegewide directions. While Lane has not achieved the recommended 2 percent expenditure, the college budget includes $175,000 for organizational development.

Training is planned by the Organization Development Action Team (ODAT), which includes representatives from the separate faculty, classified, and management development teams, as well as the leadership of the faculty and classified unions. The activity plan developed by ODAT supports the new Vision Statement by focusing on seven skill areas: communication, team building, problem solving, leadership, change, customer service, and conflict resolution.

ODAT utilizes a "train-the-trainer" approach. For example, six Lane staff have become certified Zenger-Miller trainers in team effectiveness. In addition, ODAT conducted a campuswide survey to identify 50 "movers and shakers," or informal leaders, who could be trained to train others. The movers and shakers represented all faculty and staff groups. In the summer of 1994, they participated in four days of intensive training in communications and team skills, and now some of them are training others. To date, more than 300 Lane personnel have participated in communications training.

The training program for conflict resolution is illustrative of the format adopted by ODAT. It consists of short training units on nonadversarial bargaining, formal third-party mediation, and informal conflict resolution between individuals. Likewise, training on communications skills covers interpersonal and group skills, and includes consensus building, decision making, and problem solving.

An important support for the new vision at Lane is the evaluation process. The evaluation system for managers has been revised to place more emphasis on collaboration, teamwork, use of technology, personal growth, and other factors necessary for the development of the learning college. For faculty, the direction has been toward more frequent and systematic evaluations. In fact, one faculty member is using daily student feedback in her classes in place of the traditional once-per-term student evaluation process.

As might be expected, some managers have been perceived as having difficulty making the transition from "bosses" to "coaches." A useful tool for resolving conflicts between managers and their staff has been formal mediation, conducted by a professional mediator. By enabling managers and employees to define exactly what they need from each other and by securing commitments from each to meet the other's needs, mediation has improved relationships and performance of departments in most instances. Lane has also found mediation a useful means of resolving many other kinds of conflicts and is currently in the process of hiring a mediation service on a longer-term, contractual basis.

Fortunately, not many managers have actively resisted the new vision. The manager of one of the most inherently bureaucratic departments, Personnel, recently reorganized her staff into a team structure, as has the Student Services vice president, the vice president for College Operations, and others. The success of these ventures is attracting the attention of other managers, and the team approach seems likely to spread.

In fact, Lane's top administrators recently eliminated the traditional "Executive Cabinet" in favor of an "Executive Leadership Team" (ELT). The ELT includes the president, vice presidents, and the heads of the personnel and public relations offices. Responsibility for facilitating the ELT's weekly meetings is rotated, as is responsibility for developing the agenda. The ELT strives to work at a policy and strategy level, and to delegate operational matters to other campus teams.

Technology

The new Lane is creating a demand on campus for more and better information, and technology is helping to meet this need. A collegewide network now links most staff with each other via e-mail and with the Internet. Many staff have taken the e-mail and Internet classes taught by college instructors exclusively for staff.

New uses of technology also are serving students. A touch-tone telephone registration system—already the service rated highest by students—has been enhanced to give student callers their grades, thereby saving mailing costs. The college has experimented with broadcasting the class schedule "live" on cable television so that students can monitor open and closed classes as they register by telephone. The use of a bar code system in the bookstore is beginning to eliminate long lines. Kiosks built throughout the campus provide students with personalized information, such as their schedules, grades, and transcripts; and with general information, such as campus maps. Counselors and advisors are developing systems to aid them in serving students, and the library system has been computer automated.

The Student Activities office replaced the traditional student identification cards with rudimentary "smart cards." These cards have great potential to hold information about students, such as their class schedules and the services they use, and to function as credit cards, perhaps eliminating treks to the cashier's office. Currently, the cards are used to access the library and kiosks. Future plans include use of the card by the cafeteria, bookstore, and student accounts as a debit/charge system; and perhaps by the admissions and records office as a portable, interactive student record.

An Instructional Technology Center has been developed especially for faculty who want to test and/or create new forms of computerized instruction. The center provides cutting-edge equipment, software, and technical counsel to all faculty. Increasing numbers of faculty are using the center on a drop-in basis, and faculty who wish to pursue major projects may apply for support through Instructional Technology Initiative grants.

As the major projects described above moved forward, the same obstacles to change were encountered again and again. The college's facilities and equipment simply were not adequate to support the new vision of the future. Therefore, in March 1995, Lane asked district taxpayers to approve $42.8 million in general obligation bonds to replace obsolete instructional equipment and construct new classrooms and labs with state-of-the-art technology. Taxpayers approved the request and gave an important boost to Lane's efforts to create a learner-centered college.

Instruction

With the new structure in place, instructional clusters began working on initiatives such as revising the curriculum, improving the class scheduling process, and integrating K-12 education reform. Substantial amounts of money were made available to faculty for curriculum projects. These "mini-grants" were awarded on a competitive basis and enabled the college to make significant progress in areas such as developing new certificate programs. The class scheduling process was analyzed by outside consultants, who recommended a number of changes to improve efficiency and service to students. The new instructional cluster structure proved to be effective for working with area high schools to implement and coordinate education reform and tech-prep programs.

One of the most promising new instructional initiatives to be implemented was the Fast Forward Program, a learning community in which a cohort of students pursues a multicultural/interdisciplinary series of courses leading to the Oregon Transfer Degree. The courses are offered by a team of transfer instructors representing disciplines such as English, philosophy, Spanish, ethnic studies, social sciences, mathematics, and the sciences. The students and instructors work together throughout the day in one classroom, and the disciplines are interwoven around thematic or historical segments. Instructors and students report that the Fast Forward Program is superior to traditional instruction as a means of developing skills in communication, critical thinking, and teamwork.

The response of the faculty to the new vision is interesting. Not especially resistant to the learning college concept, faculty have tended to embrace such tasks as developing new curricula and outcomes measures, and experimenting with new technologies—all the while tending to stay with tried-and-true methods in their classrooms. Some faculty express skepticism about technology-based instruction, collaborative learning, and other "new" methods, but there are signs that this attitude is changing. Faculty who have tried new techniques in the classroom attract the interest of their colleagues, and faculty who are experimenting with new techniques, such as computer-based instruction, are forming interest groups. It is expected that these "islands of innovation" will gradually spread throughout what has traditionally been a very innovative faculty.

The *Future Faculty Task Report*, written by faculty, envisions a faculty that will

- Demonstrate experience or potential for innovation and creativity in both the classroom and related educational duties. Apply theories of educational research and attempt novel strategies.

- Challenge established patterns of instruction and curriculum when they were created for convenience or neglected the needs of learners.
- Remain current in the occupational needs of the community and develop curriculum that supports these needs (Barber et al., 1995, p. 7).

Process Redesign

Another major focus that will support all the others is process redesign, the formal rethinking of work processes. In 1995–96, despite level funding from the state because of equalization, the college invested nearly half a million dollars in process redesign in the belief that it would accelerate meaningful change. The funding was to cover the hiring of consultants, payment for temporary staff to free up regular staff for redesign projects, and purchase of developed materials.

The first step in process redesign was to conduct a thorough technology assessment to describe Lane's technological environment and to identify the level of technological investment, training, and redeployment that will be required to improve college services and operations. In both college services and instruction, technology promises to be the key to providing high quality services despite decreased funding. Yet the college is struggling with how to fund technological improvements and how to administer the technology.

At Lane, administrative and instructional computing are served by the same mainframe computer and campuswide network, but administered separately. In 1994, the college employed an outside consultant who recommended that all computer-related services be combined under one manager, but the recommendation proved to be difficult to implement. In connection with process redesign, the college had another group of outside consultants conduct a technology assessment. Again, the recommendation was to align computer resources across campus. The consultants also recommended that Lane commit to a campuswide computing strategy, defining and communicating the services to be provided and who would provide them.

While the college is still debating how to administer computer services, progress has been made towards a more customer-oriented approach with the development of a help desk to assist Lane personnel with computer problems and by clarifying which services are provided by administrative computing personnel and which by instructional computing personnel. In the 1996 *Technology Planning Work Team Report*, a technology project team summarized the technology issues facing the college and proposed a governance structure for technology planning and a work agenda for the new structure. College leaders have enthusiastically accepted the work team's proposal to create a new strategic team, the Technology Advisory and Coordinating Team (TACT), and to make that team the facilitator of all technology planning processes and decisions.

This initial focus on technology has laid the groundwork for process redesign. The Lane approach has three basic components.

- A project leadership team that addresses communication, training, and change management issues.
- A process evaluation and selection team that defines core processes within the college, collects data that define the process steps, and recommends processes for redesign.
- Process teams that study and make changes in key processes.

To date, the Process Evaluation and Selection Team has identified opportunities for improvement in six core process areas: student services, planning/budgeting, facilities, grants and contracts, personnel/payroll, and procurement. After careful study of these processes, the team recommended that initial efforts at redesign focus on services to students that "provide information, enroll students, maintain records, promote success, and aid transition to lifelong learning." The second priority they identified is planning/budgeting. Only the student services redesign, called Students First!, has been developed thus far.

The Students First! team's workroom provides a glimpse of the redesign process. The walls are covered with yellow sticky notes that list in minute detail the steps involved in various student services processes. The team's overall goal is to develop a completely new process that provides the best possible services to students at the lowest possible cost. Even in its initial analyses, the team has discovered instances of duplication and activities that add little or no value to student success. Elimination of these steps will enable overburdened staff to focus their efforts and operate more efficiently and effectively.

In July 1996, the *Students First! Final Report* was published. It contains 12 major recommendations for redesigning student services based on cross-functional teams, more extensive use of technology, and streamlined processes. The proposed changes will be phased in over the next two years.

Meanwhile, process redesign in the student services created parallel interest in redesign of instruction. Throughout the 1995–96 school year, instructional leaders discussed how the faculty could be supported to move toward a stronger focus on learning. A team of faculty and managers was formed to develop a plan for a Strategic Learning Initiative. The initiative will consider the entire range of instructional and learning processes and will be planned and implemented through a partnership between instructional managers and leaders of the faculty union. The shared goal is to produce changes that are long-term, systemic, and strategic. Specifically, the leaders hope to apply the latest research on learning and motivation, the latest advances in technology, and the best possible information on student needs to 1) enhance faculty learning about students and instruction and 2) achieve cost efficiencies that maximize resources to advance student learning. The initiative is in its very early stages, but there is cautious optimism that it will strengthen the learning environment.

LESSONS LEARNED

While "grand plans" have totally transformed some community colleges, the culture of Lane Community College is averse to such systematic, top-down schemes. The best way to achieve change at Lane has proven to be gradually, through groups and individuals who champion a cause and spread their enthusiasm to others. The champions of the learning college have included the president, vice presidents, and staff in various roles throughout the college. The college has tried to achieve *shared leadership*, so that any of these staff members can lead at any given time.

An illustration of shared leadership is the classified employee who decided that the play *Oleanna* would make a wonderful learning experience for Lane personnel in place of the traditional opening day speeches. This play about a professor and student, set entirely in the professor's office, addresses power relationships in academe, a topic that the classified employee felt all Lane staff could benefit from exploring further. She convinced the president, secured funding from the training budget, hired professional actors, selected and trained after-the-play discussion leaders, and directed the play—all in addition to her regular duties as an office manager in the health department.

Not everyone loved the play. While most people praised it, seeing it as a powerful statement about power relationships between teachers and students, others thought it treated the subject of sexual abuse insensitively. Nevertheless, the staff member/leader received the college's first annual risk-taker award and was treated with great respect by all.

The lesson learned is that it is important to create a climate of trust in which people can lead and fail without recrimination. The learning college cannot exist in a cautious, careful, fearful college community. A learning community supports risk-takers and rewards grand failures as well as grand successes.

A second lesson learned is the difficulty of overcoming bureaucracy. Most community colleges started out as top-down bureaucracies. Movement toward a vision-driven learning college requires that confining rules and regulations be de-emphasized in favor of values, vision, and variety. Problems should bring forth student-centered solutions, not more rules and regulations. People should be given the flexibility to work outside their jobs, even outside their departments, if the work will benefit the college and its students. The bureaucratic tendency toward treating all staff and all students the same should give way to a celebration of diversity and differences. Leaders must realize, however, that such change requires constant vigilance to identify and eliminate the bureaucratic tendencies in all of us.

A third lesson learned is that not everyone will be able to embrace the concept of the learning college. Managers who are not able to change their management style, students who only want to learn in traditional classrooms in traditional ways, and instructors who resist change must all be treated with care and respect. The learning college can accommodate a variety of values and styles and need not create an atmosphere of educational correctness or doctrinaire inflexibility. Gentle persistence has proven to be superior to heavy-handed control in producing an atmosphere where everyone at Lane can learn to change.

A final lesson learned is that the learning college cannot exist without extensive use of technology in offices and in classrooms. Most colleges, like Lane, have not yet learned to deal with technology as well as they need to, nor can most colleges afford to provide the technology necessary for student success. Many university departments of education are beginning to turn out graduates who are at home with technology, but the vast majority of existing community college personnel will have to receive their computer training on the community college campus.

On its journey toward becoming a learning college, Lane has encountered many obstacles. Level state funding is making it difficult to create more learning options for students. The accreditation visiting team praised the college for its new venture, but requested an interim written report on the progress of the learning college. Technological change on campus has at times seemed to produce chaos. Day-to-day tasks seem always to postpone movement toward the learning college ideal. Staff often seem more willing to accept empowerment than responsibility, while leaders sometimes seem more willing to give up responsibility than power. There is a great deal of role confusion among groups and between individuals. Working in teams does not come naturally to educators socialized to be strong individualists, suspicious of movements and groups.

Still, despite these challenges, Lane is learning to be a learning college, and learning takes time and patience.

ONE PRESIDENT'S VIEW OF THE FUTURE

The Lane of the future will be a learning community where people with diverse needs and abilities will be able to learn at their own pace through a variety of means tailored to their learning styles. They will be given many options: when to start, when to finish, what kinds of learning experiences to join, and what learning goals to achieve. Programs of study will be geared to the learner's needs, not to the bureaucratic needs of the organization. Learners who prove unable to meet their goals will be provided with an individualized, customized plan for gaining the skills to rejoin their chosen path and to succeed.

Students and staff of the future Lane will enter and leave the college with their diversity intact. We will respect their origins and their destinations and will learn how to assist them in meeting their learning goals. The college will manage the learning environment to meet the needs of individual learners whose origins, abilities, and interests are diverse.

Students and instructors working together will be empowered to make decisions about what educational experiences are appropriate. The student who wants to become a surgeon may pursue a different biology curriculum than the student who wants to operate a greenhouse. The artificial boundary between college and work will be lowered, so that students can learn inside and outside the college, in the classroom and in the greenhouse.

All of this movement will be orchestrated with the assistance of technology. Learners will travel through their learning experiences the way people travel around the world today—with the assistance of the computerized travel agency/college. The passport will be a "smart card" used to gain entrance to learning experiences and to record those experiences for future use. Learners will be discouraged from traveling through the college without gaining proper preparation or enough learning resources to complete the journey, and travelers' aid stations will be located at strategic places along the way to find and assist students who lose their way. There will be no failures, only challenges.

The college will continuously monitor the learning and will adjust the system as needed to better serve individual learners. Learning, not contact hours or dollars budgeted, will be measured. Faculty, staff, and managers will focus on one goal: helping learners better complete their learning journey. All proposed activities will be evaluated in terms of their value to the learning process. Faculty, staff, and managers will pursue systematic learning plans for themselves so that they can grow and develop as facilitators of learning.

The Lane of the future will be directed squarely at learning. Everyone at Lane—students, staff, faculty—will be a learner. Everyone at Lane will be a valued member of many caring groups. Everyone at Lane will be cared for and will care about the success of others. Everyone will share in the vision of quality learning experiences in a caring environment.

REFERENCES

Barber, Bob et al. *Future Faculty Task Report*. Eugene, OR: Lane Community College, Fall 1995.

———. *Technology Planning Work Team Report*. Eugene, OR: Lane Community College, January 1996.

Bridges, William. *Managing Transition: Making the Most of Change*. Reading, MA: Addison-Wesley, 1993.

Mamet, David. "Oleanna." Dramatists Play Service, 1992.

Roueche, John E., and Baker, George A., III. *Access & Excellence: The Open-Door College* Washington, D.C.: American Association of Community Junior Colleges, 1987.

Students First! Final Report. Eugene, OR: Lane Community College, July 1996.

CHAPTER 9

Becoming a Learner-Centered College System at Maricopa

Paul A. Elsner

INTRODUCTION

C ommunity colleges have enjoyed a reputation for being agile, responsive, flexible, and adaptive to their communities. They have fared better than other segments of higher education in recent years, as public confidence and resources have eroded.

However, in the face of a disconcerting call to transform government, corporations, hospitals, and universities—virtually all segments of life in this latter part of the twentieth century—community colleges are hardly immune. They have a well-founded reputation for being responsive to their communities, but even these adaptable institutions will fail if they do not respond to the significant changes currently facing American society.

If community colleges are to meet the challenge, they must forge a satisfactory methodology for change, transform their priorities and procedures, develop mechanisms for continuous improvement and self-reform, and utilize the benefits of new technologies. This chapter presents such a challenge. It is about Maricopa Community College's struggling efforts to become a more learner-centered college. It is also a story about how very successful organizations cannot stand on their past achievements. Change for a successful organization may be harder. Inclination toward stasis is more likely when an organization has been successful in the past. Maricopa is a successful organization, and its staff is well aware of the special challenge of making changes at a successful organization.

The Maricopa Community College District (MCCD) began its long quest toward becoming a more learner-centered college by including such a goal in its Vision Statement. This statement was developed only after wide discussion and participation of Maricopa's internal community. The adoption of the Vision Statement by the governing board followed months of debate about wording and final concurrence by most of Maricopa's key leaders.

Placing a statement of desire to become a learning organization in the Vision Statement, by itself, does not mean much, even when there is general agreement. Getting there is a long and worrisome journey.

THE ACTUAL STARTING POINT

The Maricopa Community Colleges participated as an initial partner in the Pew Higher Education Roundtable's (supported by the Pew Charitable Trusts) efforts to examine obstacles to change and transformation in higher education. Under the leadership of Robert Zemsky and others, several diverse kinds of institutions were asked to participate in this project. These institutions included land grant colleges, research universities, community colleges, and liberal arts colleges. These colleges were assumed to have an interest in participating in a national effort to assess restructuring and transformational strategies.

Maricopa participated in two roundtables with the Pew Charitable Trusts' staff in examining options for bringing about institutional change. Some of Maricopa's leadership had participated in earlier policy discussions about the state of higher education. These earlier discussions were summarized in a series of publications called *Policy Perspectives.*

One of the striking results of the early Pew policy studies was that although many institutions had faced serious financial crises and had made strenuous budgetary adaptations to respond to the resource crunch of the late 1980s and early 1990s, most had failed to improve their financial or political situations. In a policy report distributed by the Pew Higher Education Roundtable, these institutions presented themselves as

> battle weary veterans, survivors of the assault on their institutions' budget. Around the presidents' table they regaled the visitor with tales of the hills stormed: the modest but painful reductions in staff; postponed faculty appointments; salary increases that did not keep the pace with inflation; investments in Total Quality Management to bring greater efficiency to their administrative procedures. They had even succeeded in keeping the annual tuition increase within the general range of those imposed by peer institutions. To secure their future, they had taken their first steps toward the planning of a new and vigorous capital campaign. (Pew Charitable Trusts, 1993, p. 1)

Unfortunately, the Pew analysts felt that none of the steps taken by these institutions had material impact on the well-being of the institutions. More surprisingly, throughout all the agony and pain, these institutions had barely made an impact on their budget crises. The policy analysts and the Pew Higher Education Research program reported that the institutions described were, at best, only tinkering at the margins.

Few, if any, colleges among those summoned to participate in the roundtables, although reputed to be innovative like Maricopa, had undergone deep and necessary structural change. It soon became clear to roundtable participants that higher education, including those institutions most visibly concerned about change, had not experienced fundamental transformation.

Colleges that agreed to participate in the Pew project had to commit to a dialogue process, referred to as "The Roundtable." The roundtable was to be locally organized and facilitated by Pew staff, eventually to be turned over to local leaders with the hope that it would take on a life of its own.

In organizing its roundtable, the Maricopa Community Colleges chose to load it with faculty. In fact, the early roundtable was dominated by instructional, student service, and faculty personnel, but included the chancellor, two board members, and local citizens.

One of the early issues placed before the Maricopa Roundtable, which still remains with us, is the question: What would make a difference? What would have the greatest leveraging effect on the general nature, structure, and purpose of a college or university?

Ironically, in early conversations of the Maricopa Roundtable, there seemed to be little debate as to why Maricopa needed to pursue restructuring. As reports indicated, the colleges were faced with some of the same challenges that have shaped the restructuring of other American enterprises. Faculty seemed very aware of these changes. There have been assertions by some leaders that faculty are not aware of these major forces, but that is not true of Maricopa faculty.

Maricopa's faculty seemed especially aware of the growth of competitive suppliers and private sector competition. They had experienced the impact of declining state, federal, and local support. They were also aware that customer dissatisfaction and erosion of confidence in higher education could place community colleges in the same predicament as the public schools that suffer under the yoke of school reform efforts. Faculty and staff also seemed very aware of the globalization of business and politics. And they were keenly aware of the impact of technology and other market forces.

DIALOGUE BEFORE FOCUS

Maricopa's early roundtable discussions required a genuine commitment to conversation and dialogue before participants could arrive at what appeared to be a focused discussion.

Facilitators from Pew emphasized that collective conversations must occur before any patterns of consensus were likely to form. This was wise counsel. In a college committed to learning, dialogue is an essential but often neglected skill. Maricopa actually began a series of training and facilitation efforts to assist and inspire its members to communicate in meaningful dialogues. One of the major problems in higher education is that policy leaders, faculty, and staff in many of our institutions do not know how to talk to one another. The language of the CEO is embedded with references to control, competition, and protection of territory. The CEO is often a primary barrier to open communication, to real talking, real sharing, and real exchange.

The following excerpts from Maricopa's handbook for conducting dialogues offer some perspectives on what can happen when real dialogue takes place:

- Small groups of thoughtful, concerned citizens can change the world. Indeed, it is the only thing that ever has.—*Margaret Mead*
- Dialogue can occur when a group of people see each other as colleagues in mutual quest and deeper insight and clarity. What is necessary going in is the willingness to consider each other as colleagues. In dialogue, a group explores complex, difficult issues from many points of view. Individuals suspend their assumptions but they communicate their assumptions freely. The event is a free exploration that brings to the surface the full depth of people's experience and thought, and yet moves beyond their individual views.—*Peter Senge*
- Dialogue is the art of free play, a sort of collective dance of the mind that . . . has immense power and reveals coherent purpose. —*David Bohm* (*District Office Steering Team QQ Dialogues,* 1995)

As Maricopa marches toward becoming a learning organization, it follows the road of dialogue. Dialogue precedes focus. Focus precedes a coherent vision.

Rather than talking about global structural changes, the faculty and the leadership agreed that the area of teaching and learning, particularly bringing the institution around to a learner-centered focus, was a direction the faculty could support and rally around. Moreover, the faculty agreed that tangible changes such as greater collaboration and elimination of vertical structures and bureaucracies in the organization needed to follow commitments to a learner-centered philosophy. To leverage structural change, Maricopa agreed that changing the learning paradigm from a traditional one to a current, more learner-centered approach was the vehicle to more comprehensive, and even profound, structural change.

Participants in the early conversations of the Maricopa Roundtable also acknowledged the challenges of discussing such a new paradigm, one of which was a lack of common vocabulary for the 3,000 full- and part-time faculty and staff at Maricopa. An early step involved creating a taxonomy of the old learning paradigm and the new, or more desired, and hopefully more effective, learning paradigm.

Maricopa was not far into these conversations before roundtable members agreed that using the word "old" to describe the past and the word "new" to describe the desired paradigm were not fully operational terms. What constituted the old or traditional may still be desirable, and what constituted the new already existed in several places at Maricopa. The issues of time, desirability, good, and new, had to be sorted and clarified as operational terms. To quote from an early report

> The time sequence was important to us. We felt the need to acknowledge that Maricopa was doing a number of things that would be characterized as "good" things in the desired learning paradigm; at the same time, Maricopa was still teaching and learning in ways that would be characterized as "not good" in the desired learning paradigm. At that point we concluded that Maricopa had tinkered with change; and Maricopa had to embrace change in order to improve learning. Change could not be isolated in one corner of Maricopa, nor could it be "top-down." Also, the change we envisioned required a new vocabulary and shared language which all of us must work to develop. Finally, we knew it was time to stop talking about change; we had to commit to bringing about that change. (*Maricopa Roundtable Policy Perspectives*, 1994, p. 4)

In the discussions that took place regarding what is now referred to as a "traditional learning paradigm" and a "desired learning paradigm," many Total Quality Management (TQM) processes were used. These early conversations provided a critical departure point from other restructuring efforts in higher education, which often focus on fixing the current system instead of replacing it. Maricopa began to work from a vision that placed learning first, providing a clear focus for restructuring efforts

Donald Norris and Michael Dolence's impressive text distributed by the Society for College and University Planning, entitled *Transforming Higher Education: A Vision for Learning in the 21st Century* (1995), reinforces the need for such a vision. They note that higher education's greatest dilemma in facing the twenty-first century is that colleges and universities have not been able to construct a vision for learning in the face of so much swift technological change, external forces, budgetary crises, and political and global shifts.

Maricopa's vision for structural change is embedded in changing the learning paradigm. The roundtable group delivered this revelation and shared it districtwide in a *Maricopa Roundtable Policy Perspectives* 1994.

The roundtable participants created a comprehensive dissemination plan consisting of a series of policy discussions on each of the campuses with key faculty leaders, staff members, and students. The participants attempted to explain Maricopa's involvement in the Pew Higher Education Roundtable Restructuring Project. They attempted to inform all staff members about the characteristics of the traditional and the desired learning paradigm. They also discussed the key components of the desired learning paradigms. The roundtable participants sought input from all others concerning the characteristics of both the traditional and desired learning paradigms. Maricopa hoped to reach a consensus on a desired learning paradigm from these policy discussions. In its major dissemination product, which reached all colleges and virtually all staff and faculty of the Maricopa Community Colleges, the following primary (and contrasting) elements were reviewed:

> **First, learning is a process which is lifelong for everybody and should be measured in a consistent, ongoing manner focused on improvement.**
>
> The *traditional learning paradigm* is most concerned with individual courses, the content of the courses and individual grades. Quantity, not quality, is important. For example, the number of students in class, the number of hours faculty teach, the number of books in the library, are the important measures of learning. Learning involves memorizing the content of courses with a great amount of energy focused on getting good grades, not learning. Learning involves the teacher giving knowledge or information to the passive, receiving student. Learning is competitive. The Bell Curve is required for grades. Who can get the best grade? and, What will be on the exam? are some of the most frequently asked questions by students. The assessment method is currently the traditional course-content testing system conducted at specific times during the year (e.g., "midterms" and "finals") which is not an accurate measure of competencies, strengths or skills; it is often merely a measure of hours or days in the classroom.
>
> In the *desired learning paradigm*, learning is both a product and a process. Learning occurs throughout the institution, not just in classrooms. Learning comes not just from textbooks or lectures. The curriculum can be flexible, relevant and responsive to students. Experimentation is rewarded. Data are collected on the needs of students on

a regular basis. All students can learn. Each learner's needs are met. Students and teachers learn from each other and from everyone within the institution and the larger community. Learning is connected from class to class and experience to experience. The larger community is directly involved in the learning process. Everyone is learning how to learn and facilitating learning. Faculty staff and the larger community are models of lifelong learning. The institution is a model learning organization. The results of learning are measurable and achievement-focused. Student performance is outcome-based. The student's performance evaluation leads to continuous improvement. There are appropriate, authentic, flexible patterns of evidence for evaluating student learning. The purpose of measurement is not to find defects; it is to encourage improvement.

Roundtable comments: We believe—passionately—that the student is the center of learning. All of our thinking and actions must reinforce and support this belief. We must make whatever changes are necessary to ensure that the student is the center of learning.

Second, everyone is an active learner and teacher through collaboration, shared responsibility and mutual respect.

The traditional learning paradigm is a production-line model which treats all students as if they were the same. It is a model that is faculty-centered in the classroom. It is often more responsive to the needs of faculty and administrators rather than students. The student must fit into the institution created and maintained for the convenience of faculty and administrators. For example, the curriculum is determined by what the faculty want to teach and by the attitude of faculty and administrators that "we know better" what students need. It is a homogeneous atmosphere with little diversity. Faculty, administrators and students function as independent actors. Each actor is a single individual operating in a singular environment without regard for the larger environment of family, work or different learning styles.

The desired learning paradigm is characterized by a responsibility shared by the student and the institution through its faculty and staff and the larger community. That responsibility is lifelong learning. Collaboration occurs in and out of the classroom and competition is reduced. Students, faculty, staff and the larger community are partners in the teaching and learning processes. There are incentives and rewards for experimenting with teaching and learning processes. Diversity is considered a strength. The institution reflects the reality of the world's cultures and mirrors society in its increasingly complex nature. Everyone is truly open to sharing with each other, learning from each other, and understanding each other.

Roundtable comments: Everyone is responsible for personal learning and change, and we are responsible for sharing with each other.

Third, the learning process includes the larger community through the development of alliances, relationships and opportunities for mutual benefit.

The traditional learning paradigm is generally not aligned with K-12 and all sectors of higher education and the larger community. There is limited involvement in higher education on the part of the community and employers. The community may not understand all the college has to offer. Overall the community is not involved in learning; learning occurs on campus.

The desired learning paradigm finds the institution seeking a greater understanding of the needs of the community and meeting community needs. A strong, supportive relationship exists between the community and the institution. There is a better understanding of the institution by the community, and greater financial and other support from the community results. The larger community is directly involved in the learning process. Collaboration among education, business, industry, government and all community groups is the key to learning and working for a lifetime. K-12 and all sectors of higher education are tightly connected, including connections among all of the Maricopa Colleges.

Roundtable comments: Everyone must think and act in a more collaborative fashion with the larger community of which we are only a small part.

Fourth, learning occurs in a flexible and appropriate environment.

The traditional learning paradigm finds learning restricted to the classrooms in buildings on the campus. Typically the faculty member is at the front of the room, lecturing. Class time equals credits. The classroom is apt to be hierarchical and authoritarian. The classroom is rigidly structured—even in its looks. There is limited state-of-the-art technology. Textbooks, pencils, paper, chalk and transparencies are common.

In the *desired learning paradigm* appropriate technology enhances teaching and learning processes and is integrated into learning processes. Different learning delivery systems are encouraged to meet the unique needs of the larger community. The larger community is directly involved in the learning process.

Roundtable comments: Everyone must open his/her mind to embrace new forms of learning and delivery systems. (*Maricopa Roundtable Policy Perspectives*, 1994)

Initially the roundtable consisted of 28 members, 11 of whom were faculty and one a citizen from the community. Even though the roundtable included a balanced representation from the Maricopa system, participants wanted widespread commitment. To secure that commitment, a series of campus-to-campus policy discussions ("mini-roundtables") were held involving a wide range of faculty and staff on each of Maricopa's ten campuses. Refinements to the desired learning paradigm were incorporated from these discussions.

STRATEGIC CONVERSATIONS

Another feature of the dissemination process was the governing board's commitment to hold strategic conversations rather than formal study sessions. Strategic conversations were structured discussions about key strategic issues. Most board meetings cover legal, financial, and personnel issues, and board members seldom engage in discussion on strategic thinking. These strategic conversations replaced much of the routine business. They were well-structured, well-facilitated, and better researched sessions than previous governing board meetings.

Throughout 1994 and 1995, a number of strategic conversations covering significant strategic topics were held. Much of the process for committing to the movement toward a more learning-centered college came from these strategic conversations. In addition, the Maricopa Policy Perspective Roundtable was a critical topic in the board's strategic conversations. The following list of strategic conversation topics (Figure 9-1) illustrates the variety of issues addressed:

- Strategic Issues Associated with Diversity
- Strategic Issues Associated with New Learning Paradigms
- Strategic Issues Associated with Non-Traditional Education
- Popcorn Session: Viewing of the Film Mind Walk/Panel Discussion
- Service Learning
- Strategic Issues Associated with Financial Planning
- John Cleveland Presentation on Chaos Theory
- Strategic Issues Associated with the Bond Issue and Facility Needs of Colleges
- Margaret Wheatley Presentation on Leadership and the New Science
- Strategic Issues Associated with Marketing MCCD
- Strategic Issues Associated with Full Time Student Equivalency
- Strategic Issues Associated with Leadership and the New Science
- Strategic Issues Associated with System Unity
- Strategic Issues Associated with the MCCD Internal Community
- Strategic Issues Associated with Student Transfer
- Student Needs in a Rapidly Changing World
- Assessment of Student Academic Achievement
- Strategic Issues Associated with Faculty and the Maricopa Community
- Strategic Issues Associated with Continuous Quality Improvement Efforts

---

MARICOPA GOVERNING BOARD STRATEGIC CONVERSATIONS 1994–1995

FIGURE 9-1

A NEW CULTURE IN WHICH LEADERS LEARN; LEARNERS LEAD; AND COLLABORATION RULES

For a number of years, Maricopa has been developing a culture in which leaders learn and learners lead. The experience in the roundtables helped confirm this basic value and develop it even further.

The strategic conversations provided an excellent laboratory to practice this value. Customarily, sessions of the board are led by the chancellor or executive staff. Strategic conversations, however, are often led by faculty, classified staff, students, or key staff members involved in coordinating some of Maricopa's strategic directions.

As a result of Maricopa's emphasis on helping leaders learn and learners lead, several hundred staff members have become qualified in group process and communication skills to facilitate discussion. This outcome is one of the characteristics of the desired learning paradigm in which we learn from one another.

This value has evolved especially through the work of Maricopa's quantum quality effort. Several years ago the district created the Quantum Quality Commission, which has trained facilitators from all ten campuses to apply TQM approaches for change and transformation within the institution. In fact, the first 40 hours of training in the quantum quality effort were conducted by two faculty members from Rio Salado Community College, who facilitated a comprehensive session involving the governing board, ten presidents, the faculty leadership, four vice chancellors, the chancellor, and other administrators and support staff. This was an excellent example in which leadership does not come from the top down but emerges from the competencies and commitments of involved faculty and staff. The quantum quality effort at Maricopa has played a key role in helping the district move further down the road to becoming a more learner-centered college and to preparing leaders to learn and learners to lead.

The installation of a new mid-rise tower at Rio Salado Community College also provided an excellent laboratory for the illustration of this core leadership value. Rio Salado, a nontraditional college that relies heavily on outreach and distance education, proposed a state-of-the-art technology-production center in a new building. In the spirit of collaborative planning, Linda Thor, president of Rio Salado, invited residents and staff from the other Maricopa colleges to participate in a day of dialogue and planning. Every participant was a high-ranking executive within the Maricopa Community College system, but the key facilitator was a staff assistant on one of the campuses.

In keeping with its commitment to collaboration Maricopa's trained facilitators now lead a number of groups beyond Maricopa's campuses. Staff members have been called upon to facilitate important governance and planning processes, including statewide retreats of community college presidents, meetings of Maricopa's governing board, and sessions of Maricopa's Think Tank involving representatives from local schools, community-based organizations, and area colleges and universities.

These collaborative processes and activities are consistent with the goals of the desired learning paradigm. As stated in the roundtable report, "the larger community is dually involved in the learning process. Collaborations among education, business, government, industry, and all community groups is the key to learning and working for a lifetime. K-12 and all sectors of higher education are tightly connected, including connections between the Maricopa Community Colleges" (*Maricopa Roundtable Policy Perspectives*, 1994, p. 8). By combining its values of leaders learn and learners lead with its commitment to collaboration in its community, Maricopa has developed a base for major structural change and transformation in the institution.

LEARNING ORGANIZATIONS AS SYSTEMS

At Maricopa the goal of becoming a more learner-centered college is supported by the college's commitment to become a learning organization. According to Peter Senge (1990), a learning organization is one in which all employees are involved as continuing learners to improve the practices and programs developed to achieve the purposes of the organization. Maricopa leaders have worked hard to create a learning organization in the institution that provides a solid foundation on which to create a more learner-centered college.

A learning organization requires that all parts, all entities, and all people in the organization function as an interrelated system. To achieve this interrelatedness, organizational leaders must overcome the historical perspective that views an organization as a series of programs, functions, or departments. While colleges are made up of distinct units, a learning organization always views these units as interrelated and connected. Systems thinking has been developed by many theorists, but Fritjof Capra, through his book, *The Turning Point: Science, Society, and the Rising Culture*, has had a major influence on organizational thinking at Maricopa. Capra (1988) wrote:

> The new vision of reality we have been talking about is based on awareness of the essential interrelatedness and inter-dependence of all

phenomena—physical, biological, psychological, social, and cultural. It transcends current disciplinary and conceptual boundaries and will be pursued within new institutions. At present there is no well-established framework, either conceptual or institutional, that would accommodate the formulation of the new paradigm, but the outlines of such a framework are already being shaped by many individuals, communities, and networks that are developing new ways of thinking and organizing themselves according to new principles. (p. 284)

Margaret Wheatley, who has visited Maricopa several times and who has been a consultant to The National Institute for Leadership Development, a FIPSE- and Ford Foundation-supported project based on the Phoenix College campus, has assisted Maricopa's staff in thinking about organizational culture. Wheatley suggests that most current thinking about organizational behavior is inherited from the seventeenth century. Newtonian physics and Cartesian conceptual frameworks about the universe have been the basis for the current emphasis on planning and analyzing, and the preoccupation with the parts of whole systems.

This philosophy has greatly influenced modern organizational behavior, which means that specific trouble spots in a college or university are usually targeted and analyzed as a source of difficulty. The solution has usually focused on fixing the part rather than reviewing the entire system for systemic flaws. In this model, institutions of higher education usually dismiss a personnel director, a purchasing agent, or a registrar because that particular function is not operating efficiently. In systems thinking, leaders examine the entire system to determine whether or not the overall system has been poorly conceived and whether or not the roles and functions of individuals in the system are clear and connected. Individuals who fail in an organization often do so because the overall system itself is flawed.

Wheatley believes that we currently think of "the world as a great clock," a machine that can be analyzed, taken apart, and repaired. The leader's role is to be able to spot the problems and fix them. Wheatley suggests that this is a naive model of organizational functioning and of leadership.

Contemporary organizations, like Maricopa and other colleges and universities, are living organisms. Organizations have an innate ability to find their own solutions and self-organize around shared and agreed upon purposes and larger visions. Wheatley believes that an organization must have its own sense of self, and that it has to be able to respond to the questions: What are we about? Why are we here? To what purpose and to what end do we function? When individuals in an organization begin to work together to answer these questions, the outcome often results in creative self-organization and change.

Regardless of the scope of the organization or the task—building a new Boeing 777 or leading ten Maricopa colleges—individual members of an organization are powerfully motivated when they know they can be involved in their own improvement and when they can organize their work to provide better service. It is one of the primary tasks of the leaders of such organizations to encourage and provide opportunities for employees to understand and participate in the larger view of the organization. Such involvement is difficult to achieve, because, again historically, individuals have usually functioned in fragmented and isolated units structured in vertical and hierarchical frameworks.

As Maricopa has undertaken a massive effort to move to becoming a learning organization, collaboration has emerged as a key value in overcoming the compartmentalization of old structures. Peter Senge suggested that collaboration is the fundamental underpinning of transformational change in an institution. According to Senge, the greatest single obstacle to speeding up change in an organization is the resistance to collaboration. Furthermore, he says that change is about speeding up the process of evolution. Evolution, however, is a very slow process. Senge noted that it took 3 million years to grow a lung, another 20 million to walk upright, 60 million more years to grasp a spear, and 10 million more to light a fire. He described change as fast forwarding organizational evolution. Failure to collaborate is what slows down the change process. Collaboration is not yet a natural behavior for most organizational members. As Senge stated "In America, we shoot collaborators!" (1995).

At Maricopa, two significant enterprises have emerged as the primary mechanisms to ensure that Maricopa becomes a learning organization and a system of learning colleges. The two enterprises are the Learner-Centered System Steering (LCS) Team and the Organizational Analysis Team (OATS). These two teams have different paths, different goals, and different processes, but they constantly interact and change their goals and processes related to their interaction with one another. These major efforts at collaborative change are subsumed under a broader organizational banner commonly referred to at Maricopa as "Project Apollo."

The Learner-Centered System Steering Team

The Learner-Centered System Steering Team coordinates a fairly massive reengineering effort by identifying, analyzing, and recommending the various steps or cycles that students experience from registration through graduation or completion.

Many staff members at Maricopa have reservations about the term "reengineering" because to many people it implies layoffs and restructuring, all too familiar behaviors in the corporate world. The word "reengineering" is also frequently confused with TQM, restructuring, and automation, all of which may have negative emotional meanings for members in an organization.

As Ron Bleed (1996), Maricopa's vice chancellor for Information Technologies, stated in his paper, *Perspective on Project Apollo*, from a positive point of view the word "reengineering" represents "improvements in innovation, flexibility, service to the customer, cost effectiveness, and adding value" (p. 6). On the negative side, "reengineering" means layoffs and loss of place or role.

To determine what an ideal learning support system would be for students, the steering team conducted studies to identify critical cycles students would experience in a learner-centered system. Twenty-eight representatives from 22 departments formed a design team, chaired by a student, to analyze these cycles.

Over the spring of 1995, members of this group reviewed all the activities the Maricopa Community Colleges hope to accomplish to support learners' completion of a community college program. Student focus groups gathered student input about activities and issues associated with learner support. These activities led to the identification of 17 cycles that were placed in priority by the team and grouped into four broad categories or cycles. Each would be reengineered.

The four categories included 1) the Learning Plan; 2) Financial Aid and Support; 3) Scheduling; and 4) Curriculum Approval and Articulation. All LCS cycles will eventually be automated.

To arrive at the reengineering strategies for these four cycles, cross-functional teams met two days a week for over six months with the assistance of a private consulting firm, Axiom, Inc., to perfect the methodology for designing these new systems. Members of each of the teams had expertise in the content and processes of the cycles under investigation. Internal staff were used to facilitate these processes. Most of the teams included ten members or more and were truly cross-functional and integrated with multiple functions at the colleges. It was the first time that Maricopa engaged such a wide range of integrated, cross-functional owners of these processes in the reform effort. Normally such tasks are accomplished through vertically structured bureaucracies examining their own processes, which often leads to protectionism and safeguards against reconstitution and renewal.

Engaging in these cross-functional processes with a view to improving learner-centered systems caused MCC not only to create new classifications of teams and employees, but it also gave the Maricopa system a vocabulary of renewal not thought possible before engaging in the LCS effort. The experience gained in these cross-functional processes proved to be a watershed for Maricopa. When cross-functional teams in a large, complex institution like Maricopa work together to create a new focus on learner-centered systems, creative opportunities for change can be the result.

From these experiences, Maricopa developed a vocabulary of common mental models (images, beliefs, and assumptions that individuals carry around in their heads regarding people, places, and processes) that helped the players track their history. The mental models also helped to clarify relationships and connections. The participants in these cross-functional teams and others who followed were surprised about how many concepts of the learning college were already embedded in their views. Once these individual views were seen in clear relief in the mental models, members realized they had developed a common vocabulary for their learning organization. The mental map in Figure 9-2 is an illustration of the many conceptual descriptors and connectors that emerged from a strategic conversation held at a recent board meeting involving approximately 50 participants.

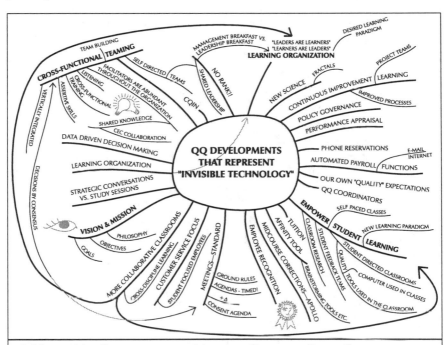

A Mental Map Resulting from a Maricopa Governing Board Strategic Conversation January 1996

FIGURE 9-2

Success of the cross-functional teams and the outcome of a common vocabulary were related in part to Maricopa's use of Renewal Analysis Teams (RATS). These in-house teams, trained to assist groups across the colleges through the renewal process, functioned as external facilitators who brought an objective view and skill to examining issues and challenges. In addition to these in-house teams, private consulting firms provided expertise in organizational analysis and innovation and provided another layer of observation from the outside. Experts in the student learning cycles under examination in such areas as advisement, admissions, registration, and articulation were also brought in to share their views and to encourage participants to create new learning-centered structures and processes. This approach worked quite well at Maricopa because of its long history of using combinations of staff across the colleges to develop programs and its experience in the use of external consultants and experts.

With assistance from the Renewal Analysis Teams, the members of the Learning-Centered System Steering Team began to examine their assumptions about student success in the college as they studied the cycles students went through from initial registration to completion. In the past, staff members responsible for advisement and student placement had assumed that students came to the Maricopa Community Colleges with a fairly clear view of what they needed in math, English, vocational preparation, and transfer courses. Students were introduced to a cafeteria array of courses from which they built their schedules with little overall preparation of a learning plan. As a result, students often selected discrete courses for a short-term purpose, overlooking their long-term goals and the advice the college could provide to assist them in meeting those goals.

In some cases, students were placed in 16-week math courses that were largely irrelevant to their real learning needs. Advisement did not center on developing a learning plan for students but on enrolling students in specific courses. There was often very little relationship between the specific courses and an overall learning plan. In this situation, students often accumulated many credits without any plan of where these courses would lead.

As the work of the LCS Team emerged, it was clear that Maricopa needed to reexamine the processes it used to engage the student in maximum learning opportunities provided by the college. With a new focus on a learning-centered system, the district is now fully engaged in developing new programs of assessment, advisement, placement, and related functions to ensure that each student develops an overall learning plan. With the application of new technologies, a refocused set of procedures and practices, and a renewed staff effort, the future is bright indeed for students who matriculate at the Maricopa Community Colleges.

The Organizational Analysis Team

To complement the LCS Team and its various subcommittees, consultants from the Oracle Corporation and the Axiom group worked with renewal coordinators and business experts to create a methodical organizational analysis as it related to the LCS effort. This analysis is currently ongoing and functioning under the title of the Organizational Analysis Team (OATS).

The Organizational Analysis Team's task is to analyze the impact of change on Maricopa. The tasks to be accomplished by the team include:

Assess Current Environment—Understand and define the culture. This will include a variety of tools and techniques, including surveys and discussions with key managers of various levels to uncover barriers to effective communication and discover patterns that might foil improvement attempts. This will facilitate the identification of stakeholder impacts.

Stakeholder Impact Analysis—Determine how innovations to the cycle areas will affect stakeholders and investigate how stakeholders will react to innovations.

Evaluate Human Resource Requirements—Educate the Human Resources Department regarding the organizational impact that will result from the planned innovations.

Develop Change Management Plan—Determine how the innovations will be rolled out to stakeholders during the Design and Implementation phases.

Develop Education and Communication Plan—The plan will guide the process of telling the MCCD community stakeholders about the Apollo Project and the Learner-Centered System Innovation phase.

Obtain Executive Approval—Obtain agreement of sponsors and key executives regarding the general nature of the innovations and changes.

The Organizational Analysis Team consists of many leaders, policy analysts, presidents, consultants, faculty, deans, and staff at all levels of the Maricopa organization. It is very challenging for members of an organization to understand and respond to the many changes that will come with implementing a new learner-centered system. For that reason, it is vitally important that as many staff and faculty as possible are involved in early processes to understand what is going on. At Maricopa, over 700 faculty and staff are involved in this process, and the numbers increase daily.

Two of the most important functions of OATS are to run interference and to translate the meaning of ongoing changes in the institutional environment to faculty and staff. The team acts as a cushion and interpreter of change, which makes it easier for the players to understand what is going on. This does not mean, however, that everything is easy. As

Maricopa continues to move forward with major changes, there is increasing organizational anxiety and difficulty in translating the overall Apollo Project. Even though the processes used at Maricopa are rational and despite untold opportunities for individual participation and collaboration, tremendous resources to move the changes along, and a common vocabulary and commitment, there is still some widespread resistance and discomfort in pockets of the organization about moving to a learner-centered system and becoming a learning organization. It has become clear to all involved that change is never easy in complex institutions.

TECHNOLOGY'S IMPACT ON LEARNING ORGANIZATIONS

The Maricopa Community College District is recognized as one of the country's leading institutions of higher education in applying technology to improve teaching and learning and institutional management. The district has been cited by CAUSE, one of the most important information technology associations in higher education, and other organizations for its networks and for its innovations in technology. The leaders at Maricopa recognize that technology is only one of many forces impacting on their colleges, but they recognize that it is a very powerful force with which all community colleges and institutions of higher education must deal.

In a learner-centered institution, technology plays a major role in assisting students to navigate more of their learning options. Although the pedagogy may not be keeping up with practice at this point, many faculty at Maricopa are using electronic forums and Internet protocols as the central learning scaffold to build a cyber-learning system. Such a world is fast and very hyperactive. It defines and redefines itself every day. If not managed properly, technology could undo much of what educators value and upset many of their functioning traditions.

Even the most aggressive advocates of technology find themselves bewildered by its patterns, its rapidly forming trends, and the commerce it creates for itself. It is clearly one of the major forces that is guiding Maricopa's efforts to create a learning organization and a learner-centered institution. Technology is pushing the district to a learner-centered world, and the district is struggling to adapt to this world as fast as it can.

The district has attempted to track the introduction and development of new applications of technology throughout its history as a way of visibly communicating the impact of this powerful force. Maricopa is well along the path of a major journey toward using technology to become a learning-centered institution. The technology is helping to drive the college to becoming a learner-centered system as networks expand, workstation capacity increases, and learning options become richer and more varied through the information highways.

SYSTEMS, CHAOS, AND ORDER

Once in a while, there are periods in the development of an institution that can be called the "defining years." Maricopa is in such a period. In fact, all of American society is facing a period of new definition. What we do and how we think about ourselves will chart the future of Maricopa for the early twenty-first century and perhaps even longer.

Margaret Wheatley (1995) said in a presentation to the faculty and staff at Maricopa Community Colleges, "Organizations are like living systems. We go through chaotic evolutions but eventually self-organize. Events like DNA recombine to produce an order, an arrangement. These arrangements, however, are not fixed—they are constantly moving and reshaping themselves."

Higher education, including community colleges, has been in a fixed place for too long. Institutions of higher education must be shaken out of their comfortable roles if they are to deal with the changes other social institutions are facing. In the Maricopa presentation Wheatley (1995) said: "We seek stability in our lives, a regular, predictable life. To be absolutely stable, completely predictable is a prelude to our deaths." At Maricopa, the goal is to be at the first stages of rebirth and renewal, not the first stages of demise.

What are the renewing forces at work now? Peter Senge, Russell Ackoff, Margaret Wheatley, Peter Drucker, and Fritjof Capra all share similar views. They look to a broader environmental context for the definition. The "part" cannot carry the whole. What is happening in the broader community to our youth? To the aged? To companies? To basic institutions? To families? Senge says that collaboration is the key to finding answers to these questions. Change in a collaborative process, however, is slow and evolutionary—like growing a lung.

Leaders are struck with how chaotic system life really is at Maricopa. There are many agendas to be managed, perhaps a couple of hundred in this large and complex organization. If a survey were made of only the "major" projects going on in Maricopa's ten colleges, it would take days to review the variety of reports of projects going on simultaneously. In this period of "defining years," the times call for multiple and complex responses characteristic of the hyperactivity going on at Maricopa. Supported by the views of a number of well-known consultants and by the trust in its own values and processes, Maricopa believes that these many events will self-organize, form their own patterns, and place themselves in their own particular order. An order is emerging out of the chaos going on in Maricopa, and that order is moving the district toward a learning organization and a learning college.

LESSONS LEARNED AT MARICOPA

Maricopa's efforts to create a learner-centered system and to become a learning organization are an important journey for this institution. What is going on at Maricopa is a microcosm of what is happening across the higher education system, the corporate world, and the government of the United States.

So what have we learned? First, we have learned that collaboration and cross-functional team processes require incredible amounts of support. While collaboration is the central underpinning of a learning organization, and is the preferred model and methodology for change—as Senge and others have pointed out—it is extraordinarily slow and difficult. Collaborative models, however, promise tremendous benefits worth pursuing.

Robert Stanley (1994), president of the Stanley Foundation, in an address at Arlie House, stated that "It is not centralized hierarchies and top down arrangements that forge our destiny, it is the dynamics of collaboration and consensus building that move mountains." He went on to say that "Where nation-states might fail, collaboratives and collectives have often prevailed on contemporary issues."

When Maurice Strong organized the Rio Conference on World Environmental Issues, it was not the nation-states that forged the agenda and figured out ways to address the seemingly unsolvable issues. The collaboratives, cooperatives, and voluntary associations that were brought together at the Rio Conference were far more powerful than the heads of states who are often frozen to act—including President Bush who only at the last minute elected to attend the conference.

A new methodology for responding to change and transforming institutions is emerging. It is far from perfect. When common, cross-functional, collaborative interests come together at gatherings such as the Cairo Population Conference or the Beijing Women's Conference, new destinies are forged. Municipalities, learning organizations, corporations, churches, and government units are all testing out the methodology of collaboration. Those who perfect such models will enjoy great success and power in the future.

Maricopa's efforts with Project Apollo to create and design a new learner-centered system are all part of the search for a new learning paradigm. In this search, collaborative methodologies have been applied at every level of the institution and have been designed to reach the smallest unit—a neighborhood, an elementary school, a family, a department head, or a student.

Collaborative processes have proven to be more useful in creating change because they are 1) more effective at achieving focused results; 2) they touch the smaller units of organizations; and 3) the hierarchical "top-down" approach has proven to be less effective in responding to the complex changes facing modern society.

Second, we have learned that the CEO plays an important role in creating a learner-centered institution. The CEO must endorse and support the vision of a learner-centered institution and constantly reinforce that vision through commitment and resources. When the going gets rough, the CEO must be there to provide moral support and to translate organizational changes and support organizational redirection. Change for an institution as complex as Maricopa is a decades-long process, and there will be constant setbacks and issues of territory to be negotiated by the CEO.

Third, we have learned that it is critically important to involve students in the change processes. Maricopa always attempts to consult students first in terms of any changes that might be planned. Students will continue to be part of the deliberative process.

Fourth, we have learned that it is also critical to involve faculty at every step of the long process. Even though one-half of the members of the original Pew Higher Education Roundtable were faculty, we have had to continually work on involving faculty in the committees, conversations, task forces, and projects. There is no easy solution to achieving full faculty participation and commitment to the changes currently underway in the Maricopa district. It is clear, however, that without faculty involvement, participation, and commitment, substantive change cannot occur.

Finally, we have learned that Maricopa must rely on both internal resources and external consultants to assist with creating a new learning-centered system. It is clearly a long process that will require considerable internal and external support. Maricopa is fortunate in that it has sufficient financial resources to pay for this support. A $386 million bond has provided $87 million for technological development and $20 million for network infrastructure. To date, only 3 percent of those funds have been spent related to the development of a learning-centered system. With these resources, Maricopa is well positioned for the long haul in its commitment to create a true learning-centered institution.

There are tremendous changes going on in American society in preparation for the twenty-first century, and many of these changes will impact higher education. The free market will destabilize defined roles, and students will shop the free market for the best customer services available.

Technology will make learning accessible to anyone, anyplace, anytime. In this environment, the Maricopa Community Colleges are positioning themselves to become a learning-centered system of learning colleges, whatever the future.*

REFERENCES

Axiom Management Consulting, Inc. *Business Renewal*, A Reengineering Methodology, 1994.

Bleed, Ron. *Perspective on Project Apollo.* Unpublished document. Tempe, AZ: Maricopa Community Colleges, Information Technologies Services, 1996.

Capra, Fritjof. *The Turning Point: Science, Society, and the Rising Culture.* New York: Simon & Schuster, 1988

Dolence, Michael G. and Norris, Donald M. *Transforming Higher Education.* Ann Arbor, MI: Society for College and University Planning, 1995.

District Office Steering Team QQ Dialogues. Unpublished report. Tempe, AZ: Maricopa Community Colleges, 1995.

Maricopa Roundtable Policy Perspectives. Unpublished report. Tempe, AZ: Maricopa Community Colleges, 1994.

Pew Charitable Trusts. "A Call to Meeting," *Policy Perspectives, The Pew Higher Education Research Program*, section A, February 1993.

Senge, Peter. *The Fifth Discipline.* New York: Doubleday, 1990.

———. *Transformational Change*, Lecture at the Ritz-Carlton. Boston, MA, 1995.

Stanley, Robert. Presentation at the Global Conference on Lifelong Learning. Warrenton, VA, December 1994.

Wheatley, Margaret J. *Leadership and the New Science.* Presentation to the Maricopa Community Colleges, 1995.

---

*Leaders interested in following Maricopa's progress can do so by accessing the following Web address: http://www.maricopa.edu/

CHAPTER 10

The Palomar College Experience

George R. Boggs and Diane G. Michael

Significant discoveries often have their roots in the dynamics of a particular time and place. Caring people, often with a diversity of backgrounds and points of view, come together to solve common problems or to chart a course for the future. Such was the case in the early 1900s when educators began the first junior colleges, starting what would become the largest and most responsive system of higher education the world has ever known—the American community college. Just as the beginning of the twentieth century was a time of invention and the beginning of the community college movement in America, at Palomar College, 1989 was a time for rediscovery. Discussions about the future of the college led to a new focus on student learning and the invention of the "learning paradigm."

INTRODUCTION

Palomar College is a public, comprehensive community college in southern California. Founded in 1946, the college grew over the years to serve a geographic area of over 2,500 square miles in northern San Diego County. The college had long prided itself on the comprehensiveness and quality of its programs and its collegial shared governance system. Starting in 1978, however, with the passage of the California property tax limitation initiative (Proposition 13) and subsequent state actions such as the defunding of courses considered frivolous by the state, the enactment of uniform student enrollment fees, and the state-imposed enrollment caps, the college was swept into changes beyond its control.

Challenging Times

In the fall of 1985, the new college district superintendent-president was faced with many challenges. The college, like many other community colleges in California, was going into its fourth consecutive year of enrollment decline, employee salaries had been eroded by inflation, the college was in need of updated instructional equipment and facility improvements, and the district financial reserves had fallen to the point that the new president received a warning letter from the state chancellor's office. The year before, a consultants' report described the college as suffering from a proliferation of committees, which were contributing to distrust, politics, divisiveness, and factionalism.

In his first address to the faculty and staff, the new president asked the college faculty and staff to join him in "gaining control of our own destiny." He talked about the importance of viewing the student as a customer, the need to make students active participants in their learning, and the necessity of setting high expectations for students. He explained how everyone at the college must care about students, and why the college must find ways to maximize and document student success.

In the ensuing years, the college instituted many programs intended to raise standards while providing support for students. A new tutorial program was initiated. Serious efforts were made to spread writing and critical thinking across the curriculum. A matriculation program was designed to assess students for their basic skills abilities, to advise them as to proper course placement, and to monitor their progress. Articulation programs with area high schools were strengthened.

Institutional Effectiveness

From 1987 through 1989, the president of Palomar College served as chair of the Commission on Research for the California Association of Community Colleges (CACC). Serving with him as staff was his director of Institutional Research and Planning and a commission member who, in 1990, would become the vice president for Instruction at Palomar College. A major focus of the commission in those years was institutional effectiveness. In 1988, CACC published a report of the research commission, *Indicators and Measures of Successful Community Colleges*, and in 1989, CACC published *Criteria and Measures of Institutional Effectiveness*. Although the reports did not focus solely on learning outcome measures as the most important indicators, it was clear that community college leaders in California were determined to develop methods to document the effectiveness of their colleges.

By 1989, Palomar College had made significant progress. The budget had been stabilized. Student enrollment reached an all-time high of 22,000. The college received a report from the California State University (CSU) system revealing that transfers from Palomar College actually received higher grades after transferring than did CSU native students. The college had just developed a new shared governance system and was beginning to update its policies and procedures. A new flexible academic calendar and a new professional development program for faculty (which would be nationally recognized in 1992) had been implemented.

Pressures to Reform

At the state level, a legislative committee had just concluded an exhaustive review of the California community colleges resulting in the passage of comprehensive community college reform (AB 1725) in 1989. As a result, funding for community colleges in California was now centralized and program-based, and the colleges were being asked to be accountable for the expenditure of scarce resources. At the national level, the American Association of Community and Junior Colleges had just issued, in 1988, the report of its Commission on the Future of Community Colleges, *Building Communities: A Vision for a New Century.* This document called on the colleges to expand access, to improve retention of students, to form new partnerships and alliances, to develop a core of common learning, and to build a climate of community.

At the local level, Palomar College found itself in a dynamic environment. The communities it served were among the fastest growing in the country. College leaders and the governing board were challenged to find ways to make classes accessible to the people of the college's large and rapidly growing district without overburdening the San Marcos campus. In addition, the California State University system had chosen to build its twentieth campus just two miles from the San Marcos campus of Palomar College, raising concern about the impact the new university would have on Palomar's mission.

The nature of the college's student body was also changing, becoming, on the average, older, more female, and more diverse. Assessment tests revealed increased weaknesses in basic skills abilities. English as a Second Language classes and developmental courses in mathematics, reading, and English became the fastest growing. Everything around the college, from the local, state, and national environments to its students, seemed to be changing. The questions being asked by Palomar's leaders were whether the college would be prepared for the future and how it could influence what that future might be.

Formation of the Vision Task Force

It was in this environment that the college president convened and chaired the Vision Task Force. The charge for the group was to develop a proposed vision statement for the college, to look into the future, and to envision what the college should be in the year 2005. This 16-member task force was composed of representatives from all segments of the college and one community member. The vice president of the Associated Student Government and a member of the governing board joined faculty members, administrators, and other staff members in an adventure that would last 18 months.

The founders of the college, which had opened its doors in 1946 to 198 students, probably would not have imagined that it would grow by 1989 to enroll 22,000 students in nearly 130 different degree and certificate programs at the San Marcos campus and at seven Education Centers and more than 60 other locations scattered throughout a district larger than Rhode Island or Delaware. Too often, institutions are so busy keeping up with the demands of the present that they are not able to see a future that is any different. The charge of the Vision Task Force, however, was to do just that: to imagine what the college would look like 16 years in the future.

THE INITIAL REFORM PROCESS

The Vision Task Force began its work by studying documents about the challenges and roles of community colleges and about the economic and social trends in the country, state, and communities served by the college. The members read *Building Communities*, the reports that led to the California community college reform act, articles on strategic planning, and articles on classroom assessment. They reviewed vision statements from businesses and from other colleges and universities. They surveyed and interviewed faculty, staff, students, and selected community members. They asked business owners in the communities served by the college how many new employees they would need in the next 16 years and what skills future employees would need. They interviewed presidents of local colleges and universities to see what plans neighboring institutions of higher education had for their futures.

Environmental Scan

Data were also gathered from local, county, state, and national governments; public schools; and local planning agencies. The task force was interested in population projections and in the special needs of that population. The members wanted to know whether potential students would need English language or citizenship skills, whether there would be more single-parent households, and what the age and ethnic mix of the population would be. The task force members were also concerned about changes in transportation arteries. Based upon what was found, the task force developed a set of assumptions about the environment in the future.

Next, the task force critically assessed the college's strengths and weaknesses. The members wanted to know both what the college did well and what could be done better. The task force members discussed at length their own values and their own aspirations for the future of the college, how the college did its work, and the nature of its contributions to the community and society. After 18 months of study, discussion, and work, the task force issued its proposed Vision Statement and a revised Mission Statement to the college community. Having concluded its work, the task force was disbanded.

The Vision Statement

In the foreword to the Vision Statement issued in 1991, the college president wrote, "Readers of these statements will note that they reflect a subtle but nonetheless profound shift in how we think of the college and what we do. We have shifted from an identification with process to an identification with results. We are no longer content with merely providing quality instruction. We will judge ourselves henceforth on the quality of student learning we produce. And further, we will judge ourselves by our ability to produce even greater and more sophisticated student learning and meaningful educational success with each passing year, each exiting student, and each graduating class. To do this, we must ourselves continually experiment, discover, grow, and learn. Consequently, we see ourselves as a learning institution in both our object and our method" (Boggs, 1991, p. 1).

The new Mission and Vision statements clearly established Palomar College's goal to become a learning college. The five themes of the statements—empowerment, learning, evaluation, discovery, and growth—all focused on student learning. Under the empowerment theme, the Vision Statement proclaimed, "Palomar College empowers students to learn and empowers our educational team—faculty, staff, and administration—to create powerful learning environments." Under the learning theme, the Vision Statement read in part, "We provide an environment where persons of diverse cultural and ethnic backgrounds become partners in learning, build on the strengths of their own cultural traditions, and respect, embrace, and learn from persons of other traditions." Under the evaluation theme, Palomar College said it "judges its work and its programs and formulates its policies primarily on the basis of learning outcomes. . . ." Under the discovery theme, the Vision Statement committed Palomar

College to discovering "new and better ways to enhance learning." And under the growth theme, the college said it will continue "to build on its strengths and shape its growth to promote more efficient and effective learning."

When the proposed Vision Statement was presented to the college constituencies, it was approved without much discussion or even realization of its significance by the Faculty Senate, the Administrative Association, the Associated Student Government, and the Council of Classified Employees. On February 12, 1991, the governing board adopted the Vision Statement and the new Mission Statement as official college policy.

A Paradigm Shift

Members of the Vision Task Force were surprised to find such easy acceptance of such a dramatic change in the college mission and direction. The task force was asking the institution to take responsibility for student learning, not just for delivering instruction, and there was no opposition! Some members speculated that people thought that the Vision Statement would find a comfortable resting place on a shelf, and business would continue as usual. Or perhaps, people felt that this emphasis on learning outcomes was just another passing fad to be endured. What the task force members now think is the real reason for this easy acceptance of the Vision Statement came to them as they viewed Joel Arthur Barker's videotape on paradigms (1989). Task force members realized that people are blinded to the need to change because they are operating from a different paradigm of community colleges, one which college leaders have labeled the "instruction paradigm." The new paradigm envisioned by the Palomar College Vision Statement began, in 1991, to be called the "learning paradigm" by college leaders.

Palomar College leaders knew it would not be easy to change the paradigm that guided the college from one of providing instruction to one of producing student learning. But they began a series of activities to start on the path to change, beginning with the language used. As a result of the work of the Vision Task Force, the college already had a new Mission Statement that defined its purpose as student learning. Next, catalogs, publications, and job descriptions were changed. For example, the job description of the instructional deans was revised to include responsibility for creating effective learning environments for students. Student service deans are now expected to develop and evaluate the performance of assigned personnel in terms of their contributions to student learning and success.

Recruitment brochures were revised to attract a faculty and staff committed to promoting and supporting student learning. Employment procedures were revised to help select faculty and staff who shared the college's values and beliefs. Orientation programs for new full- and part-time faculty and new members of the governing board now emphasize the principles of the learning paradigm.

Student learning forums that brought together faculty, staff, and students were scheduled. These forums were based upon the conviction that if faculty and staff listen carefully to students and respond appropriately to their suggestions, student learning and student success can be improved. For example, in 1993-94, there were three of these forums at Palomar College. The first was facilitated by students who focused on positive and negative classroom and campus experiences and successful techniques that helped them learn.

The second student learning forum was facilitated by faculty and the college president. Its goal was to review the negative experiences identified in the first forum and to develop suggestions to counteract them. The ESL faculty facilitated the third forum, "How to Engage Your Students from Day One," which focused on techniques for assessing student understanding from the first day of class and on skills for improving communications with students.

External Validation

External validation of one's ideas is often helpful. Starting in 1993, Palomar college staff members began to write about the learning paradigm and to present their ideas at conferences. Bob Barr, Palomar's director of Institutional Research and Planning and a member of the Vision Task Force, wrote articles for the Association of California Community College Administrators (1993), the RP Group (1994), and the League for Innovation in the Community College (1995). John Tagg, a member of the English faculty and also a member of the Vision Task Force, joined Barr in an article in *Change Magazine* (1995). Barr's ideas have also influenced the Commission on Educational Policy of the Community College League of California.

The college president, George Boggs, has written articles for the National Institute for Staff and Organizational Development (1993), the California Higher Education Policy Center (1995), and for the American Association of Community Colleges (1993, 1995). Since 1993, Palomar College staff members have made more than 15 presentations about the learning paradigm at individual colleges and at conferences, including three keynote presentations. Palomar College staff participated in two national video conferences on the learning paradigm in 1995.

Feedback from these outside presentations and articles has helped college leaders to clarify their thinking. It has also reinforced the belief in the need to shift to the learning paradigm. An added benefit has been the effect on the reputation of the college. Faculty and staff members who attend conferences are frequently asked by colleagues from other colleges about the innovations at Palomar. When they return, they are not only proud of what is being accomplished at Palomar, but they are even more committed to the paradigm shift.

As a result of a newspaper editorial written by John Tagg on the effective use of technology to improve learning outcomes (1995), Palomar College was asked by Encyclopedia Britannica to be the first community college to pilot-test its Britannica-On-Line service. Faculty members have been experimenting with the potential of the Britannica-On-Line database since the fall semester of 1995. In the spring of 1996, the database was made available to students in selected classes through the Internet.

District Goals

Just prior to the endorsement of the Vision Statement by the governing board, the board identified and distributed district goals for the 1989-90 academic year. The goals were good ones, but there was not any mention of student learning outcomes. The board was concerned about employee salaries, campus appearance, enrollment growth, student parking, policy manuals, and communication. By 1991-92, the district goals were significantly different. At the outset of that goals document, the board stated its commitment "to setting all of its goals in the context of the Palomar College Vision Statement. The college exists to provide and support student learning. The themes of empowerment, learning, evaluation, discovery, and growth, as identified and discussed in the Vision Statement, should guide the college in its decision making and planning." The board's goals included development of the Educational Master Plan, staffing and staff diversity, student diversity, fund raising, and shared governance, all framed within the context of contributions to student learning.

Persistence

Each year since 1991, the governing board has recommitted itself to the Vision Statement by referring to it in the development of the annual district goals. In the 1995-96 district goals, the board calls upon the faculty and staff to identify important learning outcomes and to set goals for improving those outcomes. In that document, the board also states its intent to foster "an attitude which encourages innovation and provides a learning environment that significantly improves student learning and success outcomes."

The college president has made the Vision Statement or the learning paradigm the theme of his annual address to the faculty and staff every year since 1991, recognizing the efforts of innovative faculty and staff members who are contributing to the paradigm shift at Palomar College. Presentations to adjunct faculty members have also emphasized the new direction for the college. Each year, new faculty members are given a three-day intensive orientation to the college and its culture and values. After the college president finished his remarks at the 1995 new faculty orientation, one of the new faculty members was overheard saying, "Now I know why I was hired here."

The 1995 fall Orientation Day for faculty and staff was a unique experience. Returning faculty members were not told that they would become students-for-a-day until they arrived on campus. After a continental breakfast, faculty and staff members were off to their first of three classes patterned after learning communities. The teachers used active-learning methods to involve their "students" in learning. The experience also gave the college president the opportunity to get back into the classroom as a chemistry teacher, allowing him to demonstrate some methods of involving students in learning chemistry. Evaluations of this activity were very positive. Some faculty members commented that it was the best Orientation Day ever at Palomar College.

The president also has an established practice of taking each new faculty member to lunch or breakfast in the first year of employment to see how the faculty member is adjusting to Palomar and to reinforce the college values. New board members experience similar orientations. The values of Palomar College are living and are constantly communicated and reinforced.

The Planning Process

The Vision Statement now guides Palomar's planning processes. But it has not always been easy. Early resistance was encountered in some of the planning committees as exemplified by statements such as, "We should first correct some of the glaring deficiencies in the current system before we conclude that it doesn't work," and "(w)e should simply hire well-educated, high-quality teachers, give them a place to work and a place to be creative, get out of their way and don't work them to death."

After six years of consistent work, however, the learning paradigm seems to be an accepted part of the Palomar College culture. For the first time in 1995, the Goals of the Palomar College Faculty Senate state a commitment to enhancing student learning. College personnel are moving ahead deliberately to make Palomar College a learning institution in both object and method.

TOWARD A NEW LEARNING COLLEGE AT PALOMAR

Among the things one can expect the learning paradigm to promote are collaborative learning; learning communities; focus on learning outcomes; better use of technology; recognition of the importance of everyone's role in promoting, supporting, and facilitating student learning; and a new unity of purpose among all the college's people.

The College's People

Everyone is familiar with the story of the two bricklayers who, when asked what they were doing, responded very differently. One answered that he was laying bricks. The other responded that he was building a cathedral. The second bricklayer saw himself as an important contributor to the outcome. Likewise, at Palomar College, the goal is for all employees to see their roles as important to the mission of producing student learning. Everyone, from the groundskeeper to the teacher to the librarian to the president to the student, is there for one purpose—student learning.

In the instruction paradigm, the faculty members are the most important people at the college. Their role is to deliver the instruction, primarily by lecturing. The staff is there to support the faculty and the teaching process. Students, all too frequently trained by 12 years of being passive in class and being competitive and individualistic outside class, come to receive the instruction. Administrators and board members set and implement the policies of the college. In the learning paradigm, however, the most important people at the college are the learners. The faculty members are primarily designers of learning environments and methods. The staff is responsible for supporting student learning and success. Students are active participants in their learning. They form study groups and cooperate outside class. College decisions and plans to support student learning are developed through a shared governance system.

Learning Communities

In the fall of 1992, Palomar College offered its first learning community. It was not an idea original to Palomar. The faculty learned of its potential from some colleges in Washington state. To build learning communities, students enroll in a block of classes that are linked by a common theme. The students and the faculty members involved become a community of learners, partners in the examination of important issues from different perspectives.

The first Palomar College learning community, offered in the fall of 1992, had as its theme "Love, Gender, and Sex." The linked courses examined what it means to be a woman or a man; how this society and other societies think and have thought about gender, sex, and sexism; how men and women communicate with each other; and how they learn. Students were awarded credit in speech, English, philosophy, and psychology.

Students and faculty in this first learning community attended all class meetings, read books from a broad interdisciplinary perspective, and engaged in lively discussions in seminar groups. The students wrote extensively to formulate and advance their own thinking and to present their views to others. The discussions proved to be lively as faculty and students alike found their basic beliefs challenged.

Subsequent learning communities at Palomar College have included: "Entrepreneurship—Doing It Right," composed of linked courses in business, speech, and reading; "Persuasion in Popular Film," composed of linked courses in philosophy and speech; "Scholar Athletes," composed of linked courses in English, speech, health, and college success skills; and "Reading, Writing, and Wrenches," composed of linked courses in mathematics, speech, reading, and automotive technology.

"The Reading, Writing, and Wrenches" learning community ran into some unanticipated problems due to the differing math and English backgrounds of the automotive students for whom the learning community was targeted. This problem, however, was somewhat offset by the unanticipated positive outcome of causing the mathematics faculty to redesign Palomar's basic skills mathematics sequence. The result is a one-track, applications-based, technology-supported, seamless mathematics curriculum that takes the students through intermediate algebra and prepares them for transfer courses in mathematics. This new integrated basic skills curriculum now makes it unnecessary to designate specific class sections as emphasizing trade-oriented applications.

Research on the learning communities at Palomar College has shown that they increase student critical thinking skills, and that they improve students' self-assessment of motivation, writing skills, and comfort level in relating to members of different racial/ethnic groups. Student retention has been much higher in the learning communities.

Learning communities are now flourishing at Palomar College. Recent additions include a pairing of the study of Spanish language and culture with natural history studies in Costa Rica; one designed for non-native speakers of English to develop reading and writing skills through exploration and analysis of themes in psychology; and a third combining courses in graphic communications, photography, and English designed to help students learn the principles of mass communications theory and techniques. This last learning community actually produced the college's award-winning literary magazine in 1995.

The college's most ambitious learning community to date began in the spring of 1996. Because of its scheduling, it was called "Afternoon College." This learning community linked English, mathematics, study skills, and supplemental instruction (tutoring). Afternoon College was especially designed for entering first-semester students to ensure that they begin their college experience in a structured and supportive environment and that they enroll early in courses which will help them throughout their college experience.

Afternoon College is similar to a highly successful program called "Starting Blocks," offered through Palomar College's Extended Opportunity Programs and Services (EOPS). Starting Blocks has been offered to 25 students per semester for the past three years. Linked courses for these students include English, college success skills, mathematics, and reading. Students in the Starting Blocks program had a higher retention rate and a slightly higher grade point average than EOPS students in a control group.

Departmental Leadership and Innovations

The mathematics department has perhaps made the most significant changes to its entire curriculum since the inception of the learning paradigm. These changes were facilitated by the acquisition of two computer laboratories through grant funding and by the free time given to several department members to initiate the changes. Even at traditionally off-peak times, visitors to the open-entry math lab find a room full of students working on self-paced assignments. Students check themselves into and out of open labs at Palomar College by swiping the magnetic stripe of their Personal Identification Card (PIC) through an automatic reader.

Across the curriculum, instructors are developing ways to balance lectures with active learning, including group activities. In addition to the changes in basic skills courses, the mathematics faculty has revised its transfer-level curriculum to include a coordinated lecture-laboratory format that takes advantage of technology and allows students to develop higher level cognitive skills.

Math classes frequently begin with a review of the assigned practice sets focusing on the problems that presented difficulties for the students. Having the students "walk through" the solution to the point of confusion or error assures that they have actually attempted the material and reinforces successful approaches to problem-solving. Instructors frequently use class collaboration in working through the steps of the solution. This approach has the dual advantage of acknowledging students for having learned the material, and of reinforcing their learning as they explain the solution to their classmates.

Once a new topic is introduced and one or more examples are worked through by the instructor, work groups are assigned problems to complete together. The instructor moves around the room, listening to the interactions but intervening only when asked and only after the group has made a sincere effort to solve the problem on its own. The group might be asked to choose a spokesperson to put the solution on the board and to explain it to the rest of the class.

In the Life Sciences Department, an anatomy instructor recently developed a series of questions for each unit of the course. Students were randomly assigned to groups to research certain of these questions and to present answers to the entire class. There are rules governing group activities: all members of the group must speak during the presentation, a visual aid must be used, at least four essays related to the material must be presented, and each member of the group must rate the performance of each of the other members and be able to explain the rating.

In the anatomy class, the instructor found this active-learning approach led to higher grades, but attrition was also higher than it would have been in a more traditional course. Students for whom English was a second language had the most difficulty with this approach. The instructor feels that these students were intimidated by the reading assignments and, given the course structure, could not compensate for their difficulties. In future classes, the instructor plans to assess student abilities earlier and to be more assertive in recommending that they receive needed help.

The Palomar College English writing laboratories afford students the opportunity to compose their out-of-class writing assignments on the computer. The access to computers has led to more and better writing because students can easily revise their papers without major retyping. Composition classes are also scheduled to meet in one of the computer labs one hour each week. This hour affords instructors the opportunity to foster small-group collaborative work. For example, one instructor divides students into "conferences" of five or six students to work on writing assignments related to reading material that will be discussed at a subsequent class session.

When composing a group paper, all students in a given conference are networked so that they are working on a common document. Students initial their individual contributions to the composition. The instructor circulates throughout the class, making comments and suggestions as warranted. The students use the resulting paper as a basis for a class presentation. The instructor has found that this group learning experience leads to more insightful analysis, greater participation in class discussions, and greater substance in subsequent individual writing assignments.

In addition to these innovations, instructors at Palomar College are experimenting with new technology to supplement class material, to produce multimedia programs, and to communicate with their students electronically. As this technology becomes more accessible, instructors hope to have students do more collaborative work outside class by assigning electronic mail groups to work on assignments.

Several departments have developed outcome-based criteria for evaluating student work. The art department includes fellow students in the critique and evaluation of projects. The director of the campus art gallery also plays a role in the selection of two projects per class to be displayed in the annual student art show.

The English Department has a holistically graded final examination for one of its courses. Before any grading of exams begins, the entire department reviews a selection of student papers. The criteria by which the papers are to be judged are discussed, and then all members of the group must agree on a grade for each sample paper within one point on a six-point scale. Only then does general grading begin. Each paper is read by two different graders and by a third if the spread between the two grades is greater than one point.

The instructor for the biology majors course is anxious to try new methods in his class. He is concerned, however, that he currently has no way of measuring whether a new technique really improves student learning. As a result, he is developing a comprehensive final examination that he hopes to use in the future as a benchmark against which to evaluate the new methods.

In another example of active learning, a business education teacher has developed a marketing internship class in partnership with General Motors (GM). She provides initial direction and guidance to the class but, before long, changes her role to that of a consultant. The students form a company and develop a complete promotional campaign for a local GM dealership. The students elect a coordinator who actually runs the class, meeting with the instructor as needed for guidance. At the end of the course, the students confidentially rate themselves and their peers in relation to both the role they played and their contribution to the learning experience. These ratings are assessed by the instructor and are considered in the final grade. An important component of the final grade assigned by the instructor is the ability to work effectively as a team member.

Many faculty members at Palomar College are now using the classroom assessment techniques advocated by Angelo and Cross (1993). In addition to providing immediate feedback on student learning, instructors have found these techniques helpful because they are forced to identify clearly what it is they want their students to learn. New techniques can be tested easily to see if they enhance student learning. The use of classroom assessment also demonstrates to the students that instructors are concerned about student learning.

Student Services and the New Technology

Palomar College has also worked to make its student services more user-friendly and more supportive of student learning. Even prior to the development of the Vision Statement, Palomar College Student Services staff adopted the motto, "We support student success." Use of technology has extended college resources and has provided better and faster support to students. For example, in 1990, Palomar College was one of the first community colleges in California to develop a telephone registration system. Then, in 1992, Palomar College developed the Palomar Automated Student Self-Service (PASS) stations. These ATM-type kiosks allow students to access information about the college and their personal academic records through a touch-screen monitor. Students use the magnetic stripe on the back of their Personal Identification Cards (PIC) to access information about grades, class schedules, and course placement recommendations based upon assessment test scores. For security reasons, a personal identification number (PIN) is assigned to each student, without which access to confidential information is denied.

Because students can register for classes over the telephone and can look up their own grades and even print a copy to go, these functions are now rarely performed by staff over the counter. In the fall semester of 1995, more than 14,000 students registered for classes over the telephone. Over 18,000 students each year utilize the three PASS stations in the Student Services Building lobby. These repetitive, staff-intensive transactions are being handled more efficiently for students by using technology, freeing the staff to deal more effectively with less common student needs and concerns.

Palomar technicians are currently working on a system that will allow students to access grades and other information over the telephone by digitizing the database into a voice modality. The paper files are being scanned into an imaging system that stores and retrieves records electronically. With a network CD-ROM, the National College Catalog collection is now online, and the college began transmitting transcripts electronically in 1996. All these efforts are intended to make it easier for staff to provide students with the services and information they need in a quick and efficient manner.

The Counseling Department has made use of new technology in the recent development of a multimedia orientation program. New students are oriented to the college and are informed of its services and requirements through an interesting visual presentation.

The Counseling Department has also employed other innovations to help students. To keep students on track with their learning objectives, the department sends letters to students who have at least 15 units of credit and have not yet declared a major. A Career Center helps students who have not yet decided on a vocational objective, and a Transfer Center helps students who intend to transfer to an upper-division college or university after Palomar.

Other student services intended to support students in accomplishing their learning objectives include student health services, tutorial services, financial aid, job placement, veterans' services, child care, peer advising, services for students with disabilities, and services for students with economic disadvantages. The Student Health Center, for example, provides medical support, physician and nurse care, inoculations, family planning counseling, and low-cost medications to 16,000 students annually. Palomar College has borrowed from an African expression, "it takes an entire village to raise a child." At Palomar, it takes an entire college to retain and support the success of a student. The Student Referral Assistance Guide, which outlines and describes all of Palomar's student support programs and lists local referral agencies, is now distributed to all faculty and is discussed in orientation sessions for new employees.

THE CREATION OF A LEARNING COLLEGE CULTURE

Providing leadership in refocusing a college on learning is not an easy task. Most community colleges have been in existence for a while and have strong, established cultures. All too often, universities are viewed as models for what community colleges should become. In a university, the responsibility for learning is usually considered to be the student's and not the university's. The criteria for judging the quality of universities are almost always based upon inputs and process measures rather than outcomes. Factors such as selectivity of student admissions, number of library holdings, size of the endowments, and number of doctorates on the faculty are commonly used to rate colleges and universities. Perhaps it is time for us to seek a paradigm in which community colleges will be the models, in which colleges will be evaluated based upon their contributions to student learning and success.

The Starting Point

Unless a leader is starting a community college from scratch, it will be necessary to gain support for any new direction. The best way to start is to bring together a group of visionaries and campus leaders from all segments to review and update the college's mission and vision statements. At Palomar College this group was called the Vision Task Force, and it met for 18 months. It studied and argued until consensus was reached about the future of the college. This process cannot be rushed. It is easy to pick up a nice, attractive vision statement from another college and modify it slightly, but it will never be owned by the college unless it is developed from scratch by the people of the college. Educators can learn from what colleagues at other institutions do, but they must shape everything to fit the unique environment of their own college.

Some college leaders may wish to bring in a consultant to work with the group, especially in the beginning. It may be helpful to have someone outside the college set the ground rules of group operations. Other colleges may wish to have an expert on strategic planning help the group discover the steps to take in developing a long-range plan or vision for the college. Colleges that are further along in the learning paradigm may also be able to provide help in the early stages of development of a new vision. Staff members from Palomar College have worked with other colleges to get them started on the path toward developing their own vision statements.

The task force must come to understand the needs of the communities that the college serves and to anticipate what those needs will be in the future. Census data, information from planning agencies, and survey information from area businesses and other educational institutions will be important for the group as it develops environmental assumptions about the future and compares them with the future abilities of the college.

Once the new vision and mission statements that focus the college on the future needs of the communities it serves and that define it as a learning college are prepared, it is important to get official endorsement from all college constituencies before taking them to the governing board for approval. If this new work is to be a truly shared vision and mission, every segment of the college must approve. The effort to iron out problems at this early stage will pay off later.

The Importance of Language

In Bob Barr's 1994 study of California community college mission statements, he found virtually no focus on learning. "When it was used, it was almost always bundled in the phrase 'teaching and learning' as if to say that, while learning may indeed have something to do with community colleges, it is only present as an aspect of teaching" (p. 1). Language is important in American society. College leaders need to be sure they are saying what they intend to say.

College catalogs, schedules, and other publications should all mention student learning as the college's primary purpose. Job descriptions should be revised to make it clear that student learning is everyone's job. Employee recruitment brochures should be unambiguous in stating that the college is interested in receiving applications from individuals committed to student learning. College or district goals should refer to improving student learning outcomes, and they should reinforce the vision and mission statements.

Promotion of the Vision

If the new vision and mission statements are to be taken seriously, they must be actively supported by the CEO and the governing board. If the faculty and staff come to believe that the vision and mission statements are just rhetoric and that there is no real commitment from the top, there will be no progress. The CEO and the chief academic officer must be especially visible and persistent supporters of the new learning mission of the college.

College leaders may experience strong resistance on some fronts, and their message may seem to be ignored at times, but they must never give up. The leaders should use every opportunity to communicate and reinforce the student learning mission of the college. Annual speeches to the faculty and staff, annual "State of the College" messages, "Year in Review" reports, and orientation sessions for new employees and new governing board members are ideal times to discuss the college's commitment to student learning and success and to assess the progress toward realizing the college's vision.

There will, of course, be some people who will never accept the change. These are generally people who are comfortable with doing things the way they always have been done, and perhaps, they are the people who distrust administrators to start with, especially if they try to change things. Not much can be gained by focusing too much energy on this group of people. Instead, the CEO should support the leaders and the innovators and should celebrate their successes at every opportunity.

Although a leader may not have a chance to start a college from scratch, every new employment decision is, in its own way, a new start. The leader should be sure that every new faculty and staff member understands and agrees with the values of the college. For student learning to be the college's mission, it must be every employee's mission. Hiring people who do not want to accept responsibility for contributing to student learning will result in a significant setback.

The CEO can continue to communicate the importance of student learning to new faculty and staff members by personally taking part in new employee orientation sessions. Other members of the staff can explain some of the details about how the college operationalizes its values, but the

CEO needs to spend some time with this group and needs to communicate that new employees are expected to take risks and to try new ideas, which might produce better and more student learning. A college is only as good as its people. They must be selected carefully, and they must come to understand the values of the institution and the expectations they must meet.

One of the best ways to bring new people into leadership positions on the learning mission of the college is to invite them to join the leaders in making a presentation at a conference or at another college. The experience at Palomar College is that the faculty and staff members who have been involved in these presentations have become the greatest supporters of the paradigm shift. This should not be surprising to those of us who have been teachers. When one teaches something, one really has to know it.

THE COLLEGE OF THE FUTURE

The college of the future will have a mission statement which clearly communicates that the college exists to promote and support learning. Indeed, it will take responsibility for the success of its students. Courses, programs, and departments will give way to cross-discipline learning communities. The college staff will be as concerned about the success of a diverse group of students as they are about access.

The criteria for a successful college will also change. Instead of input measures like enrollment growth and participation rates, the college of the future will base its success on the success of its students. The focus will be on constant improvement of student learning outcomes. Both the students and the college will be held to high standards.

The college of the future will not necessarily have the traditional one teacher per classroom. Faculty, instead of being primarily lecturers, will become facilitators of learning and designers of learning environments. Staff, instead of being seen as supporters of the faculty and of the instruction process, will be perceived as important contributors to an environment which promotes and supports learning. Instead of acting independently, faculty members will be part of a learning team that includes all of the college's staff and the students.

The use of new technology and flexible learning systems means that classes will not all necessarily start and end at the same time as most do now. Neither will learning be location bound. Students will be able to make use of new technology to communicate with teachers and fellow students from education centers, work sites, and their homes.

Students, in the college of the future, will not be seen as passive vessels receiving knowledge that the teacher dispenses in lectures. Instead, students will be active constructors of knowledge. Rather than being individualistic and competitive, students will be cooperative and collaborative. They will be partners in a community of learners.

College leaders will move away from the idea that any expert can teach and will acknowledge that empowering learning is a complex activity that requires its own share of research and development. The college of the future will itself be continually learning how it can improve its systems to produce more and better student learning.

A degree from the college of the future will represent more than just time spent in class and accumulated credits. It will mean that the graduate has demonstrated specified skills and knowledge.

Obstacles

Despite the increasing calls for accountability, there are many obstacles to overcome before America's colleges can become responsible for student learning outcomes. As discussed earlier in this chapter, there will be resistance to change on the part of faculty, staff, and students. Faculty will have to make a significant adjustment as they move from being dispensers of knowledge to being facilitators of learning. Staff will have different and increased responsibilities. The Learning Paradigm also requires changes in student behavior. Although public school reform is leading to a more active learning environment, higher education institutions may still receive students who have had 12 years of training to be passive in class and individualistic and competitive outside class. These students may have difficulty adjusting to an environment which requires them to be active participants in a community of learners.

A major obstacle in some states like California is the detailed and prescriptive nature of the Education and Administrative Codes. These laws and regulations seem to be designed to protect and perpetuate the Instruction Paradigm. Most state funding formulas for institutions of higher education are enrollment driven. What really counts under this system is how many students are sitting in class at census week. It does not matter whether the students complete the class or whether they even learn anything. They may even drop out of college completely, but as long as they are replaced by new students so that the seats are occupied when the next census is taken, the college is seen as successful. Funding formulas must change, as they have in some states, to reward learning outcomes.

Another obstacle is the fact that there are not yet very good methods to measure learning outcomes. In fact, most colleges have not addressed which learning outcomes should be measured. This should not be a surprise; learning outcomes are not important in the Instruction Paradigm.

When learning outcomes become important, colleges will find ways to identify and measure them.

Leading the Way

These are challenging times when good leadership can make significant differences for colleges and universities. Colleges can choose to proceed along the same path as always, honoring the sacred traditions of academia and fighting a continual battle for a larger share of diminishing public resources. The alternative is to realize that the present mission of America's colleges no longer fits the needs of today's society and to transform them into the learning colleges of tomorrow.

REFERENCES

Angelo, Thomas A. and Cross, K. Patricia. *Classroom Assessment Techniques: A Handbook for College Teachers, Second Edition.* San Francisco: Jossey-Bass, 1993.

American Association of Community and Junior Colleges. *Building Communities: A Vision for a New Century.* Washington, D.C.: AACC, 1988.

Barker, J. A. *Discovering the Future: The Business of Paradigms* (2nd Ed.) Videotape. Burnsville, MN: Charterhouse International Learning, 1989.

Barr, R. "From Teaching to Learning: A New Reality for Community Colleges," *Leadership Abstracts,* Mission Viejo, CA: The League for Innovation in the Community College. March 1995, Volume 8, Number 3.

————. "A New Paradigm for Community Colleges," *News. The RP Group.* The Research and Planning Group for the California Community Colleges. February, 1994.

————. "New Paradigms for Community Colleges: Focus on Learning Instead of Teaching," *Ad Com* (Newsletter of the Association of California Community College Administrators). Sacramento, CA: ACCCA, October 1993.

Barr, R. and Tagg, J. "From Teaching to Learning—A New Paradigm for Undergraduate Education." *Change,* Washington, D.C.: American Association for Higher Education. November/December 1995.

Boggs, G.R. "Community Colleges and the New Paradigm." *Celebrations,* An occasional publication of the National Institute for Staff and Organizational Development (NISOD), Austin, TX: NISOD, September 1993.

————. "Focus on Student Learning." *Crosstalk,* San Jose, CA: California Higher Education Policy Center, April 1995, Volume 3, Number 2.

————. "The Learning Paradigm." *Community College Journal,* Washington, D.C.: American Association of Community Colleges, December/January 1995/96.

————. "Letter to Colleagues and Friends." *Palomar College 2005: A Shared Vision.* San Marcos, CA: Palomar College, Spring 1991.

————. "The New Paradigm for Community Colleges—Who's Leading the Way?" *The Catalyst,* Westminster, CO: National Council on Community Services and Continuing Education, Fall 1995, Volume XXV, Number 1.

————. "Reinventing Community Colleges." *Community College Journal,* Washington, D.C.: American Association of Community Colleges, December/January 1993/94.

California Association of Community Colleges. *Criteria and Measures of Institutional Effectiveness*. Sacramento, CA: CACC, 1989.

————. *Indicators and Measures of Successful Community Colleges*. Sacramento, CA: CACC, 1988.

Tagg, J. "It's Time to Put Education On-line." *The San Diego Union-Tribune,* March 9, 1995.

Wingspread Group on Higher Education. *An American Imperative: Higher Expectations for Higher Education,* Racine, WI: The Johnson Foundation, Inc., 1993.

CHAPTER 11

The Community College of Denver Creates a Climate for Learning

Byron McClenney

From my perspective of 24 years as a faculty member at the Community College of Denver (CCD) and more than a decade of service as CCD Faculty Council Chair, it is evident that the current leadership has worked hard to create a collaborative decision-making atmosphere at the college. I have also had the opportunity to compare CCD with other institutions through my role as the faculty representative on the State Board for Colorado Community Colleges and Occupational Education and on the Advisory Council to the Colorado Commission of Higher Education, and I have come to recognize that we have a unique administrative/faculty partnership at CCD.

Helen Kleysteuber
Professor, Business Technology, Chair, Faculty Council

Before one school year, faculty members of the Community College of Denver (CCD) gathered for a Fall Convocation and were asked to respond to a set of possible goals for the future development of the institution. Some were surprised and some were skeptical, but they all used a five-point scale to rate the extent to which they could agree with each statement. Results were printed in the first internal newsletter for that new year. What any discerning reader could see was that the people of CCD agreed on the type of institution they wanted to develop. It was one in which students and learning come first and one where collaboration would be the way to do the work. The year was 1986, and a decade-long journey to create a "learning" college was underway.

INTRODUCTION

It was serendipitous that the college was engaged in the self-study process leading to the reaffirmation of accreditation. The steering group was designated as the Planning Council and was asked to do what today might be called an environmental scan of the service area and to take a hard look at the movement of students through the institution. A series of background papers was developed by appropriate faculty and staff members. These papers were distributed to all personnel with the indication that they would be the basis for the Spring 1987 Convocation.

At the convocation, faculty and staff met in a hotel ballroom in small groups to discuss the implications of the papers. The groups produced tentative strategies on how the college would move forward in light of what had been learned about the institution and its service area. The Planning Council took the results of the day and created the first set of "Strategies" for the future and "Priorities" for the next year (1987-88). This activity became an annual cycle that has allowed the faculty and staff to learn from the results of the previous year and to plan for the next steps in developing the type of institution envisioned.

The early work on developing the climate for learning focused on student outcomes. A great deal of work was involved in determining what students should know and be able to do as they complete a program. The starting point was the occupational or career programs. By the end of 1988, faculty members and program advisory committees had made enough progress to issue guarantees by program to cover the competencies to be demonstrated by all graduates of the occupational programs. Subsequent work has led to the identification of competencies for all courses and programs.

The effort to create competencies for courses and programs raised other key questions: How is achievement of competency to be determined? What strategies work best in helping students achieve the competencies? Which students are most likely to succeed? What kind of "support net" needs to be provided for those students who need more help?

Confronting all these questions, the college became aware of the need for a set of values to guide the work to create a climate for learning. Faculty leaders paved the way for an institutionwide discussion of values. The faculty council identified faculty members who were willing to work with the vice president for instruction and the instructional deans to lead the discussion. Draft documents of value statements went through several iterations, and open forums were used to solicit feedback from faculty. The "Statement of Values for Teaching Excellence" emerged from these discussions with broad support. The statement indicates that Community College of Denver faculty are committed to a teaching/learning process that

1. Enables students to become independent learners.
2. Demonstrates a commitment to student outcomes (job readiness, skill levels, mastery of subject matter).
3. Provides an opportunity for critical thinking and problem solving.
4. Provides linkages between instruction and real-world applications.
5. Demonstrates an excitement about teaching and learning.
6. Maintains high but realistic expectations.
7. Demonstrates appreciation of a diverse student population.
8. Encourages growth in students' self-esteem.

At the same time faculty worked on a statement of values, they also worked on assessment and accountability issues. Impetus for this effort was boosted by the passage of a Colorado state law requiring accountability reports from all public institutions of higher education. The combination of internal initiatives and external mandates has, over a period of years, led to significant changes in the way CCD does business.

KEY CHANGES

The annual planning cycle that evolved from the activities in 1986, further fueled by the first collegewide data collection on student outcomes in 1989, provided the means for a transformation in the way the Community College of Denver worked with its students. By the early 1990s, CCD was well on its way to being transformed into a learning college. The transformation has been extensive and is illustrated below in a number of key areas.

Guarantees

The faculty agreed upon exit competencies for all certificate and degree programs in the college and agreed as well on how to assess exit competencies for all programs. As a result, the college now guarantees job competencies to employers for all graduates and guarantees the transferability of all of its AA and AS courses. The review and revision of exit competencies for all programs are now a part of the regular program review process.

Academic Advising

The academic advising system at CCD has been completely overhauled to place the needs of the learner first. All undecided/unprepared students are channeled into a centralized educational advising center where they receive special attention. A computerized, entry-level basic skills assessment instrument that includes survey and demographic data was designed to help identify at-risk students at the point of entry. As a result, first semester students most at-risk are now identified on faculty rosters so that faculty can provide special attention and support.

A key change in policy and the addition of two new services also expanded the academic advising function. In the past, students were allowed to select major programs based upon their interest. A new policy requires students to apply for programs, which means they must understand the nature and requirements of a specific program before they can be accepted into it. As a result of this policy change and the tracking of student success by program, new data on the success of program majors have been very helpful in assisting students to plan their futures.

The advising center also established a transfer center to increase the amount of information about transfer for students and to assist them in making decisions about transfer. In addition, the tutoring center expanded its intake process to identify external barriers to student learning, such as lack of financial aid and child care support. All these changes reflect the CCD faculty and staff's commitment to creating an academic support system that can ensure student success.

Retention

As the college expanded its academic advising and other support services, more attention was paid to how the college could increase the retention of its students. A Title III Grant provided funds for a computer-assisted math lab, a computer-assisted English lab, and a computerized early alert system designated "project success." The early alert process provides a letter to each student which includes feedback on progress in each course after six weeks. Included are referrals to support services which can be visited on a specific day when all classes are suspended to facilitate the connections. In addition, a Title III Grant has been used to develop models for improving retention rates and general college-level skills of Hispanic students attending the college.

Critical Skills

Continuing efforts to develop a learning-centered institution, faculty focus groups studied accountability reports and recommended that the college initiate projects to teach writing, reading, computing, speaking/listening, and valuing diversity across the curriculum. Advisory committees from the faculty established critical skill levels for various programs, and the Teaching/Learning Center coordinated the development of a handbook to help faculty incorporate critical skills in the various programs.

The college also initiated a series of "learning communities" to bring together faculty from various disciplines to plan experiences that would integrate critical skills. Learning communities or federated communities generally include the integration of two to three courses in which students earn six to nine credits. In the spring of 1996, the college offered learning communities in general psychology and English composition, introduction to computers and planning for success, and introduction to computers and basic mathematics review.

Staff Development

Staff development has been the key to assisting faculty and staff in creating new programs and in learning how to implement and assess these programs. The Teaching/Learning Center provides staff members opportunities to innovate and to apply new ideas. One of the most successful of these new ideas has been the faculty evaluation plan. With support from the faculty council, the center created a classroom observation instrument to be used in faculty evaluation based on the eight teaching/learning values that guide the college's efforts to become a learning-centered institution. Student evaluation instruments now allow students to rate faculty members on the extent to which they fulfill the teaching/learning values in the class. Faculty on probation are provided special opportunities to increase their understanding and application of the core institutional values.

The faculty evaluation program has been so effective that the State Board for Community Colleges and Occupational Education approved the plan for faculty credentialing. A faculty merit pay plan has also been developed by the faculty with 80 percent of merit pay based on measured teaching effectiveness using the core values.

The Teaching/Learning Center also encourages staff development through a mini-grants program that supports classroom research and a variety of projects designed to increase student learning, student retention, and student completion of programs. Mini-grants range from $500 to $1,500 and are awarded to faculty based on institutional priorities that focus on increasing learning and retention.

EVIDENCE OF STUDENT SUCCESS

The program initiatives noted earlier have been supported and influenced by the development and refinement of a process of accountability reporting. From the first collegewide data collection on student outcomes in 1989 to the first complete accountability report in 1990, the purpose has been to provide feedback on student success. The evolution of this process may be instructive.

1991   CCD set goals based on baseline data and produced the second accountability report that included tracking of two special populations: minorities and students taking remedial classes.

1992   CCD began collection of data by program and by additional groups of special populations: physically handicapped, learning disabled, limited English proficient, educationally disadvantaged, financially disadvantaged, etc. CCD produced a third accountability report.

1993   CCD's ongoing practice of merging accountability data and institutional planning formed the basis for a "special emphasis" self-study for a North Central Association accreditation. CCD produced a fourth accountability report.

1994   The North Central Association's reaffirmation of accreditation led to a glowing report and 10 years of accreditation with no special reports or focused visits. To quote from the report, "One of the strengths of CCD's assessment process has been and is the participation and acceptance of the program by the faculty. . . . As a result, the accountability and effectiveness measurements are part of the College fabric. . . . Frankly, the team was pleased to evaluate a college that undertook the planning/accountability/assessment activities in the spirit in which they were meant. The college decided to take a look at itself and to improve. . ."

1995   CCD continued its annual process of using data, planning, and budgeting to improve institutional performance and initiated different reports targeted at different audiences: students, faculty and program advisory committees, the general public and the Colorado Commission on Higher Education.

The annual accountability report provides a visible measure of institutional success by documenting progress in efforts to foster student success. Examples of student success published in the College Catalog include the following:

- Between 1987 and 1995, CCD increased the total number of graduates by 98 percent.
- Between 1987 and 1995, people of color as a percent of total graduates and transfers increased from 13 percent to 42.5 percent.
- Studies show degree-seeking students who start with remedial courses are as likely to graduate as other degree-seeking students.
- The average cumulative GPA of CCD transfers at four-year colleges is 2.9 on a four-point scale.
- Of vocational graduates who completed their educational goals, 98 percent either continued their education or were employed within one year.

The institutional climate has developed to the point where people look forward to the feedback on how well CCD is performing. The expectation is that the systematic review of accountability and planning data will routinely lead to improvements in program delivery and student support. The annual plans developed by the instructional and student service divisions now routinely reflect what has been learned through the evaluation of the previous year.

In addition to the accountability reports required by the state, the institution has initiated its own annual evaluations asking for feedback from students. A report card on how the college and its staff are doing is printed in the spring schedule of classes for all to see. (See Figure 11-1.)

1995 CCD REPORT CARD

CCD administered student evaluations of faculty to a majority of classes during Spring Semester, 1995. Over 4,700 students responded as follows:

	On a 5 point scale
Instructor was available in and out of class	4.4
Instructor cared about my learning	4.5
Instructor was well-organized and prepared	4.6
Instructor provided useful, current information	4.5
Overall, I would grade the instructor	4.6

CCD administered a survey to random classes during Spring Semester, 1995. 815 students responded with the following ratings for CCD:

	Percentage of Students Rating CCD as Satisfactory to Very Good
Instructor's knowledge in his/her field	100%
Content of classes	98%
Quality of instruction	97%
Class size	96%
Academic advising by faculty	94%
Services provided by computer labs	94%
Services provided by academic support center	92%
Services provided by admissions/registration office	92%
Availability of classes	91%

1995 CCD REPORT CARD

FIGURE 11-1

In addition to institutional data about student progress and these high ratings by students, external validations confirm the college is on the right track. CCD was one of the first colleges among public institutions in the state to be recognized by the Colorado Commission on Higher Education for an exemplary annual accountability report. Existing criteria, measurements, and support for teaching effectiveness then paved the way for CCD to be the first community college approved by the State Board for Community Colleges and Occupational Education to conduct its own teacher certification. Finally, additional validation came when a North Central Association Evaluation (October 1993) found "exemplary planning and accountability activities" that are "a part of the college fabric."

A climate that places learning first at the Community College of Denver has been created by adhering to a common core of values for teaching excellence and by measuring student success on an annual basis. The college takes annual stock of the extent to which it is meeting its goals to increase and expand student learning, and furthermore, this information is made public to faculty, students, and community leaders. This open process of sharing the outcome measures has created a climate in which every staff member at the Community College of Denver wants to perform well and is proud of the performance of the institution.

The college has worked for some time to develop a system to provide individual feedback to faculty members on the success of their students by individual class and program. The college has developed a sophisticated program that provides a great deal of specialized data for faculty with emphasis on characteristics of students who succeed in the various programs. All faculty receive a package of this information on an annual basis from the vice president of instruction, and faculty use these data to improve the performance of students in their classes.

EXPANSION OF THE CLIMATE FOR LEARNING

In the coming years, the college will continue to expand and develop programs and activities that will create a supportive climate for learning at the Community College of Denver. This process will be driven by the annual cycles of accountability and planning that have become embedded in the culture of the college. Each year the board reviews and confirms the achievements of the previous year and provides support for the priorities set for the coming year. This annual process of reviewing the past year's accomplishments, and using those experiences to set the priorities for the coming year, is an institutionwide process that has created a student success model in which each person and each unit of the college commits to support student learning. Through this annual review process, the college staff and faculty work as one to conserve institutional resources and apply them to the most effective programs and activities.

One of the most dramatic examples of how the process works is reflected in the creation of a system of campus technical education centers. Community needs assessment clearly demonstrated the importance of specific outreach efforts to serve residents of the poorest neighborhoods in Denver. In response, CCD decided to build the technical education centers in those neighborhoods, and these centers are now located in four areas in Denver, representing the poorest neighborhoods in the community. The centers are open-entry/open-exit and self-paced operations focused on remedial instruction and one-year certificate programs in career fields. Case managers follow each student and work with faculty members as part of the team to support learning. Faculty members function in an open lab environment which, in most cases, is a computer-assisted learning approach.

These centers have been so successful that the 1996 Planning Council encouraged the college to expand the technical education center concept at one of the campuses of CCD, the Auraria Campus. The Planning Council also recommended that the faculty on the Auraria Campus begin using the case management approach and that they begin offering more open-entry/open-exit programs to their regular students. In addition, the council recommended more collaboration among the various sites of this comprehensive, multi-campus district. A key factor in the continuing expansion of these various student-centered programs is the stated priority for 1996-97 to offer a more diverse "menu" of offerings that will give students more choices to match their learning styles.

As the college expands its commitment to placing learning first, leaders will examine how and why they seek outside funding. In the future, external grants will be pursued if they support established strategies and priorities, rather than on the basis of their general availability. A major priority for future external grant support will be in the area of programs to assist the more educationally disadvantaged students to become successful.

The Academic Support Center has already received such a grant, the purpose of which is to completely eliminate the gap between ethnic groups on the variables of student success. A 1995-96 report has already demonstrated an 83 percent success rate among more than 1,000 students who have participated in the program designed to provide tutors, mentors, learning lab support, and intense advising. This is a higher success rate than the rate for students at large. This news is encouraging given the fact that people of color are disproportionately represented among the educationally disadvantaged. At the Community College of Denver, the ethnic composition of educationally disadvantaged students needing special services from the Academic Support Center breaks down as follows: 36 percent Hispanic/Latino, 28 percent White, 23 percent African American, 11 percent Asian American, and 2 percent Native American.

Data have indicated that Hispanic students have been less successful than other ethnic groups, which led to a special external grant to support a project called "LaFamilia." The learning community concept is being used to develop a family or community on the campus for Hispanic students. Hispanic professionals from the community are recruited as mentors, and college services are coordinated across division lines to create the "family" for the LaFamilia students.

New programs and activities in the future, and particularly activities that involve external funding, will reflect the priorities set in the annual planning cycle. The 1996 Planning Council agreed on the following "strategies" for future development as most representative of the vision to create and expand on the current climate of learning:

- All CCD award-seeking students will receive adequate training in emerging technologies.
- Success rates of students of all races, classes, and cultures will be comparably high.
- The five critical skills (reading, writing, computing, speaking/ listening, and valuing diversity) will be taught across the curriculum.
- Internal and external customers will be satisfied with the learning and working environment.
- All employees will be trained in customer service and computing.
- The college will employ advanced informational and instructional technology to provide state-of-the-art learning, teaching, and working opportunities.
- CCD will be noted for its success with special populations.
- Systematic evaluation of accountability, assessment, and planning information will routinely lead to improvements in program delivery and student support.
- The number and proportion of CCD students transferring to Colorado four-year institutions will continue to increase.
- Scholarships, internships, and jobs for CCD students and graduates will increase.

THE TOUGHEST CHALLENGE

The latest development that reflects CCD's commitment to creating a climate of learning is illustrated in the creation of a pay-for-performance process for faculty. Stimulated by legislative leaders who were working on quality indicators and supported by the State Board for Community Colleges and Occupational Education, this initiative presents a tough challenge. As motivation, a major boost in salary of 12 percent for faculty was made available for the 1996 fiscal year for institutions willing to develop a pay-for-performance program.

The faculty of CCD rose to the challenge. A 25-member task force of faculty and administrators led the development of the CCD approach to pay-for-performance. The task force worked on the approach during 1995. Papers were written, forums were held, and focused retreats provided refinement and a chance for administrators and faculty to interact. The philosophy for the pay-for-performance model sets the tone for the entire process.

> The Community College of Denver's process and standards for faculty appraisal, advancement, and salary adjustment are designed to reward and promote teaching excellence.
>
> The process and standards are a means of focusing our collective attention on teaching effectiveness, examining our assumptions, and creating a shared academic culture dedicated to continuously improving the quality of instruction at the Community College of Denver.
>
> The Teaching Faculty Job Description and Annual Performance Appraisal describe expectations for quality teaching that are explicit and public; procedures for systematically gathering evidence on how well performance matches those expectations; guidelines for analyzing objectively and quantitatively the available evidence; and directions for using the resulting information to document, explain, and improve performance.
>
> The establishment and measurement of both process and standards for performance appraisal are performed in a collegial manner and through collaborative processes.

Figure 11-2 shows the breakdown of the categories used to evaluate faculty, and the weight given to each category.

The faculty position description, designed to be consistent with the teaching/learning values, is tied to the performance appraisal process and the pay for performance process.

Criteria have been established for each of the summary ratings of outstanding, highly successful, satisfactory, needs improvement, and unsatisfactory. Salary distribution (X) is to be determined each year and is to be consistent with the summary evaluation. There will be no increase for an unsatisfactory rating, 0.5X for needs improvement, 1.0X for satisfactory, 2.0X for highly successful, and 3.0X for outstanding.

According to board policy, two consecutive years with less than satisfactory evaluations (ratings of "Needs Improvement" and "Unsatisfactory") may result in nonrenewal. Faculty rated in these categories are provided opportunities for improvement through the Teaching/Learning Center.

Teaching/Equivalent Responsibilities (80%)
  • Student Evaluations (40%)
  • Performance Goals (20%)
  • Classroom Observation (12%)
  • Job Elements (8%)
Service (10%)
  • Job Elements (5%)
  • Performance Goals (5%)
Professional Responsibilities (10%)
  • Job Elements (5%)
  • Performance Goals (5%)

POSITION DESCRIPTION CATEGORIES AND PAY PLAN EVALUATION PERCENTAGES

FIGURE 11-2

Accountability really begins to mean something when the paycheck and contract renewal rest on the outcome of a performance review process. Development of the policy would not have been possible without all the other "building blocks" and the extensive involvement of faculty and administrators in a very interactive process. The challenge of making the pay-for-performance process work is daunting, but the potential reward is enormous.

While most faculty saw the process as a logical next step in the creation of a climate for learning, numerous questions were raised. Will the process properly reward those who are most effective in fostering student learning, or will it foster negative competition among the faculty? Is it possible to get consistency across the many instructional divisions? Will there be enough money to make all the effort worthwhile? These and many other questions were yet to be answered as CCD prepared to implement the process for the first time.*

THE FUTURE

The collective commitments to the community, to becoming a quality institution, to student success, and to one another bode well for the continued development of CCD. The people of CCD do not pretend to have perfected the "right" formula or to have created more than a work in progress. There is a belief that any plan for institutional improvement must be built on the keystones of inclusion and collaboration.

---

*The implementation process will be monitored and evaluated as part of a doctoral dissertation conducted by a student in the Community College Leadership Program at The University of Texas at Austin.

The agenda to develop a "learning" college has evolved over a period of years. It has been an agenda driven more by internal initiatives than by external mandates, which is the more desirable way to foster transformation. There are processes in place to systematically define "gaps" between the ideal and current levels of functioning. The engagement of the faculty and staff of the institution will continue to be crucial and will require constant tending by the president and other institutional leaders.

The more changes the institution incorporates, the more it encounters barriers to continued development. The fact that more than 20 percent of the instructional effort is open-entry/open-exit and competency-based means more struggles with an auditor who wants to see "seat time" documented in traditional ways. The fact that more than 20 percent of the faculty no longer teach specific class sections on a specific schedule creates problems in workload reporting. Because the enrollment changes on a daily basis, CCD frustrates those who want enrollment reports on a census date. But despite these obstacles, what is known to all concerned is that the institution will not return to the way things were last year or ten years ago.

The vision and strategies for the future call for providing more options in the way learning opportunities are made available to students. The online courses will increase, the telecourses will increase, the number of sites will increase, the use of technology will increase, and the amount of "seat time" will become less important. The focus on competencies to be developed and strategies to engage learners will drive the choices to be made. This focus on outcomes will continue to drive people and processes. The faculty and staff are engaged in the process of creating more options with the promise of helping more students be successful. It is understood that technology is not the "answer," but technology will play a key role in supporting the "answer." The future will continue to combine "high tech" with "high touch" as illustrated in earlier comments.

The implementation of a pay-for-performance plan for faculty is seen by many observers as high-risk behavior. There could be a setback, or there could be a breakthrough to a higher level of effectiveness. Whatever problems result from the first round of implementation, the approach will be based on problem-solving skills and processes that have become well established. The deans of the various instructional units will be involved with faculty leaders in an interactive process to improve procedures for 1997. The faculty and staff of CCD are confident that the climate of trust and collaboration will make the process work.

Each year when the time comes to allocate resources, there is a conscious effort to fund priority plans. Improving the climate and support for learning has been, and will continue to be, a priority. Given that assertion, the resources will be allocated and reallocated to keep the institution moving on the desired path. As indicated, more options, more flexibility in the use of time, multiple uses of technology, more locations for learning, and different patterns of work for faculty are in the future for CCD. Everyone who will be impacted will be involved in developing the "new" institution. The belief that all students can learn if given the proper climate or approach will continue to provide the impetus for new initiatives and better coordination of existing efforts.

A 1996 review of presidential performance, which included an anonymous survey of all college personnel, indicated 84 percent of the faculty and 96 percent of the administrators believe the institution effectively plans and allocates resources on the basis of its plans. That is not to say there is ever enough money or space, but it is to say people believe wise choices are being made.

What one should glean from the CCD experience is that transforming the way an institution operates requires a collaborative process undertaken over a period of years. Hard work motivated by a collective vision can produce more positive learning outcomes for students. The desire to put students first requires constant reinforcement. It is also crucial to have a mechanism in place to tend the ongoing process. The planning and accountability cycle provides that opportunity in the life of CCD. The routine feedback received from students and alumni tell the people of CCD that the institution is on the right path. It is a journey without an end, however, because full satisfaction will not be final until all students who come to CCD find a way to be successful.

CHAPTER 12

Launching a Learning College

T he basic thesis of this book, noted by example and reference in each of the first five chapters by the author and repeated by the authors of the next six chapters, can be summarized briefly:

American society is in a key stage of transformation from the Industrial Age to the Information Age, and all social institutions are—or will be—affected by the change. Many institutions, especially those of business and industry, have been actively involved in responding to these changes for some time; others, such as educational institutions, have begun to respond only recently and in most cases with a reserved enthusiasm. It appears that considerable benefit will accrue to those educational institutions that can successfully navigate the change while those that do not may atrophy or be consigned to the "rubbish heap of history."

The vast majority of educational leaders, as well as rank and file faculty, will not disagree with this basic thesis. Disagreement will come rather quickly, however, regarding the pace of change required for education to make the transformation to the Information Age. Is it going to be evolution or revolution?

The 1995-96 chair of the board of directors of the American Association of Community Colleges, Daniel Moriarty (1996), favors evolution: "[C]hange and organizational development will be much less traumatic, much more incremental, and largely dependent on more homespun virtues that have traditionally served community colleges so well" (p. 3). Moriarty makes the compelling case that community colleges have innate characteristics, such as strong ties to the community and an "inspirational sense of unique mission," that will work to their advantage in this period of change.

In the same issue of *The Community College Journal*, Richard Alfred (1996), a prolific writer on community college issues, favors a more rapid pace of change. First, he notes that "community colleges have become inflexible, slow to innovate, and resistant to change" (p. 18). Then Alfred suggests that "When community colleges lose their proprietary advantages, speed—the capacity to change quickly to meet or get ahead of the market—will be what matters most" (p. 18).

Every community college leader recognizes the need to address social change from an institutionwide perspective. Every journal, every newsletter, every conference sounds the call to begin the transformation. Cutting-edge colleges, including those whose stories are detailed in chapters 6 through 11 in this book, set the pace and provide the benchmarks other community colleges will feel compelled to reach. The pressure on leaders to make a move is increasing, but some feel impotent to act. Many feel caught between Moriarty's caution to move slowly and Alfred's appeal to move quickly. A few consider hunkering down in hopes that the reform movement will soon subside, as it has in past reform efforts; but they cannot ignore the changes going on in the larger social framework, and retirement may be too far away to leave the inevitable to others.

So how does an institution begin the long and complex process of changing its culture to one that helps students make passionate connections to learning? What can leaders do to launch a learning college? George Keller (1996) says, "We need an outburst of utopian schemes and inventive thinking. If schools and colleges are to be redesigned, we must begin massive efforts of brainstorming and creative thinking, grounded in political, psychological, and financial realities. Only then will we be able to build anew" (p. 14).

Each leader and each institution will determine the appropriate approach and the appropriate pace "to build anew," but all will be engaged in creative and inventive thinking as various forms—some utopian and some practical—of the learning college begin to emerge for the twenty-first century. While no universal guidelines exist to chart the course of change for institutions of higher education, there is a growing body of experience from which guidelines and suggestions can be derived. The remainder of this chapter consists of suggestions and guidelines adapted from the literature on TQM and learning organizations, the literature on education reform, the experiences of the six community colleges described in this book, and the author's own experience of 38 years in education, the last 20 spent as the executive director of an organization whose members have been among the most significant change agents in all of higher education.

FINDING THE TRIGGER EVENT

Most educators are familiar with the concept of "the teachable moment." That moment is a specific point in time when everything comes together for a teacher and a student, and learning occurs in an extraordinary way. There is a confluence of forces, in magical language an alignment of the planets, that prepares the way for "the teachable moment." The outcome for the learner is an "aha moment," an insight, an understanding, that transcends everyday learning. The moment is a powerful experience and a powerful motivation for more experience.

For presidents and other leaders thinking about launching a learning college, it will be important to take advantage of an existing event or to create an event something like "the teachable moment." A more accurate reference is "the trigger event," an event that releases energy and creates opportunity, an event that leaders can use to focus thought and to rally troops to action. The following scenarios suggest some ways leaders can use or create trigger events in their institutions.

Capitalize on a Natural Trigger Event

A number of natural activities that constantly unfold in the life of a college can be used for "the trigger event." Most often these are not dramatic events. Most often some project or process has been underway for months when a leader begins to see that the activity can provide leverage for channeling a vision that is much larger than was originally intended. Natural trigger events are usually messy until a leader transforms the event or events into a call for action. In retrospect, leaders create an anecdotal history of the event that makes it appear to be a planned process thoughtfully connected to the new focused energy. In reality, most trigger events are not planned steps of action, but awareness of the key role trigger events play in the change process may assist leaders in creating and using such events or at least increase their ability to recognize them when they do occur.

External forces often combine with internal events to create situations that can be turned into trigger events by visionary leaders. When the Pew Charitable Trusts invited the Maricopa Community Colleges to join the Pew Higher Education Roundtables to examine their institution and to make plans for the future, the trigger was in place. A number of other natural activities also came into confluence at Maricopa to create a propitious moment for expanded action. College staff had been engaged for several years in a major quality initiative to create more effective operations and more collaborative communication. For over a decade, Maricopa had been experimenting with applications of technology to improve teaching, learning, and institutional management, which made it the leading community college in the nation in the use of technology. Furthermore, Maricopa had created an institutional culture in which innovation and creativity were championed and supported.

Thus, when members of the roundtable began their conversations, they came with a history that had prepared them for substantive change. Given the opportunity to examine the kind of future Maricopa needed to prepare for, the roundtable participants chose to launch a long-range project to create a learning-centered institution. The roundtable became the trigger event that would change Maricopa's future forever; the first steps of this process are detailed in chapter 9.

Along with Maricopa, many community colleges in the United States and Canada are currently engaged in exploring applications of Total Quality Management or Continuing Quality Improvement. Some of these colleges are also experimenting with ideas and processes adapted from Peter Senge's "learning organization," which complements quality processes. Experimentation with these processes helps create a mind-set for change that can serve as a trigger event to launch a learning college. Most colleges begin experimenting with quality processes at fairly low and safe levels, a wise move given the propensity in education to suspect major change efforts, especially those borrowed from business and industry. Early success is directed toward improving services such as mail delivery, and eventually it may lead to improving communication and even to decentralizing decision making. At some point, often identified in retrospect, a leader or group of key stakeholders seize the opportunity to move quality processes to a new level and a new dimension. Thus a vision is born from processes and activities already in place, processes and activities that can serve as a triggering event.

That is exactly the way it happened at Jackson Community College in Michigan (see chapter 7). Jackson had been applying Continuous Quality Improvement processes since 1990 and had found them quite useful. In fact, the president of the college at that time was so impressed with the potential of quality processes that he played a key role in creating the Continuous Quality Improvement Network, a network of approximately a dozen community colleges committed to quality processes. In 1994, staff members at Jackson were still applying Continuous Quality Improvement processes but with no special focus directed to redesigning the college to become a learning college. On March 16, 1994, a trigger event occurred that dramatically changed the focus of the college's quality effort. Staff were in a training session, involved in exercises to learn about systems design, when a staff member leaned over to the president and asked, "Wouldn't it be great if we could design the college for real, rather than as an exercise?" In this case, the trigger event was fairly dramatic and specific, but it took place within the context of ongoing processes. A visionary president seized the opportunity, and in a few weeks, the college had launched a major initiative to become a learning college.

For the leaders who want to make their institutions more learner-centered there are a number of natural and ongoing activities that can be molded into a trigger event. Every community college is struggling with how to bring technology into the institution. Technology is a natural boundary-breaker, a natural change agent, and it can become a trigger event. In developing the college's long-range technology plan, someone has to raise questions about the purpose of the technology. The first conversations are likely to focus on how technology will impact teachers and teaching. At some point, however, the discussions will turn to how technology will be used to improve and expand learning, and this is the propitious moment for the leader or leaders to launch a larger vision.

Even the question of whether or not to construct a new building raises key issues that can trigger new directions for the college. Although few colleges have the resources to construct new buildings these days, those that do must review the need for buildings in terms of the opportunities created by distance learning technologies. Few institutions of higher education have examined the issue of distance learning for its long-range impact on their programs and practices. Such an examination, triggered by plans to construct new buildings, could in turn, trigger an examination of the college's overall philosophy and mission. Buttressed by information related to national reform efforts and challenged by examples of a growing number of colleges transforming into learning colleges, leaders can use opportunities created by planning for new buildings to broaden and expand the college conversation about needed change.

Institutional crises have always provided opportunities for initiating change efforts. A number of the colleges described in this book launched their initiatives to become learning colleges because of sharp enrollment declines or dramatic reductions in resources. When a new president replaces a fired president, the potential and expectation for change may reach its highest point. Less dramatic, but longer-range crises, such as the "graying" of the faculty and the changing nature of the students and communities, can also serve as triggers for action when these changes are orchestrated by effective leaders who see the big picture.

In summary, major initiatives to transform community colleges into learning colleges do not suddenly spring full blown on the agendas of educational institutions. Institutional history, culture, and current and ongoing activities provide the bedrock from which a new vision must be chiseled. The vision that will guide the college into the future will be connected to a trigger event embedded in the daily life of a college. The leader or leaders who want the college to move toward a new model of learning will be sensitive to the opportunities for change that already exist in the college, and they will capitalize on these trigger events to lead the college in new directions.

Give the Faculty a Test

In those colleges where natural processes and activities do not readily suggest trigger events, leaders may have to be more active in creating a climate that encourages change. One way to create such a climate is to involve all college constituents in an assessment of current values, missions, programs, needs, processes, and structures. If Socrates was right that the unexamined life is not worth living, there may be some built-in motivation on the part of faculty or staff to examine college life, especially if there has not been such an examination in recent years. In some unhealthy colleges where tensions between administration and faculty or among groups of stakeholders focus all activity on faculty and staff concerns rather than on learner needs, such assessments will not work. But in healthy colleges, an institutionwide assessment on some key issue or issues or dimensions tailored to the specific needs of the college may assist in triggering action that can lead toward an expanded model of learning.

In *An American Imperative*, the 1993 reform report referenced in earlier chapters, there is a self-assessment instrument specifically designed to raise awareness about the college's commitment to placing learning first. It is suggested that all college staff and faculty, including trustees, begin with the following "First Questions":

- What kind of people do we want our children and grandchildren to be?
- What kind of society do we want them to live in?
- How can we best shape our institutions to nurture those kinds of people and that kind of society?

These questions, taken from Howard Bowen's 1982 book, *The State of the Nation and the Agenda for Higher Education*, are core questions that help create a common base for communication and that help to transcend everyday issues which encourage contention and division. A college that gives sufficient time to examining these questions seriously and substantively by a great majority of its members is preparing the way for major initiatives leading to significant change. These core questions are followed by a series of questions under the headings "Taking Values Seriously," "Putting Student Learning First," and "Creating a Nation of Learners."

This assessment, if it can be introduced into the institution in an appropriate way—and that strategy will be different for each college—can become a powerful trigger to unleash pent-up concerns and commitments that can translate into action toward becoming a learning college.

Another assessment designed specifically for the community college can be found in the author's 1994 book, *Teaching and Learning in the Community College*. The final chapter is a set of "Guidelines for Auditing the Effectiveness of Teaching and Learning" (O'Banion, p 301). The author makes the following case:

> The teaching and learning climate is the visible product of a particular institution's invisible values. What faculty, administrators, board members, and staff truly believe about students and their abilities to learn, and about teachers and their abilities to teach is reflected in the climate of teaching and learning. It is a case of yin and yang in which values influence climate, and climate, in turn, influences values. The values and climate are made most visible in the written policies and statements, practices, and related behaviors of the stakeholders in the institution.
>
> An audit of the policies and statements, practices, and related behaviors is an important first step for leaders who wish to make teaching and learning the highest priority of the community college. (O'Banion, pp. 304-05)

A series of questions about institutional values and practices related to teaching and learning are clustered under each of the following general areas:

- Institutional Policies and Statements
- Student Success Policies
- Curriculum Review and Development
- Instructional Innovation
- Information Technology
- Faculty Selection and Development
- Institutional Effectiveness

A number of community colleges have purchased multiple copies of the book; some have purchased copies for the entire faculty, and the topics have become themes for year-long staff development programs. A few colleges have reported good results in their use of the guidelines to audit teaching and learning practices

This teaching and learning audit can serve as a trigger to distill an institution's core values from its policies and practices. This information, in the hands of effective leaders, can be used to launch initiatives to place learning first.

The assessment instruments from *The American Imperative* and *Teaching and Learning in the Community College* are specifically designed to measure the extent to which a college places learning first. As such, these approaches may be too direct for some colleges still unsure about leaping wholeheartedly into explorations of new learning paradigms. For colleges that need to move more slowly but that want to use an assessment approach to trigger new action, there are numerous instruments on institutional climate and institutional effectiveness that may better serve their purposes. A checklist (Armes and McClenney, 1990) derived from the report *Building Communities* encourages evaluation and discussion of a number of issues that surfaced in this key report from the Commission on the Future of the Community College. The report has been widely circulated in community colleges, and the checklist raises important issues that can gradually lead to discussions regarding new learning paradigms and learning colleges.

All community colleges are periodically accredited, and the accrediting process is another ideal opportunity to examine a college's commitment to placing learning first. In the past, accreditation processes did not directly address learning as the key mission and value of an institution, but more recent emphasis on student outcomes helps to redress this oversight. A college that wishes to move more aggressively toward the new learning paradigm, however, will need to expand and enhance the accreditation process to tailor it to its own purposes. The accreditation process can be designed to focus more directly on learning by incorporating some of the questions from the first two instruments described above. In this way, the accreditation process can be used to trigger the institution's initial move toward becoming a learning college.

Round Up the Innovations

Since their beginning almost 100 years ago, community colleges have been institutions given to innovative practices and programs. In fact, "The community college as an institution is one of the most important innovations in the history of higher education" (O'Banion, 1989, p.1).

The 1960s were the "Golden Age of Innovation" for community colleges. "Driven by the demand for access, the community college of the 1960s grew rapidly and experimented constantly in response to new roles, new needs, and new students" (O'Banion, 1989, p.7). The League for Innovation in the Community College was born during this period as a reflection of the innovative spirit of this rapidly expanding sector of higher education. However, "During the middle 1970s and into the early 1980s, interest in innovation declined as complex social and economic forces altered the environment in which innovation had flourished" (O'Banion,

1989, p.7). Cross (1981) observed at the time "that the late 1970s and early 1980s represent a plateau between two periods of high energy and a sense of mission in the community colleges" (p. 113).

That plateau was not to last for long. "As the 1980s passed into the 1990s, innovation returned to center stage. At every level of education, in all parts of the country, and for a variety of reasons, there is a renaissance of innovation" (O'Banion and associates, 1994, p. 10). The resurgence of innovation in the community college began in the middle 1980s, reflecting the energy generated by the reform movement initiated by the 1983 report, A Nation at Risk.

> Shocked out of the doldrums of the 1970s by dozens of national reports on the decline in the quality of education, community colleges, along with other institutions of higher education, are committed to overcoming the problems of the past decade. College leaders and faculty are beginning to recognize, on the one hand, the lack of quality in their programs, and, on the other hand, the need for increased quality if the very nation is to flourish. These factors are driving forces for innovation. (O'Banion and associates, 1994, pp. 10-11)

So while reform was being advocated, community colleges were going about their business "reforming" practices by introducing a variety of innovations, including classroom assessment, learning communities, distance learning, tech-prep, business and industry services, distinguished teaching chairs, and a host of others. These innovations, however, were not cast in a framework of major reform. They emerged in isolation, each with its champions, and were implemented as stand-alone innovations disconnected to the emerging reform efforts to place learning as the central activity of the educational enterprise.

At this point, no leader has attempted to mobilize the range of innovations that currently grace the education landscape and use these to support and guide the development of a learning college. Such action, however, could be a trigger event leading to substantive change.

The following innovations could provide the building blocks for constructing a learning college:

- active and contextual learning as expressed in tech-prep, school-to-work, and service learning;
- collaborative learning as expressed in learning communities, electronic forums, and in study groups such as those pioneered by Triesman;
- improved and expanded approaches to assessment and outcome measures as expressed in personal portfolios, experiential learning, and skills standards;

- increased focus on the customer as expressed in customized programs, service kiosks, and learner-centered advising;
- expanded and more flexible structures as expressed in open-entry/open-exit, distance learning, information networks, and differentiated staffing;
- improved teaching as expressed in classroom assessment and distinguished teaching chairs;
- application of Continuous Quality Improvement processes to flatten organizations, increase collaboration, and empower participants;
- application of technology to expand knowledge bases, data collection and analysis, communications networks, and time and information management;
- experimentation with the allocation of resources around concepts of performance-based funding and learning-outcomes funding; and
- application of new models of decision making such as shared governance and the Carver governance model championed by the Association of Community College Trustees.

The challenge for leaders is to create a new framework from existing innovations by cobbling these innovative practices and programs into a newly assembled gestalt moving toward the learning college. This approach has the advantage of building on what many key faculty and staff in the college are already doing. It is nonthreatening and avoids the defensiveness that comes with approaches based on rejecting old paradigms and pledging allegiance to new paradigms. Rounding up the innovations that already exist in many colleges and aligning them with concepts and values expressed in learning-centered paradigms has great potential for triggering a major reform initiative.

STEERING THE LEARNING COLLEGE

Once a learning college has been launched—by capitalizing on a precipitating event, by giving the faculty a test, by rounding up the innovations, or by employing whatever means leaders may use from their store of creativity—there are key elements or strategies that must be designed and followed to steer the learning college project through institutional waters to some landmark islands where successes can be declared.

The strategies are idiosyncratic to the culture of the individual institution and the character and abilities of its leaders. The strategies are not linear or formulaic, as they often appear in written descriptions. Some are more important than others; all may be of value. Institutions need to choose and experiment with strategies that appear appropriate to their needs; strategies that do not work need to be revised or discarded. In the final analysis, institutions must create their own set of strategies for steering the learning college project. The following strategies, gleaned from the literature and from the experiences of the authors of this book, are suggestions to be considered by those in charge of steering the learning college project.

Build a Critical Coalition

Major new efforts of reform or renewal usually begin with a handful of people. In the case of the learning college, several staff members might have heard a speaker at a conference or read an article that triggers their interest. The dialogue begins and more staff members join in. The CEO may have initiated the first discussion or, at least, is soon drawn into the ever-widening circle.

At some point in these early discussions, a leader, usually the community college president or chancellor, creates opportunities for the next steps. The leader might articulate the broader theme embedded in these early discussions and encourage their continuing development, or if the leader is more aware and committed to change, she or he might capitalize on a trigger event or initiate some activity that will move the agenda forward. In any case, once it is clear that the elements of a renewal effort are beginning to emerge, the leader must create a critical coalition of other key players to achieve a critical mass that will sustain further action. The coalition must include the institution's senior administrators. "All the quality experts agree that if any quality program is going to succeed, it must involve the top. Without the commitment of senior management, nothing gets better" (Dobyns and Crawford-Mason, 1991, p. 8).

John Kotter (1995) of the Harvard Business School describes how the coalition works in business.

> In successful transformations, the chairman or president or division general manager, plus another 5 or 15 or 50 people, come together and develop a shared commitment to excellent performance through renewal. In my experience, this group never includes all of the company's most senior executives because some people just won't buy in, at least not at first. But in the most successful cases, the coalition is always pretty powerful—in terms of titles, information and expertise, reputations and relationships. (p. 62)

In the community college, the coalition is most often convened by the president or chancellor and will likely include vice presidents; key staff in technology and staff development; and key leaders from the faculty, trustees, and students—and perhaps key representatives from the community. In very small community colleges the coalition may include four to six staff in the first year; in large community colleges the coalition needs to include at least 20 to 30 key representatives.

The critical coalition becomes the first laboratory for testing out processes that will be used later in institutionwide efforts. Care must be taken to build a sense of trust and community among the members of the coalition, and special attention must be given to ensuring that each member understands the need for the project and the concepts involved in a learning college. A great deal of reading is required. Retreats of two to three days are helpful in building a sense of community and in planning strategies. The coalition that is to guide the learning college project must be powerful enough in its representation and in its understanding and commitment to withstand the forces that resist change, which will soon emerge. This early coalition may change at a later time when other structures and processes have emerged, perhaps taking on an oversight role, but in the beginning its formation is critical to success.

Create an Emerging Vision

Early in the project a written statement of the institutional vision for becoming a learning college must emerge. The vision statement for the learning college is the guiding star by which the staff will steer their activities. The vision statement is brief—usually no more than one page—and is a clear and vivid account of what participants want the learning college to become. "The power of vision derives from its ability to capture the hearts and minds of an organization's members by setting forth a goal that is both feasible and uplifting" (Wilson, 1996, p. 5). Answers to "First Questions" suggested in an *American Imperative,* such as "What kind of people do we want our children and grandchildren to be?" can help provide responses for framing the values statement.

Wilson (1996) defines vision as a "coherent and powerful statement of what the organization can and should be some set number of years hence" (p. 3). He notes that vision differs from, but complements, mission and philosophy.

> *Mission* states the basic purpose of the organization, defines its relationships to other organizations and constituencies, and sets general objectives. *Philosophy* articulates the values that should guide organizational behavior, defines the character of relations with stakeholders, and sets the style and culture of the organization. *Vision* builds on these statements to describe the future size, shape, and texture of the organization (that is, one should be able to get a good feel for the future organization

from the vision statement); it sets specific goals and, more important, drives and guides action to achieve those goals. (Wilson, 1996, p. 3)

The critical coalition often drafts the first vision statement relying on one or two wordsmiths who are always present in educational groupings. The first draft is often murky and has an unfinished quality, but it begins to rally support and commitment from the coalition team. Over a period of months the vision evolves with more stakeholders involved until key ideas begin to hold up through each iteration.

The process should not be hurried for this is the stage in which individuals are examining their own values and exploring the outer limits of positions others will tolerate and support. The process must address the criticisms of cynics and the dreams of visionaries. A balance must be struck between the ideal and the practical. Eventually, perhaps after a year or more, the vision statement is formed and agreed upon by the stakeholders.

Involve All Stakeholders

In a community college, the key stakeholders include administrators, full-time faculty, support staff, and trustees. Depending on the culture of the institution and its capacity to manage complexity, the college may also include part-time faculty, students, and community representatives as stakeholders.

The new "science" of management and leadership that prescribes flat-tened organizations, open communication, and empowered participation makes a strong case for involving all stakeholders in major reform efforts. Margaret Wheatley, a consultant on organizational change to many institutions including the U. S. Army, says, "Any change program that insists on defining how things ought to be done, that tries to impose a structure on everyone—without their involvement—works against our natural tendencies" (In Brown, 1994, p. 24). Wheatley believes that

> Change is a capacity built into nature and, I would add, a capacity built into human nature. . . . People are not inert, resistant lumps. We have had years and years of believing that without our efforts people will do nothing; without our plans and designs, our organizations will fall apart. But this is not the world we live in. Organizational leaders need to realize that complex systems can emerge, not from their designs, but when individuals interact with one another around some simple, straightforward principles of interaction and purpose. (In Brown, 1994, p. 24)

Wheatley goes on to say

> You need deep and meaningful involvement of the whole organization. This seems like an insurmountable barrier, to involve the whole

organization, but I believe the starting point for real change is to focus energy and direction on this one key question: "Can we involve the expertise and experience of *everyone* in the organization?" We can't ignore that question. We've got to figure out how we can avoid the temptation to design things for people instead of engaging them and creating their own responses to change. (In Brown, 1994, p. 26)

Few community college presidents will argue against the importance of involving all stakeholders in the process of creating a learning college, but many will be challenged by how to do this. It is more practical to set a goal of involving all stakeholders who want to participate and to provide numerous opportunities for their participation. Stakeholders can participate in institutionwide convocations, workshops and seminars, and special training sessions. The staff development program can be reengineered to focus on activities related to the learning college. In-house newsletters can provide important information regarding the learning college project. In some cases, a special publication will need to be created to carry the message, as was the case with Miami-Dade's Teaching and Learning Project. Copies of key documents, such as the vision statement and later documents such as new policies for assessing students or selecting faculty or for rewarding and promoting support staff will need to be sent to every stakeholder for review and response. Universal agreement is not the goal; universal opportunity to participate is, and some changes may need to be put to a vote.

Ensure Appropriate Support

Appoint a Project Manager. In addition to the continuing overall leadership of the college's CEO, a project manager should be appointed to coordinate the various activities of the learning college project. Such an appointment will signal the value the institution is investing in the project. The project manager should be a well-respected member of the college community. The staff development officer or the TQM coordinator might be considered or a faculty leader, released from teaching duties for a period of several years, might be used. The project manager will need time to catch up on the related literature in educational reform, organizational change, leadership development, brain-based research, information technology, Continuous Quality Improvement, and assessment. If the project manager is already trained in skills to facilitate groups, that experience will be a great asset. The project manager must work closely with the CEO and the coalition team to keep the learning college project on target.

Provide Support for the Project. As difficult as it is in these times to allocate resources for new projects, a modest budget should be created for project activities. In most colleges, this budget can be created by reallocating funds from current budgets in staff development, travel, and internal communications. The president's "discretionary fund" can also be tapped.

Support will be needed to train facilitators. A major change effort of the kind envisioned here, one that attempts to involve all stakeholders, will work only if many staff members participate in carefully designed sessions to increase their understanding of the issues and to elicit their participation in creating the architecture of a learning college. Building a new set of shared values across a campus community by involving more representatives of more stakeholder groups than has probably ever occurred is a monumental effort. Helping representatives from various groups learn how to operate in newly formed teams is a major task. Colleges cannot achieve these goals unless they become learning organizations with all stakeholders participating as learners.

In Lane Community College's project (see chapter 8) many teams, clusters, and groups were created to carry out the business of developing a more learner-centered organization. Cross-functional strategic teams and vertically integrated project teams do much of the basic work. These teams and groups are becoming more effective through training. At Lane, an Organizational Development Action Team (ODAT) is responsible for ensuring that training occurs in communications skills, team effectiveness, meeting effectiveness, conflict resolution, and customer service. To provide this training, ODAT identified 50 "movers and shakers," or informal campus leaders, who could be trained to train others. Through 1995, over 300 Lane staff had participated in communications training.

As Jerry Moskus, president of Lane, said "Working in teams does not come naturally to educators socialized to be strong individualists, suspicious of movements and groups." (See p. 164.) Fortunately, educational institutions have the internal resources to provide education and training for their own members, and this formidable resource must be used to help stakeholders prepare for the new behaviors required in a learning college.

Ensure Trustee Support and Involvement. If creating a learning college is a major change for an institution—and it will be—the governing board must be fully involved from the beginning. The trustees will need to participate in training sessions to begin to prepare for policy and resource changes related to philosophical and structural changes. If the entire architecture of education needs to be changed, as has been called for by a number of national task forces and commissions, the full support of the trustees is crucial.

Throughout 1994 and 1995, Maricopa Community Colleges' (see chapter 9) governing board held a series of strategic conversations on such topics as chaos theory, new learning paradigms, leadership and the new science, system unity, diversity, and Continuous Quality Improvement.

These conversations were facilitated by faculty, classified staff, students, and administrators, and served as a laboratory for illustrating emerging values of Maricopa's commitment to involve all stakeholders. Through the strategic conversations many ideas emerged, new networks formed, and new structures evolved; governing board members grew in their understanding of the issues and in their commitment to the goals of the comprehensive and complex project designed to help Maricopa become a learning-centered institution.

More and more trustees in community colleges are becoming aware of concepts associated with the learning college. The Association of Community College Trustees (ACCT) has commissioned the author of this book to assist in that process. Abstracted from this book, a "white paper" on "The Learning Revolution: A Guide for Community College Trustees" has been prepared and will be distributed to all community college trustees in the United States by ACCT in early 1997.

Create an Open System of Communication

Convening a single meeting and distributing one key paper about the learning college will doom the project to an early death. This is not a project that can succeed by tossing one stone in the pond and following up on all the ripples. Creating a learning college means tossing hundreds of stones into the pond, dumping boulders into the pond, and even filling in the pond and digging a new one. This kind of change will not occur unless the community of stakeholders is kept fully and constantly informed about what is happening and unless there are mechanisms provided whereby they can communicate across the entire community of participants. Fortunately, technological innovations now exist, and are beginning to be in place in many community colleges, that allow for a rich exchange of information and opportunities for intimate connectivity.

Wilson (1996) says "If a vision is to shape the future and drive action, then the leader—and others in executive positions—must communicate it broadly, consistently, and continuously, until it becomes an integral part of the organization's culture" (p. 5).

The message must be driven home again and again through speeches, newsletters, meetings, articles, interviews, surveys, and actions. John Kotter (1995) suggests that business executives who communicate well incorporate the message in their hour-by-hour activities:

> In a routine discussion about a business problem, they talk about how proposed solutions fit (or don't fit) into the bigger picture. In a regular performance appraisal, they talk about how the employee's behavior helps or undermines the vision. In a review of the division's quarterly

performance, they talk not only about the numbers but also about how the division's executives are contributing to the transformation. In a routine Q & A with employees at a company facility, they tie their answers back to renewal goals. (p. 64)

The project manager will have major responsibility for ensuring that the mechanisms are in place for the communication that is needed. The CEO of the college will need to take responsibility for many "official" roles in communicating about the project activities as well as many unofficial ones. As the project emerges and matures, more and more participants will take responsibility for communicating their needs and their ideas.

Consider Consultants and Established Processes

Several of the colleges engaged in creating learning colleges have made effective use of external consultants. In some cases, consultants can provide an overall perspective on educational reform and the growing emphasis on learning, and these consultants are useful in addressing the entire faculty and staff or in making presentations to the board of trustees and key community groups. Other consultants are specialists in some key areas such as chaos theory, portfolio assessment, brain-based research, or technological networks; they are useful in meetings with groups working on specific projects. There are also consultants trained in specific processes that the college will want to adapt and use. The process consultants can be brought in to train facilitators or can be used on a continuing basis to facilitate group meetings.

Consultants are educational resources and should be used wisely. They can escalate learning for stakeholders, challenge reluctant participants, help identify other resources, and serve as an informal benchmark with what else is going on across the country. But consultants do not make the same commitments to the project as do college leaders; they do not have to suffer the same consequences; and they are not in the project for the long haul. Consultants should be used for what they can offer, but they should not be expected to carry the project and shoulder primary responsibility. College leaders and staff must own the project as theirs. Responsibility for the kind of change involved in creating a learning college cannot be handed off to others, no matter how competent or highly recommended they come.

Colleges may also want to consider borrowing some of the specialized processes that have been designed for other settings. The Total Quality Management and Continuous Quality Improvement movements, for example, have designed a number of detailed processes for identifying problems, designing alternative solutions, making decisions, improving communication, assessing skills, and building community that will prove useful in changing the organizational culture of a college. These processes are updated versions of techniques that have been around for some time, but they have been improved through refinement and through application and testing in varied settings. Many of the TQM processes are refined versions of techniques described in Alex F. Osborne's *Creative Imagination* issued decades ago; current processes also reflect a great deal of experimentation with "T" groups and encounter groups that dominated processes in the 1960s.

Processes in current use have their own language, their own special names, and their own special champions. Many are outlined in step-by-step detail and are accompanied by training manuals. These processes are not magic solutions, however, and they are seldom based on scientific experimentation. In the right hands, they can usually achieve their purpose. College leaders and the project manager should review these processes carefully and select the ones that will work best in the established culture of the college. Leaders should keep in mind that every consultant will champion his or her favorite process, and that most faculty will recommend the process they have most recently experienced. Colleges must find a better way than this to select the processes that will be used in training college stakeholders in new behaviors that will be applied to create a learning college for the twenty-first century.

Pay Attention to Language

Colleges that want to become learning colleges should examine their official documents and their daily language to assess the current emphasis at their institutions. At Palomar College (see chapter 10) leaders reviewed official documents and incorporated the language of their newly developed learning paradigm in all their documents. Student learning is now a clear purpose in the mission statement of the college. Student learning is everyone's job as indicated in revised job descriptions. Recruitment brochures now indicate the college's commitment to student learning and its interest in receiving applications from individuals who share that commitment. College goals now include student learning outcomes as key elements. The president of Palomar College, George Boggs, says "College leaders need to be sure they are saying what they intend to say." (See p. 205.)

It is possible, of course, to create new language while still retaining old beliefs and behaviors. Seasoned community college educators can spot with ease those who do not "walk the talk." Faculty are fully aware of leaders who trot out new language that is not fortified with new beliefs and new behaviors. Such action is a vacuous exercise that serves only to harden existing layers of cynicism.

As community colleges explore and experiment with learning college models, there is an opportunity to create a new language about learning, a community-college specific language. In the past, community colleges have borrowed a great deal of language from universities and four-year colleges to describe their values and their practices. Currently community colleges are busy adapting language from business and industry. Surely there is a special language of learning embedded in the idiosyncratic experiences of community college faculty as they continue decade after decade to provide learning opportunities for the most challenging learners in all of higher education. Community colleges have long been, among institutions of higher education, the institutions most committed to learning. The language they use should reflect that commitment

That commitment has recently been confirmed in a study by the Pew Higher Education Roundtable (Institute for Research on Higher Education, 1996). Comparing 32 sample institutions, including community colleges, comprehensive institutions, liberal arts colleges, and research universities, community colleges exceeded all the other sectors of higher education in their concern with fostering successful learning. (See Figure 12-1.) Over 50 percent of the community colleges held this value; only about 15 percent of the research universities did so.

In a review of the most prevalent themes to emerge from the Pew Roundtable discussions, community colleges gave highest priority to "address changes in student needs." Comprehensive institutions gave highest priority to "strengthen campus community"; liberal arts colleges gave highest priority to "focus on the curriculum"; and research universities

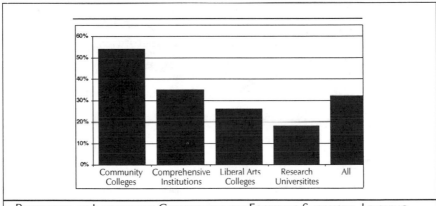

PERCENTAGE OF INSTITUTIONS CONCERNED WITH FOSTERING SUCCESSFUL LEARNING

FIGURE 12-1.

gave highest priority to "rethink faculty roles and rewards." While the sample for the study was quite small, results do reflect many common perceptions about the differences among institutions of higher education. In any case, community colleges do appear to place more value on learners and learning than do other institutions of higher education, and they are urged, in their efforts to create learning colleges, to find their own voices in the creation of a new language about learning.

Reallocate Resources

Very few community colleges, if any, operating in the current economic climate of reengineering and downsizing have the resources to support new projects, especially projects of the magnitude and duration associated with creating a learning college. In almost all cases, current resources will have to be reallocated to support project efforts, and to date, there is not a great deal of experience from which to derive guidelines.

Some creative college leaders have actually used the financial depressions in their institutions as part of the leverage to launch a learning college. At Jackson Community College in Michigan (see chapter 7), the picture was particularly bleak. The college had lost 12 tax elections in a row, equipment was obsolete, enrollment was dropping, collective bargaining agreements left no room for negotiation, and the district had lost hundreds of base manufacturing jobs over the last few years. This situation, along with the appointment of a new president, was used as a precipitating condition—a trigger event—to initiate a very successful transformation toward becoming a learning college.

There may be lessons to be learned regarding the allocation of resources from the restructuring project currently under way with support from the Pew Charitable Trusts. A number of institutions of higher education, including community colleges, have been holding roundtable discussions and designing projects to restructure their institutions for the future. Recognizing that "the need for academic restructuring owes much of its urgency to tough financial times" (*Policy Perspectives*, April, 1994, p. 8A), college participants have addressed the issue of declining resources, and a number of recommendations have emerged in the project's newsletter *Policy Perspectives*. The core recommendation relates to reducing the high, labor-intensive cost of higher education, including faculty and administrators. The following summary of these recommendations comes from the February 1993 and April 1994 issues of *Policy Perspectives*.

- Higher education remains an enterprise too often prone to define progress in terms of addition rather than substitution or subtraction (1994, p. 8a).

- A variety of institutions over the past 12 months have confirmed our sense that where institutions have succeeded most they have done so principally by imposing budget discipline in response to changes in their circumstances. Such discipline is a necessary first step in reshaping the culture of an institution (1993, p. 6a).
- The institution must establish the "priority" changes it needs to make and then set goals for substantial and lasting changes in each of these areas, sending the message that marginal changes will not be sufficient (1993, p. 6a).
- The kinds of saving and reductions in current expenditures that are required both to offset diminished revenues and to provide sufficient capital for investment in new programs cannot be achieved without setting aside the principle that personnel reductions will only be made if all else fails (1994, p. 8a).
- In times of transition the first instinct of most institutions is to protect the faculty. We believe, however, that this transition is different. Changes in how faculty regard themselves and their institutions lie at the heart of the restructuring process (1993, p. 9a).
- A substantial portion of the administrative growth of the past decade . . . has resulted from the entrepreneurial instincts of administrative staff and the sense on the part of senior administrators that it is easier to solve a problem by creating a new administrative unit than by making an established unit take on a task not of its own choosing. Accordingly, restructuring needs to begin on the administrative side of the house (1993, p. 9a).
- Given strong leadership and a sustained commitment to the retraining of current staff, we believe that a five-to-seven-year process designed to re-engineer operations can yield a 25 percent reduction in the number of full-time employees an institution requires (1993, p. 7a).
- Fundamentally, restructuring will strengthen institutions precisely because the process itself will force a sustained reexamination of functions and procedures that have grown haphazardly over the last three decades (1993, p. 7a).

This is pretty brutal stuff for most educators. This is the kind of discussion that weakens the resolve of community college leaders to lead change and that strengthens the resolve of faculty unions and administrators to resist change. This open discussion of changing the rules regarding the labor-intensive formula in higher education also flushes out into the open the faculty concern that the call for transformation and change is a thinly veiled disguise to get rid of faculty. That may be the motivation of some community college administrators—allegiance to movements is used for all kinds of purposes—*but it is not the position advocated here.* Healthy institutions will be able to deal with this issue openly and honestly; unhealthy institutions will use the issue to feed their neuroses.

There are responsible administrators, however, operating in healthy institutions today that will address this issue head-on, and these are the leaders and the institutions that will create the models of the learning colleges of the future. Chancellor William Wenrich (1994) of the Dallas County Community College District has linked the faculty productivity role with the need for a new model of learning in a statement entitled "masters of the learning environment."

> Increasing "educational productivity" relates to one of two alternatives: 1) Increasing the quality or quantity of learning by students without increasing cost proportionately, or 2) maintaining the quality and quantity of student learning while reducing the proportional cost. The key element is to make more effective use of the most critical learning resource, the full-time faculty members. (p. 1)

He goes on to define a new role for faculty as masters of the learning environment and notes that "some faculty will be unwilling or unable to adapt to this new paradigm. To the extent financially feasible, they should continue to teach in a traditional mode, but upon their departure, their replacements should be expected to exhibit the professional skills to be masters of the learning environment" (Wenrich, 1994, p. 1).

This humane and clear approach is one example of how community college leaders will implement new structures and opportunities to reallocate resources to ensure support for the creation of learning colleges.

Evaluate, Evaluate, Evaluate

Community colleges have not established strong records of evaluating their activities and assessing student outcomes, but in recent years that situation has begun to change. Along with the rest of higher education, community colleges have been strongly influenced by the assessment movement, strengthened with calls for accountability from state legislators and with new standards set by the regional accrediting associations. Assisted by improved assessment tools and new technologies such as computer-assisted assessment, community colleges are beginning to develop a positive mind-set regarding the value of assessment and evaluation in all their activities.

At Sinclair Community College (see chapter 6), interest in student assessment actually prepared the way for Sinclair's journey to become a learning college. In 1985, college staff began discussing developing learning outcomes for each of the college's programs. A number of major initiatives emerged as a result of this discussion, and by 1990 Sinclair had in place a comprehensive and exemplary institutionwide assessment program. Sinclair's president, David Ponitz, noted that "The goal for an institutionwide assessment effort was to improve student learning and the processes that contribute to effective and efficient learning." Without using the language of "the learning college," Sinclair had made a major step in that direction when it became a priority to develop "processes that contribute to effective and efficient learning."

In 1991, the pace of the Sinclair journey picked up when the college embraced Total Quality Management. In the development of a new vision statement, each department developed mission statements regarding departmental roles in contributing to learning as the central mission of the college. Because Sinclair had spent time to develop an effective system of assessment to measure student learning, it was natural for college staff to want to assess the effectiveness of their mission statements. Six core indicators of institutional effectiveness have since been agreed upon, and critical success factors have been identified for each core indicator. Sinclair is well on its way to creating a learning college that will evolve in the framework of a detailed and effective system of evaluation.

At the Community College of Denver, there has been a strong emphasis on evaluation for over a decade. Cited by the North Central Association of Schools and Colleges for its evaluation and accountability models, the college prepares annual reports on student success and prints student evaluations of the college and its faculty in its class schedules. President Byron McClenney reports that "This open process of sharing the outcome measures has created a climate in which every staff member at the Community College of Denver wants to perform well and is proud of the performance of the institution." (See p. 218.)

Creating a learning college is, in part, a journey into the unknown. Evaluating progress all along the way is necessary to gauge progress and make corrections. Only by evaluating what is happening and what has been achieved will community colleges be able to build models of the learning college that others will want to emulate. The colleges that describe their journeys in this book, and especially those that pay attention to evaluation, will serve as the beginning benchmarks for many colleges that will follow.

Commit to the Long Haul

In 1986, Miami-Dade Community College initiated its well-known Teaching and Learning Project that resulted in, among other things, the creation of 100 distinguished teaching chairs. Not anticipating that the project would become so large or take so long, president Robert McCabe began referring to the initiative as "The Project That Ate Miami-Dade" (In Jenrette and Napoli, 1994, p. 258).

Time is the enemy of all projects designed to initiate major change. Linda Thor (1996), president of Rio Salado Community College in Phoenix, notes this fact in reference to her college's total quality initiative. "If there is one simple process required to implement quality leadership in an organization. . . . It is, simply put, TIME. It will not—it cannot—happen quickly. . ." (p. 114).

In their efforts to create a learning college at Jackson Community College, Lee Howser and Carol Schwinn also note the importance of planning for the long haul.

> Making cultural changes in an organization takes an extraordinary amount of time. Whatever the original time line, double it! While there are many "NIKE'S" or changes of the "Just do it!" variety, fundamental change requires conflict resolution and substitution of old behaviors. The process just takes time. (See p. 146–47.)

Jerry Young, president of Chaffey College in California, has indicated that he worked for five years as a new president at Chaffey just to open up the system to the point where faculty could say "This isn't working." Just building an awareness of the problems will be a long effort for some colleges, and this stage must precede any meaningful action toward becoming a learning college.

Leaders planning to launch a learning college should be realistic about the time it will take to create this new educational enterprise. Changing the historical architecture designed for earlier agricultural and industrial periods will require years of destruction and construction, not to mention the time it will take to change the behaviors of those who represent "1,000 years of tradition wrapped in 100 years of bureaucracy," a description of higher education offered by Roger Moe, majority leader of the Minnesota State Senate, referenced in chapter 1 of this book.

Celebrate Changes and Accomplishments

In an effort as comprehensive and complex as creating a learning college, it is a good idea to develop a culture of celebration to recognize milestones of special achievement. Real transformation of the educational culture will take a very long time, and celebrating short-term wins will keep the momentum going. Most staff will not join the long journey unless they can see results along the way, preferably in early stages.

Some early achievements might include agreeing on a general awareness of problems and issues and a general consensus of the need for change—no mean achievement for many institutions. Institutionwide agreement on new value and mission statements is an achievement to be noted and appropriately celebrated. The creation of a new student assessment system and new organizational structure, or the addition of new information technologies may be worth celebrating. Leaders should orchestrate celebrations and opportunities for recognition around each of these milestones and use each one to vault to the next.

It is important not to celebrate a short-term achievement as final victory, declaring the war won. The premature victory celebration stops momentum and provides opportunity for traditional forces to regain territory. Each celebration should be planned as an opportunity to leverage new plans. Kotter (1995) advises business leaders to capitalize on every achievement as passage to the next.

> Instead of declaring victory, leaders of successful efforts use the credibility afforded by short-term wins to tackle even bigger problems. They go after systems and instructors that are not consistent with the transformation vision and have not been confronted before. They pay great attention to who is promoted, who is hired, and how people are developed. They include new re-engineering projects that are even bigger in scope than the initial ones. (p. 66)

One of the reasons for developing sound systems of evaluation is to be able to document institutional achievements. When learning begins to saturate the culture, and when structures and programs are designed to increase and expand learning, then the evaluation and assessment systems will document the success as a sound basis for celebration.

CONCLUSION

Colleges that change their basic systems to focus on learning by expanding learning options for students, by engaging students as full partners in the learning process, by designing educational structures to meet learner needs, and by defining the roles of learning facilitators based on the needs of learners, will create an educational enterprise that will help students make passionate connections to learning, one whose accomplishments will be worth great celebration in the institution and throughout the society. The learning college that places learning first and provides educational experiences for learners anyway, anyplace, anytime, has great potential for fulfilling this dream.

REFERENCES

Alfred, Richard and Carter, Patricia. "Inside Track to the Future," *Community College Journal*, February/March 1996.

Armes, Nancy and McClenney, Kay, "Building Communities: A Checklist for Evaluation and Discussion," *Leadership Abstracts*, February 1990.

Bowen, Howard. *The State of the Nation and the Agenda for Higher Education*. San Francisco: Jossey-Bass, 1982.

Brown, Tom. "An Interview with Margaret Wheatley," *Industry Week*, April 18, 1994.

Cross, K. Patricia. "Community Colleges on the Plateau," *Journal of Higher Education* March/April, 1981.

Dobyns, Lloyd and Crawford-Mason, Clare. *Quality or Else: The Revolution in World Business*. Boston: Houghton Mifflin Company, 1991.

Institute for Research on Higher Education. "Leaving Hats at the Door: Themes from the PEW Campus Roundtables," *Change*, May/June 1996.

Jenrette, Mardee and Napoli, Vince. "The Miami-Dade Teaching/Learning Project." In *Teaching and Learning in the Community College* edited by Terry O'Banion. Washington, D.C.: American Association of Community Colleges, 1994.

Keller, George. "Let's Move Beyond Critical Thinking," *On the Horizon*, January/February 1996.

Kotter, John P. "Leading Change: Why Transformation Efforts Fail," *Harvard Business Review*, March/April 1995.

Moriarty, Daniel F. "In Rough Seas, Stay the Course," *Community College Journal*, February/March 1996.

O'Banion, Terry. *Innovation in the Community College*. New York: Macmillan Publishing Company, 1989.

————, ed. *Teaching and Learning in the Community College*. Washington, D.C.: American Association of Community Colleges, 1994.

Policy Perspectives, Institute for Research on Higher Education, University of Pennsylvania, Philadelphia, Pennsylvania, February 1993.

Policy Perspectives, Institute for Research on Higher Education, University of Pennsylvania, Philadelphia, Pennsylvania, April 1994.

Thor, Linda. "Leadership: The Driver of the System." In *High Performing Colleges: Volume I: Theory and Concepts* edited by Daniel Seymour. Maryville, MO: Prescott Publishing Company, 1996.

Wenrich, William. "Masters of the Learning Environment." Unpublished paper, Dallas County Community College District, Dallas, Texas, 1994.

Wilson, Ian. "The Practical Power of Vision," *On the Horizon,* March/April 1996.

INDEX